Date Due			
JUL 2 '56			
AUG 2 2 '56			
NOV 1 '56			
JUL 2 4 '57			
MAY 7 '59			
AUG 1 6 '68			
MAY 6 74			
	PRINTED	IN U. S. A.	

M H C LIBRARY

VOCATIONS FOR GIRLS

REVISED EDITION

VOCATIONS FOR GIRLS

MARY REBECCA LINGENFELTER

HARRY DEXTER KITSON

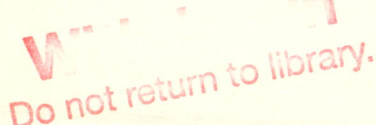

HARCOURT, BRACE AND COMPANY

New York

COPYRIGHT, 1939, 1951, BY
HARCOURT, BRACE AND COMPANY, INC.

All rights reserved, including the right to reproduce this book or portions thereof in any form.

PRINTED IN THE UNITED STATES OF AMERICA

To Nancy and Barbara

Contents

Contents

1. On Choosing a Vocation	3

I · GUARDIANS OF HEALTH

2. Nurses	12
3. Physicians	23
4. Dentists	30
5. Dental Hygienists	36
6. Osteopaths, Optical Workers, Veterinarians	41
7. Physical and Occupational Therapists	51

II · WOMEN WHO MEAN BUSINESS

8. Clerical Workers	56
9. Secretaries	68
10. Saleswomen	74
11. Girls at Machines	92
12. The Lady Boss	103
13. Personnel Workers	109

CONTENTS

14. ADVERTISERS 115
15. LADY BANKERS 125
16. TRANSPORTATION AND COMMUNICATION
    WORKERS 131

III · PEOPLE ARE THEIR BUSINESS

17. TEACHERS 142
18. SOCIAL WORKERS 156
19. LADIES OF THE LAW 162
20. RELIGIOUS WORKERS AND MINISTERS 167
21. LIBRARIANS 177
22. HOME ECONOMISTS 189
23. RECREATION LEADERS 199
24. BEAUTICIANS 206

IV · SCIENTISTS AND ENGINEERS

25. SCIENTISTS 213
26. ENGINEERS 227

V · LITERARY AND ARTISTIC WORKERS

27. WRITERS, NEWSPAPER WORKERS, EDITORS 233
28. ARTISTS, MUSICIANS, ACTRESSES, AND OTHERS 244
29. RADIO AND TELEVISION WORKERS 265

VI · FARM AND HOME WORKERS

30. LADY FARMERS	273
31. HOMEMAKERS	282
32. HOUSEHOLD WORKERS	287
33. HOBBYS AND THE STAY-AT-HOME WORKER	295

VII · WORKERS FOR UNCLE SAM

34. GOVERNMENT WORKERS, POLITICIANS, AND DIPLOMATS	300
35. WACS, WAFS, WAVES, MARINES	312
36. NEW HORIZONS FOR GIRLS AND WOMEN	321
READING LISTS	337
INDEX	361

VOCATIONS FOR GIRLS

1. ON CHOOSING A VOCATION

SINCE THIS BOOK deals with vocations perhaps we ought to answer the question, what is a vocation? The definition generally given is that a vocation is a way of making a living. But this is an insufficient answer. Let's put the question another way: why do people work? To make a living, yes; but not solely for that reason. People work partly in order to have a directed form of activity. Man is an active creature. The normal person cannot be happy if he spends his time in idleness. A vocation, with its organized tasks, provides an outlet for his physical and mental energies. This craving for activity is sometimes spoken of as the "urge for self-expression"—a desire to project one's personality into some tangible accomplishment such as knitting a sweater, writing a news story, trimming a hat.

These motives, however, do not supply the final answer. There is a still more fundamental reason why people work—to supply human needs. Human beings need food, houses, wearing apparel, recreation, transportation and a multitude of services. Someone must produce them.

In a primitive society each person, or at least each family, was able to supply his own needs. The man of the family obtained food by hunting and fishing; the woman cooked it, and made clothes of animal skins, or wove cloth on primitive looms. As man became civilized, however, he developed more and more needs. He devised a printed language and wanted books, he wanted faster modes of transportation and invented automobiles and airplanes. The wants became so numerous and the articles supplying them became so complicated that no one person or family could produce them.

At this point arose a phenomenon known as "division of labor." One man said, "I will print books." Another said, "I will make pastry." Thus each one specialized in supplying one of the items that the human family needed. His mode of supplying this became his vocation.

As needs increased in number the articles produced became more and more complicated. For example, bookmaking became so complicated that many types of specialists were needed—linotype operators, monotype operators, gatherers, binders, electrotype casters, electrotype molders, packers, stenographers, etc. This development caused a continuous increase in the number of vocations until today there are between 20,000 and 30,000.

As a girl considers her responsibility to society she asks herself, in what way shall I help to satisfy human needs? Her first thought probably is marriage and homemaking, in which case she would be making her contribution by rearing children and keeping a home. We should state here that homemaking is recognized as a vocation, an exacting and important one.

But until she gets married a girl is likely to want to work, and so she should prepare herself for a vocation other than homemaking. Even after she marries she may work in order to increase the family income or to utilize extra homemaking talents she may possess. The majority of girls expect at some time to work in a non-homemaking vocation and many of them continue in it.

How shall a girl select from the thousands of vocations

ON CHOOSING A VOCATION

one that she will call her own? We should warn you that this is no easy task. There is no nickel-in-the-slot machine that will make the choice for you. You may hear of various "vocational tests" that are on the market but we warn you that these do not work automatically. Some of them are useful to employment managers in business and industry in that they assist in screening applicants for certain jobs. But in helping an individual to choose an occupation they are not of value in the specific way you might expect.

You have probably also heard that there are vocational counselors who specialize in helping people choose a vocation and solve occupational problems, but again we should warn you that no reputable vocational counselor, no matter how skillful he is, can tell you exactly what vocation to choose. He can only suggest various possibilities. You are the one who must solve this problem. In this chapter we shall outline the steps you may take.

1. *Study the occupations.* Let us assume that you have been thinking about a particular vocation, such as becoming a reporter on a newspaper. Before making a final decision you should examine the occupation thoroughly. Here is a rough outline that may serve as a guide in making this examination.

   a. Find out what duties a reporter performs.
   b. What are his hours of work?
   c. Is the work seasonal?
   d. Are there any particularly unhealthy features about the work? Any moral hazards?
   e. How much money can one expect to earn?
   f. What are the jobs to which one may be promoted?
   g. Where are the best opportunities?

h. Is the occupation overcrowded?
i. What preparation is needed by way of:
   1. general education
   2. special training; where may it be obtained? What are the prerequisites? How much will it cost?
   3. experience, particularly work experience?

2. *Read literature on occupations.* One source of answers to your questions is the printed literature on occupations. This book is intended to give you a picture of many occupations, and through lists of suggested reading to facilitate your intensive study of individual occupations. If this book does not refer to an occupation you would like to investigate, consult *Occupational Pamphlets, an Annotated Bibliography* by Gertrude Forrester where you may find references to literature on many occupations.

An important part of occupational literature is the biographies of persons who have been markedly successful in vocations. In the reading lists at the end of this book you will find a number of biographies. They will show you how successful people have blazed a trail you may like to follow.

3. *Observe the occupation at first hand.* Visit places where the occupation is carried on. If you are interested in the vocation of reporter visit newspaper plants, and discover how the reporter's work is related to the other jobs in the newspaper business. Perhaps you would be permitted to accompany a reporter on his daily rounds.

4. *Talk with workers in the field.* A person who has served in an occupation for some years can give you much information about his occupation. Don't bother him with questions that are answered in books or pamphlets. Learn all you can through reading, then ask your questions.

Members of women's service clubs such as Altrusa, Zonta, Soroptimist, Business and Professional Women's Clubs, will be glad to devote time to answering your inquiries.

5. *Appraise yourself.* Choosing a vocation is not merely a matter of gathering information about occupations. You must also consider *yourself* in the light of the demands and requirements of the occupation. This study of one's self is a highly complicated and difficult task. To perform it you must, as it were, view yourself in a mirror and consider every phase of your equipment in the light of the information you have discovered about the vocation.

For example, must an airline stewardess measure 5 feet 3 inches in height while you measure only 5 feet 2 inches? If so, you are disqualified. The vocation of engineer requires high facility in mathematics. If your marks in that subject have been low your chances of entering a college of engineering would be slight. If you are bored or irritated by small children you would probably be unhappy as a kindergarten teacher.

Although you can't increase your height you may be able to develop certain other occupational requirements. For example, you may not at present be tactful enough to qualify as a hostess in a restaurant, but by means of self-discipline you can develop more tact. Though you may not have a good carriage you may be able to acquire this trait required of a model in a retail clothing establishment.

A sensible procedure in appraising yourself vocationally is to concentrate on your assets. Thus if you have a good carriage you have one of the attributes of a good dress model. A large circle of friends and acquaintances is an asset in selling life insurance.

In this self-appraisal a good vocational counselor may

help you, not by telling you what vocation to choose, but by making your self-inventory more detailed; by using such measuring devices as are warranted; and by showing you how to balance one factor against another.

6. *Seek try-out experiences.* One way in which you can measure yourself against the conditions obtaining in a vocation is to take a job that will give you first-hand contact with it. If you wish to test your interest in social service, volunteer for service in your local Red Cross unit. If you aspire to journalism try for a place on the staff of your school or college paper.

After you have decided on a field of work your next step is to lay out a course of training for it. Through your previous explorations you will have learned how much general education is required and what kind of special training is necessary. Now you must find a favorable institution where you can be trained. The books and monographs we have spoken of usually contain a list of institutions that give training for the occupations treated. Detailed descriptions of many institutions of collegiate grade will be found in *A Guide to Colleges, Universities and Professional Schools,* also in *Education for Professional Careers.* If you need financial aid you might profitably consult the list of aids compiled in *Scholarships, Fellowships and Loans.* (See Bibliography.)

Our discussion of the problems encountered in vocational life would not be complete without consideration of one of the most important problems—how to get a job. This task is hard enough even for workers who have had a considerable amount of experience. It is doubly hard for the novice who is seeking a foothold on the occupational ladder. She has nothing to offer but the exuberance

ON CHOOSING A VOCATION

of youth, perhaps a good education, a willingness to work, and possibly some theoretical knowledge about a certain field of work. Her task is to present her assets in such a light that an employer will regard her as a promising person to employ.

There are a number of agencies that are organized to help people find jobs. The State Employment Service is the largest which you may find in your own locality by consulting the telephone book. If no office of this service is in your town or city, ask your teacher or guidance counselor where to find the nearest one. Each state operates its own employment service program in co-operation with the Federal Government which supplies some of the funds for its operation. You should feel free to seek the help of this agency since it is supported by public funds. Many public school systems maintain a placement service, too, as do most colleges and universities.

In all cities there are employment agencies that operate on a commercial basis. They may charge you a fee amounting to one week's salary. As a rule they are pretty efficient.

The persons who can be of greatest help are generally your friends and acquaintances. Let them know you are looking for a job. Generally speaking, your chances are better in your own community where you are known than in the world outside.

One way of getting a job is to apply directly to an employer. Your application may be made by letter or in person. If you are applying by letter, study one of the books in the reading list for this chapter and follow its directions in composing an interest-evoking letter. The object of your letter will be to secure an interview. If you are fortunate enough to be invited for an interview you will need to prepare for it most carefully. Full directions are given in several of the books relating to this chapter: *Pick Your Job and Land It*, by Edlund and Edlund; *How You Can Get a Job*, by Gardiner; and *Your Work Abilities*, by Rahn.

At some stage in your quest for a job you will be asked to fill out an application blank. You should do this with extreme care—don't leave any question unanswered. Write legibly, especially your name, address and telephone number. We know of applicants who were so careless as to omit these essential data.

There is one more stage in the process of getting established in a vocation—working one's way up the ladder. If you are seriously determined to forge a career you should always keep your eye on the future. Examine the positions to which you might be promoted from your first job. For example, as a sales person in a department store the positions you might next hold are head of stock, then assistant buyer, then buyer. Find out what steps you ought to take to qualify for those positions and begin to prepare for them. This preparation will involve study of certain techniques used in these advanced positions. It will involve superior performance in every task assigned you. Most important of all is that you manifest industriousness and interest in your work.

We'd like to suggest the following advice for anyone who asks, "How can I make good and get ahead in my work?" It is included in a booklet for new employees of the F. W. Woolworth Company.

> You are our chief representative to build good will between our company and the customer. Your future in our company depends upon you. Your progress will be in direct ratio to your ability and enthusiasm toward your duties.

ON CHOOSING A VOCATION

Through personal contact between YOU and the Customer we aim to accomplish three purposes: (1) To sell more of the store's merchandise, (2) To extend special courtesies and help, (3) To create additional good will for the store. Your position as sales lady is that of a personal representative of the store. To customers YOU are the store, and whatever impression YOU create, favorable or unfavorable, is the impression customers will carry out of this store.

Much depends on *your* courtesy in personal contacts with the public which we serve and with your fellow employees. It is expected that what you do and how you do it, what you say and how you say it, will reflect credit on both you and the store.

In this chapter we have outlined the steps you must take in choosing a vocation and achieving success in it. Your immediate step will probably be to explore an occupation or several occupations. This book has been designed to assist you in the exploration. It contains brief descriptions of several hundreds of jobs, gives details that will enable you to decide whether you wish to consider a specific field as a career. When you find such a field, refer to the bibliography pertaining to it and read more intensively. Follow the steps outlined in this chapter. Don't look for a magic formula—there is none. To succeed in a vocation requires persistence, ingenuity, and a dedication of one's self to a single purpose. Finally we should warn you not to be impatient if your plans do not mature as fast as you wish. Take comfort from Josiah G. Holland's verse:

> Heaven is not reached at a single bound,
> But we build the ladder by which we rise
> From the lowly earth to the vaulted skies,
> And we mount to its summit round by round.

I

Guardians of Health

2. NURSES

SOMETIMES WE WONDER why the fascinating story of Florence Nightingale wins girl after girl to the cause of nursing. Then we realize that the "Lady of the Lamp" had, beside her spirit of adventure, all the qualities of a splendid nurse: the desire to serve other people, the will and courage to go where she could best use her boundless energy, sympathy, skill in tending the sick, a good head as well as a good heart, and a capacity for fine leadership. Without such qualifications no girl can expect to go far in the nursing world.

Other qualities needed by the prospective nurse are: good health, sunny disposition, and even temper. No sick person wants a nurse with a long face and a gloomy outlook on life. Common sense, sound judgment, and an alert mind will help you avoid many pitfalls; and it goes without saying that a nurse must be trustworthy, resourceful, and willing to assume responsibility. No giddy young featherheads will be tolerated. Unless you are naturally neat, orderly, and systematic, the precision of a hospital may be extremely irritating—and, what is worse, you won't last a week. Poise, a gentle voice, a light touch, and genuine kindness of heart are qualities every nurse needs. Possibly an only child who has always been the petted darling of her home may dislike hospital discipline, but she must learn "how to take it," or choose another vocation.

So far we have been thinking about what a nurse needs in the way of natural equipment to achieve success in this field. There is, as well, the matter of education and training. In the good old days, a high school diploma—or in some places a grade school education—was an open sesame to most of the nursing schools, but not today! If you were in the top third of your high school class you may be admitted to some training schools, but college education is a decided asset, not only for your profession but because it will make you a better-rounded person. Some schools of nursing are on a graduate basis and demand a college degree for admission.

If you want to secure the best preparation, attend a good liberal arts college and absorb all you can of biology, chemistry, hygiene, physics, psychology, sociology and economics, English history, languages, home economics. In fact, take all you can carry of everything except possibly Greek—and we are not saying that this dead language would not come in handy if you happened to be nursing an elderly archaeologist or classical scholar. Don't omit the speech courses, especially if your voice rasps or if you don't read well. Anything that will help you entertain mildly sick patients is an asset; for instance, arts and crafts, dramatics, music, and the like.

After college there will be two or three more years in a school of nursing to secure the technical training. But there are other ways of doing it. Today many universities give combined academic and nursing courses leading to a degree of A.B., B.S., or B.N., which, as you'll suspect, stands for Bachelor of Nursing. This is a popular method, but the arrangement of the five years varies in different schools. The first two or three years may be similar to the course in any college except for emphasis on the basic subjects for nursing. The final years will be devoted to a very intensive period of training.

"Aren't those years of training pretty strenuous?" you ask, "especially during probation?" Although the preliminary training period *is* stiff, it consists chiefly of study. That's why the schools are so careful to select girls with good brains.

In the first year there are lectures, classes, and laboratory work in science and theory and practice of nursing, and each student will spend some time in the wards observing and helping in the care of patients. After a probationer has passed the examinations of the preliminary period, she is admitted as a regular student and is permitted to wear the uniform of the school. Her pink, blue, or striped uniform usually indicates just how far down she is in the hospital social scale. And how she will strive to qualify for the all-white graduate uniform! The student nurse will be given more and more bedside training—under supervision, of course; she will learn the ethics of the profession and will study the history of nursing and many other subjects. The classes in medical aspects of nursing are usually taught by physicians on the staff. The time is well occupied but the students have a pleasant life in the nurses' home, with good food, a careful health program, and as much amusement as can be fitted into a busy schedule.

A school of nursing resembles a college except for slightly stricter regulations and occasional night duty. Today, however, night duty is not dreaded as it once was. The student often enjoys trying out her wings this way because she carries more responsibility and may learn more than at any other time.

"If a girl enters a school of nursing from a college of liberal arts, must she begin all over again?" you may inquire.

"That depends," is our cautious reply. "A graduate of a four-year college course is credited with one or more academic years in some nursing schools, depending upon the courses she has taken. If she has had a course in a teachers' college, a school of home economics, or any other special school, she may be given credit for certain subjects required in nursing such as chemistry, biology, and the like—that is, if she can pass the examinations with the regular student nurses. Most students prefer, however, to take the full course because otherwise they may miss some practical training that they will need to make up later.

After the nursing course is completed, the new graduate faces the State Board of Nurse Examiners to secure the right to add "R.N." after her name. "From that proud moment on," states the pamphlet *Nursing Is a Great Profession*, "the registered professional nurse becomes an essential member of a health team whose job is to protect, improve, and expand world health."

Nursing is a versatile profession, chiefly because this "R.N." opens doors to many types of nursing jobs in any community, state, or nation in the world. Private-duty nursing is the oldest and still the largest field. Under the physician's general direction, these nurses care for patients during the acute stages of illness in their homes or in a hospital.

In private practice, nurses may become specialists in certain types of illness such as orthopedic, neuropsychiatric, maternity, infant, infantile paralysis. As prepayment health plans are expanded, it is reasonable to expect that nursing care will be included in the benefits and will make available to larger numbers of patients expert and individual attention in time of serious illness.

Institutional nursing may have openings for you and here there may be more chance for advancement than in private duty nursing. There will be work in hospitals, charitable homes, boarding schools, or colleges. There are general and emergency hospitals, nervous and mental hospitals, special hospitals for eye, ear, nose and throat, tuberculosis, orthopedic, skin and cancer, maternity and isolation hospitals, as well as the hospitals attached to institutions. In all these types of hospitals there will be opportunities in the operating rooms, in the wards, and in the out-patient departments.

Among the positions classed as institutional nursing are: principal or director of a nursing school; superintendent of the hospital; assistant superintendent, supervisor, head nurse, operating-room nurse, dispensary nurse, instructor of nurses, anesthetist, social service worker, and of course the regular staff nurses.

Any girl who thinks that hospital nursing consists of looking pretty in a white cap and trim starched uniform had better guess again. There is about as much truth in that idea as in the notion that all a librarian does is read exciting stories when she is not engaged in handing out books to charming readers. In the hospital anything is likely to happen as you race up and down the corridors answering patients' signals, feeding the hungry ones or coaxing others to eat, administering doses, and giving them the other attentions they need. What if you are the only one around when a patient suddenly turns blue and stops breathing! Can you save him before other help arrives? In such emergencies you'll need all the poise, calm, and efficiency you can muster.

The following incident that occurred in one hospital indicates why knowledge and ability of a high order are needed by a registered professional nurse.

"ATTENTION!" came the call over the P.A. system. "This is Dr. Jones—Emergency Room. We're admitting a child with skull fracture. He's in severe shock!"

Nurses on the pediatric floor rallied instantly. By the time the youngster was wheeled off the elevator, blood plasma was ready, and infusions, syringes, and penicillin were on hand.

That youngster had about one chance in a thousand to live. But he did. He lived because doctors and nurses acted rapidly, as a team. *Each knew what to do.*

The private nurse in a family leads a very different life. She usually cares for just one patient and stays close to his bedside, paying little attention to the rest of the family. Except, of course, when she finds a need for teaching him and his family simple rules of health and hygiene in order to guard against future illness. In the sections of the country where the newer regulations about hours are in force, she will be saved from that old bugbear of private-duty nursing—twenty-four-hour duty, which was all too frequently exactly that. Almost half of the country has adopted the eight-hour plan—elsewhere, twelve-hour duty is likely to prevail.

Public health nursing is a splendid and growing field for the girl who must have a salaried position. These nurses are employed by town, city, county, and state departments of health; by visiting nurse associations, infant and child health associations, insurance companies, and by industrial establishments. They give bedside care to the sick in their homes; teach mothers how to give better care to their families; help teachers of public schools and employers in industry to safeguard the health of their pupils and workers. They watch for the causes of physical defects, such as poor ventilation, lack of sunshine, too hard work, not enough of the right kind of food; and they help and advise in remedying conditions and in devising ways and means for better living. Epidemics are being prevented, parents are learning health fundamentals, and children are being given the right start in life through the work of these nurses as teachers in the homes, the schools, and the workshops of the country.

The life of the public health nurse is a busy one as she travels from home to home—walking, walking, walking! The mountain climber who proudly boasted that she never had too much hiking is likely to change her tune on this job, unless, of course, she has a car in which to make her calls. And you'll have to be careful or the strain on your sympathies may wear you out. You must not let yourself become hardened to the troubles of your patients, nor dare you let them "get you down."

The work of the visiting nurse, either under public or private auspices, is certain to be filled with excitement and human interest. She reports at her headquarters early every morning to map out her calls for the day. She never knows what challenge will be in those calls or what they will bring her in pathos or amusement or opportunity; or how much satisfaction she will find in using all the social, technical, and scientific skill in her power to solve the problems she will meet.

Sometimes, if within reach, the visiting nurse returns to the office for lunch with her co-workers to talk things over and exchange experiences of the morning. At the close of the day, no matter how far away she is, she must return to write up her records. Perhaps her job calls for only seven or eight hours a day, but it often lengthens into nine or ten—or even more, if she happens to be on infant welfare or maternity work. In closely built-up sections, the visiting nurse may make as many as thirty calls a day, if she is merely checking up on her patients; but if she's actually giving treatment seven or eight calls a day will be a good average.

There are still other openings for nurses: office nurses employed by physicians and dentists to assist in office examinations and other work, anesthetists, laboratory assistants, hourly nurses, special teachers, missionary nurses, Red Cross and Veterans Administration positions, Army and Navy nurses, house mothers, social directors, and housekeepers. The job of air hostess is a possibility for the graduate nurse. However, she'll not be wise to stay in that type of work very long because there will be little chance for professional growth while she is thus employed.

How do nurses get their jobs? Particularly the private-duty ones? Some of them are kept busy by a group of doctors who call them for their patients, but the usual way is through the nurses' registries which supply graduate nurses almost on a moment's notice. These registries may be conducted by individual hospitals to care for their own graduates only, or they may be run by nursing organizations. In order to distribute the cases as evenly as possible, the nurse whose name heads the list has to take her place at the foot after she is on a case which lasts more than three days. That is, unless a doctor or patient asks for her particularly. Some years ago an hourly nursing service was established in an attempt to reduce nursing costs and divide the work more evenly. This service is a boon to people who are not financially able to pay for a full-time nurse.

For the girl of limited means, nursing may offer an excellent way to obtain professional training without straining the family finances, if she can get into one of the few remaining schools which do not charge a tuition fee. However, most of the good nurses' training schools now charge a fee of from one to three hundred dollars.

Nursing is one occupation in which there is no real competition from men. Figures indicate that the ratio of male nurses has never been as high as one in ten of all nurses, and from 1920 on, nursing has been almost entirely a woman's job. Naturally, to be successful you must be good—and, by that, we mean *very good*. No mediocre nurses can be safely tolerated.

The many advantages offered by the nursing profession must not be overlooked. Your training as a nurse will teach you a great deal about human nature so that you will learn how to handle people tactfully, a tremendous asset to anyone, whether her life work is nursing, business, or raising a family. Can you think of any better preparation for being a wife and mother than a nurse's training, especially if your husband is not as robust as he might be or if your children batter themselves up more than the average?

The interesting people you meet provide one of the greatest attractions of the nursing profession. Naturally you will encounter the usual percentage of cranks, but agreeable patients are likely to be in the majority. If some of them are wealthy and need you a long time, you may have exciting opportunities to travel. And there are many opportunities for trained nurses to go places and do things all round the globe. Uncle Sam offers jobs in his floating Naval hospitals, in Navy shore station hospitals in faraway places, in Army overseas hospitals, in the Canal Zone, and wherever large numbers of government workers are stationed. You will find additional information about this in Chapters 34 and 35.

Girls who dream of Alaska as a future home are likely to find jobs in that new state as soon as they receive their white caps. We do mean "future home," as in that land of many men and few women, nurses marry so quickly that they rarely have time to repay Uncle Sam for airplane or railroad fares.

In the chapter on *Religious Workers,* you will hear about opportunities for nurses in hospitals and in public health work sponsored by religious denominations in their foreign mission stations. Special training in schools of these organizations may be required before a nurse is permitted to go to the foreign field.

Most of the large ocean liners employ a small staff of nurses to care for seasick passengers, and to give emergency nursing care to crew and passengers in the sick bay and ship's hospital. One nurse we met on the historic *Grips-*

holm told of her experiences during the years in which that mercy ship carried Japanese nationals to their homeland and picked up Americans to be repatriated. She had helped to bring more than one Japanese baby into the world and, on our own voyage, performed a like service for an infant born after 48 hours at sea.

Friendships formed during training school days, and later with your patients, are bound to enrich your life. Every time you accept a new case, there will be a sense of adventure. What kind of person will this be and will it be the beginning of another lifelong friendship?

Nursing is not all a bed of roses, as you must realize by this time. Student training days are hard; and there are certain health risks from exposure to disease. There is also the chance that a private case may turn out to be the wrong kind of adventure if the patient is unreasonable and tyrannical. In that event you may be forced to remember your lessons in nursing ethics that you must remain until another nurse relieves you. Your own personal and social life is likely to fade into the background; the registered nurse must always be within reach of her registry and ready to take a case on a moment's notice, unless she can afford to take her name off the list whenever she feels the need of a vacation. The visiting nurse must make her rounds regardless of wind, sleet, rain, or blizzard. But always there is the feeling that you are performing real service in assisting others back to healthy, happy lives, and that you are actually carrying on the torch of the "Lady of the Lamp" as well as of all other great nurses since her time.

3. PHYSICIANS

MEDICINE FOR WOMEN! Why not? It may look like a "for men only" profession from the point of view of figures, since only about 1 in 10 physicians is a woman. Don't let that deter you. Think of the progress women physicians have made since the middle of the nineteenth century. That should give you hope for the future.

The first medical schools in the country announced almost at once that women would be barred entirely from the profession. They held to this resolution until the middle of the nineteenth century when women first began to force their way into medical schools and hospitals. In 1947 the last of the great American medical schools finally opened its doors to female applicants.

Read the life of Elizabeth Blackwell which describes the difficulties faced by this first American woman physician and her sister Emily before they finally forced their way into the medical profession. After these women won the coveted M.D. degree, no hospital would open doors to them—not even a crack.

"Very well," they said, "we'll make our own jobs." So they established their own hospital, the New York Dispensary for Poor Women and Children. In 1868 these women were granted a charter to set up a course of training for "female physicians."

"Money makes the mare go" is an old saying, but it led to the admission of women to the medical college at

Cornell. The university had to admit women medical students or lose an endowment of one and a half million dollars offered on the condition that women be admitted. After Cornell opened its doors to women, the Blackwell sisters transferred their establishment to the Cornell Medical School. Money talked likewise at famous Johns Hopkins Medical School which admitted women from the first, on the promise that a large sum of money would be raised by a committee of women.

A short time ago, a North Carolina journalist reviewed the progress made by these women in white since the beginning of the twentieth century. He insisted that "now young girls can announce that they are going to be doctors with as much nonchalance as they once announced an intention to be housewives or teachers. They still have a certain amount of prejudice to overcome. The medical schools for the most part restrict their enrollment to a rough 10 per cent, and they are still more or less confined to the practice of obstetrics, pediatrics, gynecology, and pathology, but they have won a permanent place in the profession. Through arduous years of fighting and feuding and struggling they have proved that women can be doctors—and good ones too."

If you have the proper qualifications and can afford the necessary education and training, don't let any "for men only" ideas stop you. It is all up to you.

How can you prepare for a career in medicine? First examine catalogues of various medical schools. They will describe requirements for admission, desirable qualifications, length and content of courses, and so on. Pre-medical training requirements cover two to four years and will include such subjects as biology, chemistry, physics, and other sciences, as well as psychology, mathematics, social sciences, languages, and the arts. If you can afford the time and expense, it might be wise to earn a Master's degree in one of the biological sciences before entering medical school.

After you finish your pre-medical education, there is the important business of gaining admission to a first class medical school. And that is not easy unless you have always stood at the head, or very near the head, of your class. Many fairly good students have failed to meet entrance requirements because their scholastic records were not far enough above the average. Even if your marks warrant your undertaking a medical course, you may be refused on other grounds, as you may be obliged to pass a medical aptitude test before you will be accepted. No use worrying about that, though, until you have finished college.

Four years of grueling work will follow your admittance to medical school, probably costing more than a thousand dollars a year. The course will include such subjects as preventive medicine, pathology, diagnosis and treatment of disease, and surgery, as well as anatomy, bacteriology, and other phases of the sciences.

The specific qualifications for physicians are listed in many sources: absolute integrity, joy in work, a will to serve, intelligence, good memory, industry, initiative, concentration, persistence, scholarship, imperturbability, inspiration, and, above all, good health to help you resist the germs that you'll encounter. Not only good health but actual physical strength and endurance are needed, because the practice of medicine is usually hard work. Women still need what is known as pioneer spirit to get along in this man-dominated field. You are fortunate if you have a happy disposition; then that all-important cheerful bedside manner will be easy for you and your only difficulty will be in finding the beds—with patients in them.

It's not all over when you finish the medical courses. Then comes the interneship. But, fortunately, that costs you nothing. The chief problem is finding a hospital that will accept women internes. You may be given equal opportunities with the men up to this point but it has been stated that of the seven hundred hospitals approved for interneship some do not admit women *willingly*. Although that may not be true when you are ready to be an interne, you aren't likely to fall heir to one of the choice paid interneships, unless you go into a woman's hospital.

By the time you reach the interneship you'll agree with the writer who said that the person undertaking a medical career lets himself in for the most expensive form of education there is on the market. The course is so crowded and difficult that you cannot help out with part-time work except during the summer when hospital, institution, or camp positions may be available. You'll probably spend $5,000 or more before you emerge as a full-fledged M.D.

After the interneship is the hurdle of state and national examinations for a license, but they are not likely to hold you back if you have been careful in choosing an approved school. The hospital where you did your interneship must also be on the approved list, so be careful about that.

Girls who want to follow in Elizabeth Blackwell's footsteps have a great many specialties to choose from. Among them are: private practice in the city or country; surgery; preventive medicine; specialization in obstetrics, pediatrics, mental hygiene, public health, etc.; industrial medicine; research or bacteriology; social work; or writing on medical subjects.

Private practice in the country is a most promising field for the young M.D. who has a good constitution, a keen sense of humor, simple tastes, common sense, patience to endure long hard drives in all sorts of weather, and above all a genuine love of the country. In some small communities, there is still prejudice against women physicians but it is possible to overcome that if you have the ability and force. In the country you may find an opportunity to use all your training and skill, especially if you are obliged to perform emergency operations without adequate equipment. That rarely happens now, however, in these days of fine roads and easy transportation, except in isolated spots.

Physicians are needed so badly in the country that one small town actually *advertised* for a doctor after being without one for four years. Believe it or not—the lone answer to this call for help was from one of the town's own daughters who had just completed her medical training. Not only did she return home but she brought a fellow student—her husband—with her. A brass band wasn't good enough to welcome them.

In the cities, many women are winning success as general practitioners but it is advisable to start as assistant to an established physician or to take a part-time salaried position, if you can find one, until you develop your own practice. Such positions are sometimes available in city or state health departments, in clinics and laboratories for research and technical work.

Specialization in certain fields is likely to bring success

to the woman doctor. Gynecology and pediatrics—or, in everyday English, the ailments of women and children—offer splendid opportunities for women if they have had graduate training in these specialties. The woman specialist in skin diseases is likely to be highly successful. Many women prefer to go to a woman doctor for skin treatments. Specialization in eye, ear, nose, and throat is also fairly promising for women.

Although the number of women psychiatrists is still relatively small, this is an excellent field of specialization for women as they are peculiarly fitted for treating the mentally ill. The psychiatrist's delicate job is to diagnose cases with utmost care lest she label patients as suffering from serious mental disorders which call for commitment to a mental institution, when the trouble may be merely subnormal mentality, hysteria, neurasthenia, or psychopathic personality.

After the psychiatrist has examined her patients, through chemical, physical, and psychological tests, she will recommend one or more of various types of treatment. This may include drugs or vitamins when weakened physical condition seems to be the cause of the disturbance. Today shock treatments (through use of electric current, insulin, or other powerful drugs), physical, occupational, educational, and recreational therapy may all be combined in treatments which will assist mentally ill individuals to make adjustments to normal life outside hospital or other institutional doors.

The demand for psychiatrists will continue just as long as wars, depressions, and other emergencies strain the nerves of civilians and fill our hospitals with mentally sick veterans. These specialists will be needed, as well, in public health clinics, schools and colleges as more widespread use of their services is made in promoting better mental health among our young people and those not quite so young.

There are full- or part-time salaried positions for women medical examiners in welfare bureaus, public health departments, manufacturing plants, and department stores that employ women, as well as in schools, colleges, and other public institutions. Some of these positions, often under civil service, involve pre-natal care, baby health stations, training in the prevention of contagious diseases and so on. There are some opportunities with voluntary health organizations in their propaganda against the spread of disease or in giving planned parenthood instruction. You will find complete information on these openings in *Women Physicians*, issued by the Women's Bureau, U. S. Department of Labor, Washington, D. C.

Such positions will serve to keep the wolf from the door while a practice is being developed or there may be full-time work which will give you a greater sense of security than you will have in private practice. Indeed medicine is far more hopeful for the qualified girl than the figures indicate. It is possible that the great difference in numbers means that there is really more room for women.

As a missionary the woman physician with an adventuresome spirit can find many opportunities. Read *Ho-Ming* by E. F. Lewis and *Yang and Yin* by A. T. Hobart for excellent pictures of the hardships and the rewards of medical work in the mission field.

Work in women's prisons and similar institutions might appeal to a physician who has the missionary spirit or is interested in gaining experience in treatment of social diseases.

The best paying specialties in the order named are: surgery, ophthalmology, gynecology, eye, ear, nose and throat, orthopedics, pediatrics, gastro-enterology. As a rule, women physicians rarely make gigantic incomes, but very few fail to earn their living.

But it is not money alone that repays the woman physician for her outlay. One of her greatest joys is the feeling that she is accomplishing something for the good of others even though it may be at the cost of hard work and many sacrifices. The satisfaction of relieving pain, of restoring disabled and suffering men, women, and children to health, rewards her for all that she has sacrificed. There is never any monotony; the daily work is as varied as human nature. This profession is one that goes well with marriage. The married woman doctor will win the confidence of mothers, especially if she has children of her own. In private practice there will be good feeling between the doctor and her patient because people do not come to her unless they really want to.

It is hard work, and only the woman who is physically strong and who really loves to heal should study medicine.

4. DENTISTS

IF YOU BELIEVE in figures, dentistry is still a "for men only" profession. You will find very few women in the dental schools as less than 100 women dentists graduate from dental schools each year. But you'll have a good chance for success in this field if you are anxious to engage in this form of health service. Certainly you will contribute to the improvement of health and welfare of others.

It will not be difficult for you to break into this profession, even though several dental schools still close their doors to women. That prejudice is gradually disappearing, because women dentists have shown that they can qualify for the work. This is particularly true in working with children and in certain phases of preventive treatment, such as gum diseases. There is every reason to believe that you can make a success at dentistry if you are one of the superior young women who has the proper qualifications for this particular job.

The first and foremost qualification is *patience!* That is the outstanding characteristic of every successful dentist and without it you'd be lost. Think of the temperamental, nervous patients you may have and the infinite detail involved in that exciting game of routing bacteria from minute decay spots. No matter what men say about it, women have the reputation of being more patient than their brothers and for liking details better.

An agreeable manner and a cheerful disposition are essential. No one wants to be treated by a grouchy dentist —the ordeal is bad enough without adding insult to injury. Honesty, perseverance, good health, skill in work, an attractive personality, and ability to get along well with others are decided assets. Your character must be above reproach and you'll need good business sense. Last, but far from least, is the matter of punctuality. Try to develop a time sense so that you will not keep your patients waiting. They'll be hard enough to handle anyway, if they are at all nervous; irritability will not help matters.

Graduation from an approved high school with two

years of college work is a minimum requirement for entrance to dental schools. In high school there should be emphasis on subjects which will be helpful in the professional course, such as: chemistry, physics, Latin, biology, English, manual training, and general anatomy.

Here again we hope there is a well-lined purse back of you, because preparation for this profession is about as expensive as that for medicine; probably even more if you consider the charges for use of equipment, the various laboratory fees, and so on. The full course may cost up to $4,000. Moreover, this is another of those strenuous courses that leave little or no time for part-time work which might otherwise help you through financially.

In the dental school the subjects studied will be: anatomy, bacteriology, pathology, pharmacology, oral histology, operative dentistry, biochemistry, physiology, psychopathology, oral prophylaxis, oral surgery, radiology, prosthetic dentistry, crown and bridge work, dental materials, oral diagnosis, oral hygiene and pathology, orthodontia, peridontia, public health work, etc.

The last hurdle before you are actually ready to practice dentistry is obtaining the license which is given after you have passed a rather strict examination. Then comes the problem of equipment. That is, if you are setting up in business for yourself. The cost of equipping a dentist's office has been estimated at from slightly less than $2,000 up to somewhat more than $4,000. If you cannot secure several thousand dollars or, at least, get credit for that amount, with which to purchase the necessary chair, drilling machines, sterilizers, X-ray machines, materials and office supplies, we advise you to start as assistant to an established practitioner or take a salaried position in public service.

And what will you do when you begin to practice? Anyone who has spent time in a dental chair should have some idea of the duties. You probably don't know about that exceedingly important aspect of dentistry—the making of false teeth, crowns and bridges, etc. But you have doubtless had experiences with the operative phase, which includes preparing and filling cavities, treating diseased teeth and gums, extraction, cleaning, straightening teeth, and the like.

Nowadays the preventive work of the dentist is becoming more and more important. You must educate your patients to take proper care of their teeth, to follow prescribed diets, and to come to you for periodical examinations. All this is even more vital than treating the teeth after the damage has been done.

A successful woman dentist told us how she started her practice:

"After graduation from dental school," she explained, "I took a position as assistant to two dentists who had a large practice in my city. During ten years as their assistant, I picked up many points that I had not learned in school and, at the same time, I developed a clientele of my own. When one of my employers died, I became a partner. After the death of the second one, more than 90 per cent of his patients continued with me.

"I believe women are specially good in private practice," she went on. "They have more patience than men and will often do more careful work."

Then she told about one of her patients whose bridgework was admired by another dentist—a man. When the patient explained that the job had been done by a woman dentist, he said:

"I thought so. It's just like a woman to do such fine work. Most men will not take the time."

If you have your own practice, your hours are likely to be irregular and long. It is a temptation to work beyond one's strength if patients insist that they can come only after the hour you should stop. You must be firm, however, and not let your patients run your practice.

Of course, in a salaried position, the hours will be regular—usually about forty hours a week. There will be a vacation of two weeks to a month, or even more if you are in school work.

Positions in large industries and in public school systems are likely to be good berths for the woman who has trained in a dental school. Specialists in dentistry usually earn considerably more than general practitioners. Women do very well who specialize in children's work; in orthodontia, which is the technical term for correction of irregularities; in peridontia, the treatment of tissues around the teeth; or in public health work. Other fields in dentistry are: dental mechanics (now largely dominated by men), research, and teaching. We might add, however, that there are very few women teaching in dental schools.

As in all branches of health work, the field of public health is the most promising in salaried dental positions, particularly in the Federal Service. You may secure a list of opportunities in Federal Service which will give you an idea of what you may expect if you attempt one of the civil service examinations for the U. S. Public Health Service or for any other government agency. Civil Service positions are open to women dentists in the Veterans

Administration and in the Indian Field Service.

One of the chief advantages of this profession for women is the fact that marriage is not a drawback to success. It is one of the few careers which has this advantage. The married woman dentist can have her office in her home where she can keep an eye on the maid and the children. Furthermore, she can fit her working hours fairly well to the needs of the family.

Interesting contacts with all kinds of people add to the attractiveness of dentistry as a profession, as well as the satisfaction of relieving pain and helping people toward healthier, happier lives.

The long hours of hard work at the chair are likely to be a strain on the nerves, along with the difficulties of dealing with nervous, fussy patients. The lack of confidence in women that is still evident in some places is annoying and there may be other petty drawbacks such as difficulty in making collections of fees, and the like.

According to a bulletin from the Women's Bureau in Washington, the outlook for women dentists "is good in the face of an increasing demand for service and a waning supply of trained personnel." In this bulletin it is pointed out that "women dentists seem to agree that they are apt to be too busy rather than not busy enough. There is no evidence that they fared badly even in depression years. For the young woman with a pleasing personality who combines intelligence with mechanical ability and dexterity, who likes science, and who can relate cause and effect, dentistry offers a promising career. Added to these basic qualifications, she should have enough business sense to manage an office or enough teaching ability to like the educational aspects of public health work."

5. DENTAL HYGIENISTS

BEFORE THE GAY NINETIES, dentists usually did all their work themselves. Just before the beginning of the twentieth century, however, the busiest dentists hired men called dental mechanics to help make dental plates, crowns, and bridges. Soon they found that women could help them in the cleaning of teeth—dental prophylaxis is the official title of that type of work. According to the U. S. Women's Bureau, "By 1913, the demands for women for this work had grown and a training course for them was opened in Bridgeport, Connecticut. In 1915, Connecticut became the first state to pass a law permitting the issuance of a license to practice dental hygiene. Today, there are many schools which offer recognized training for dental hygienists and all states, except Texas, New Mexico and Virginia, the District of Columbia and Hawaii have laws regulating their practice."

Soon, too, instruction in care of the teeth became a part of a dental hygienist's job. There has long been a need for teachers of dental hygiene in both cities and rural communities. Instructors are needed, as well, to give talks to school children, mothers' clubs, industrial employees, and in private and municipal dispensaries.

Suppose we see what the Pennsylvania state law relating to dental hygienists states:

A "Dental Hygienist" is one who is legally licensed as such . . . to remove tartar deposits, accretions, and stains from

DENTAL HYGIENISTS

the exposed surfaces of the teeth and directly beneath the free margin of the gums, in the office of a dentist or any public or private institutions such as schools, hospitals, orphan asylums, and sanitariums or state health cars, but under the general supervision of a licensed and registered dentist, and not otherwise, and who does not perform any other operation or work on the teeth, jaws, gums or mouth whatever.

The field of the dental hygienist has two general divisions: the teaching of mouth hygiene in public and private schools and in public health work; and the prophylactic treatment of the teeth of patients in hospitals, public institutions and in private dental offices under the supervision of a licensed dentist.

A bulletin from the University of Pennsylvania School for Dental Hygienists, at time of writing, insists that "the demand for the services of the dental hygienist is in excess of the supply, and it is likely to increase rapidly in the next few years. The nature of the work and the opportunities for profitable and useful employment offer many attractions."

In this school the course is open to women only and the number admitted is limited. Any woman of good moral character, who is able to present evidence of completion of an approved high school course including the requirements for admission to the University of Pennsylvania, is eligible to apply. In addition to a detailed list of all preliminary studies and description of these, an applicant must secure three letters affirming her good character.

What about other qualifications, training, and duties (in addition to those mentioned above) of the dental hygienists in the various fields? First of all, be sure that you have perfect teeth yourself before you undertake this work. You will need them to advertise your work. And you must be neat, cheerful, resourceful, intelligent, quick-witted, efficient, have a high degree of manual dexterity and willingness to work hard. You will be required to do just that. An attractive personality is an essential to success and you will need poise and assurance, particularly if you go into school work or the public health field. Lectures and frequent public appearances require those traits.

So much for qualifications. Next comes training. This is one of the few fields where you can secure technical training immediately after graduation from high school. The length of the course is two years. It includes: anatomy and physiology, dental anatomy laboratory, dental histology and embryology, dental chemistry, dental bacteriology, dental assisting, dental hygiene and prophylaxis, public speaking, essay writing, sociology, child hygiene, community dentistry, nutrition and hygiene, laboratory assisting, first aid and nursing ethics, dental pathology, dental pharmacology, child psychology, dental radiology, surgical assisting, and anesthesia.

In the School of Dentistry at the University of Pennsylvania, two post-graduate courses are given for dental hygienists: a six weeks' course in the combined Schools of Dentistry and Education is offered for the graduate dental hygienist who desires additional credit toward a degree, and a one-week refresher course for the graduate dental hygienist who wishes to bring herself up-to-date in her particular work.

Because of an increasing demand for the dental hygienist in the field of education, the School of Education at the University of Pennsylvania, in co-operation with the School of Dentistry, offers combined courses leading to the degrees of Bachelor of Science and Master of Science. These courses are organized to prepare the dental hygienist to qualify for teaching Dental Hygiene in the public schools and institutions of higher learning.

At time of writing, estimated expenses at the University of Pennsylvania Dental School for the would-be dental hygienist are $1,289 for the first year and $1,174 the second. There are available in the school a number of interneships for graduate dental hygienists, from any school, who desire advanced work and study.

There will be opportunities for you in four lines of work: school hygiene, public health work, in the private dental office, or in industry. The school hygienist gives prophylactic treatments to every school child and recommends needed treatment from the dentist. She encourages proper care of the teeth through toothbrush drills, teaches the proper use of foods, and gives lectures to pupils and parent groups.

The dental hygienist in state public health work may have similar duties in teaching dental hygiene to the inmates of various state institutions. This work is likely to be nerve-racking if it is in a mental hospital or reformatory. A well-balanced personality and excellent poise will be needed to carry one through the trying situations which may arise. Nervous, timid girls should stay far away from such work.

The dental hygienist in the private dental office may do all sorts of odds and ends in addition to her regular duties in prophylaxis. She makes appointments, suggests diets, assists at the chair, makes examinations, trains in the care of teeth, and may act as office girl in taking care of the business details of the dentist's practice. Very frequently she will be required to soothe a frightened child and then she will need all the tact and resourcefulness at her command.

Dental hygiene is making headway in industry as well, which may give employment to more and more dental hygienists. The duties here are examining the mouths of employees, noting infections, charting cavities, giving prophylactic treatments, and teaching the proper care of the teeth.

There are also positions in hospitals and other clinics where the duties are similar to those of the school or public health hygienist. Colleges and universities are also establishing dental hygiene clinics in the interest of student health.

You will never make a fortune as a dental hygienist. Nevertheless, this is one of those satisfying phases of health work which will give you joy in helping to prevent disease and suffering. Moreover, you'll enjoy the contacts with people. There will be a sense of security, too, in a school or government position. Fairly good placement service in the dental hygiene schools is a decided advantage, and will mean even more if overcrowding should occur. Every dental hygienist must pass a state board examination before she is granted a license to practice.

On the other hand, you may run into unpleasant situations caused by the ignorance and prejudice of older workers who have not yet been converted to the idea of preventive work. Occasionally working conditions may be very bad and you may have unpleasant experiences with unruly patients in hospitals or institutions. You may become discouraged when people fail to follow up your work with the recommended visits to the dentist or continue their careless and unsanitary habits.

Although there seem to be few opportunities for advancement in this profession, we have heard of one woman who made an outstanding success in teaching dental hygiene. She became director of a training school and was so thorough in her teaching that many of her students went out to take similar positions as heads of other training schools. Here, as in every occupation, there *is* room at the top for the superior person.

6. OSTEOPATHS, OPTICAL WORKERS, VETERINARIANS

OSTEOPATHY IS ONE of the healing arts which has been growing steadily during recent years and offers an excellent field for women. The fundamental principles on which osteopathic diagnosis and treatment are based were announced in 1874 by Dr. Andrew Still, the founder of this type of therapy. We quote from a vocational study issued by the American Osteopathic Association:

The osteopathic physician and surgeon acts upon the principle that the human body is a living machine which, given wholesome physical and mental environment, good food and water, proper exercise and pure air, will be healthy just as long as all the inter-related parts of this mechanism remain in proper adjustment. When a derangement in such perfection of adjustment is produced, the osteopathic physician searches out and corrects the maladjustment if it is possible to do so. With such correction, normal health generally results.

Just as the osteopathic physician adds all other known methods of diagnosis to his own particular skill in finding mechanical body derangement, so he adds other proved methods of treatment to his peculiar ability to correct those mechanical difficulties.

Osteopathy cannot properly be called, and it never was, a drugless school of healing. A thorough course in pharmacology is a part of the osteopathic curriculum.

In many states, the osteopath may give and prescribe drugs, do minor and major surgery, practice gynecology, psychiatry, or any other specialty. She has the same legal standing as a medical doctor.

In spite of the apparent need of great strength, women are exceedingly successful in this field. By using the patients' weight skillfully, corrections can be carried out with a small expenditure of energy; hence it is not a rigorous profession.

Dr. Beryl Goodman, a successful local osteopath, points out that "this is a career which combines well with marriage and children. The office can be in the home, patients can be taken by appointment only, and the waking hours of small children left free so that the mother need not miss her baby's play hours."

The requirements for entrance into a school of osteopathy are a minimum of two years of college work in an approved college of arts and sciences, or its equivalent, with specified courses in English, physics, biology, and chemistry. All accepted students must be legally authorized to begin the study of osteopathy by the state in which the college is registered. In addition, they must obtain a pre-professional qualifying certificate in the state in which they wish to practice after graduation. Since the individual states have different standards of preliminary education, it is advisable that all students study the laws of their states concerning professional education, including the requirements of the State Boards. In some states, the osteopath takes the same State Board examination as students of medicine. Others have a combined board—still others have separate boards.

Dr. Goodman insists that prime requisites include: "a genuine desire to help one's fellow man, true love of humanity, compassion, understanding, ability to reason from cause to effect, and a skillful combination of physical senses and intelligence. However, the six or seven years spent in training are well worth while to the woman who loves her work and, if she doesn't love it, she should choose another occupation."

The standard four-year curriculum in osteopathic colleges includes many courses in anatomy, physiology, chemistry, pathology and bacteriology, supplementary therapeutics, hygiene and sanitation, public health, practice of osteopathy and osteopathic therapeutics, surgery, obstetrics, and gynecology. Student loan funds are available for upperclassmen who need assistance and who have shown peculiar aptitude for this type of therapy. Graduates will face a stiff examination in order to secure a license to practice.

As in medicine the osteopathic physician may undertake general practice in town or city, or may become a specialist in surgery, obstetrics, orthopedics, diseases of women, mental and nervous diseases, etc. After the first few lean years—which may be less than for the medical practitioner—a skillful osteopath is likely to earn a comfortable income.

This phase of the healing arts offers special opportunity to the blind since sensitive, trained fingers are of prime importance. Read Lela T. Brown's *Osteopathy, Opportunities for the Blind in Training and Practice.* This is available from the American Foundation for the Blind.

Guardians of our eye health are oculists, optometrists, opticians and optical mechanics who combine forces for the correction of visual defects. The outlook for work in the optical field is usually very good. In fact, you should take several long looks at the opportunities here for service and good employment. Training requirements for the various phases of the work differ as to the time required for preparation, the amount of study demanded, and the skills you will need.

The oculist or opthalmologist is a medical doctor who has majored as a graduate student in the anatomy and diseases of the eye and is licensed to give drugs and perform operations. Eight or nine years of study after high school are required, plus a year's interneship, before the "eye doctor" may practice. The oculist is also trained to examine eyes. He—or she—determines the needed prescription for glasses and refers the patient to an optician. At time of writing there are a number of women in this field.

An optometrist examines the eyes to find out whether glasses are necessary, and, if so, prepares the proper prescription. This optical worker's training includes laboratory work in the optical mechanical field, so that the optometrist frequently supplies the glasses from his own prescription. In a large business, he is more likely to examine the eyes, write the prescription and let optical mechanics make the glasses. Many qualified optometrists have opened their own establishments. Others prefer paid jobs at optical centers.

A four-year course in a college of optometry is required. In the Pennsylvania State College of Optometry in Philadelphia courses include physics, chemistry, anatomy, physiology, pathology, psychology and kindred subjects as well as those in the technical field. One year of approved college courses is required for entrance.

The optometrist must be excellent in science, have a mechanical bent, an attractive appearance and manner, sales ability, and tact in large amounts. Women are often very successful in this field. Details about this work may be secured free from *Optometry*, issued by the American Optometric Association, 518 Wilmac Building, Minneapolis, Minn. Examine also catalogues of colleges of optometry.

The optician is an optical technician who has added to his knowledge through experience or study. He takes measurements, assists in the choice of a suitable frame for glasses, and adjusts the finished pair. He makes glasses according to prescription. Often he sets up his own business and either does his own technical work or employs workers to do it. A successful optician of many years' experience advises prospective opticians to take optical mechanical courses in preparation for this work. You should get in touch with the nearest office of the Guild of Prescription Opticians for developments concerning post-high-school training.

The optical mechanic is the technician who constructs optical instruments and appliances. He makes glasses and lenses according to prescription. A three-year course in optical mechanics is given at Bok Vocational-Technical School in Philadelphia and similar courses are available elsewhere. Training includes surface grinding, bench work and dispensing. High mechanical ability is needed for this work. The optical mechanic must be careful and painstaking. These workers are employed chiefly in wholesale houses and by opticians who have their own workrooms for making and mounting lenses.

There should be increasing opportunities for women as optical workers because of their success in working with children. Recent emphasis in schools on correction of eye strain will undoubtedly add to the chances for women who decide to become either oculists, optometrists, or opticians.

Are you a cat and dog lover? Then you might find a good career as a woman veterinarian since there is a definite shortage of graduate V.M.D.s in the United States. Fondness for animals is not all you need, however. You should have a knack with all animals—especially small ones—a keen mind and a decided bent for scientific subjects. Ability to get along well with people is as important as popularity with animals. After all, the people, not their pets, foot the bills.

There is also the hurdle of meeting strict entrance requirements of a school of veterinary medicine—and we mean STRICT! We know a young man who had top scholastic standing in his college but failed to make the grade for one of these schools. At the University of Pennsylvania School of Veterinary Medicine all applications are reviewed *comparatively* by a Committee on Admissions. This committee will take a small number of women if they are well prepared and have a good background of adaptability.

"Why only a small number of women?" may be your question, as it was ours.

A fair reply to this question came from the dean of the school. "Our women graduates usually marry in a short time," he told us, "and some do not go on with their work. Others are not physically adapted to all phases of the work and cannot work all hours of the day and night as well as men. All these facts must be kept in mind by the committee when students are selected. I believe sincerely that there is a definite place for women in veterinary medicine with many outlets for their talents, but we have to consider their future contribution when choosing students on a comparative basis."

In the catalogue of this school are the following admission requirements:

A candidate who has received a degree from a recognized college will be considered for admission without examination provided he has covered the required subjects listed below. He may be given credit for subjects he has studied which are comparable to similar subjects given in this school which are not used for entrance credits.

The completion of not less than two full years of work at a college or university approved by the Association of American Colleges and Universities or by one of the regional associations, totaling at least 60 credit hours, and in addition physical education or Military Science is required for admission. The two years of college work must include the following subjects: English, general inorganic chemistry, organic chemistry, physics (including a laboratory course), general zoology, general botany, social science, and electives to complete the total of 60 credit hours.

The catalogue states also that "the first-year class is limited to fifty students selected by a faculty Committee on Admissions. In making selections consideration is given the following: academic preparation, character, personality, and general fitness and adaptability for veterinary medicine. Before final selection, qualified applicants are ordinarily requested to appear for a personal interview."

After admission, you must conquer many difficult courses, such as: anatomy, histology, physiological chemistry, botany, genetics, physiology, bacteriology, general pathology, histopathology, special pathology, medicine, pharmacology, immunology, obstetrics, meat and milk hygiene, radiology, and many other special subjects peculiar to this profession. In addition, are clinical orientation courses, work in the clinics, hospital service, and the like to occupy the rest of your time. You are reminded in the catalogue that your time will be so well occupied that there will be little or no opportunity for earning part of your college expenses. The degree of Doctor of Veterinary Medicine will be conferred on you after you complete the course successfully.

Among opportunities open to graduates of veterinary schools are positions in government service—especially in the U. S. Department of Agriculture—and in state public health work as meat and food inspectors, tuberculin testers, and the like. Inoculation and vaccination of animals to prevent diseases are important phases of a veterinarian's work.

The average V.M.D. is apt to choose the phase of work which she can do best, e.g., work with small animals. Only the exceptional woman will be successful in large animal practice.

Teaching is a field that offers opportunities for the exceptionally brilliant woman V.M.D. Our dean told us about one of his graduates who continued her studies after graduation until she won a Ph.D. degree. At the time of our interview, this young woman held the post of an associate professor in bacteriology on his own staff. Another graduate teaches physiology. There may be teaching positions, as well, in pathology, pharmacology, microscopy, and other veterinary subjects. There are also many female technologists and other research workers in laboratories who have graduated from veterinary schools. Some of the best research opportunities are with biological firms which supply vaccines, anti-toxins, and the like. In fact, all phases of research are promising fields for women V.M.D.s.

In large cities, the operation of a cat and dog hospital may be a fine opportunity for the woman veterinarian to start a business of her own. She may soon earn a substantial income if she gains a reputation for successful treatment of family pets. In small animals practice, the "feminine touch" will usually count heavily in favor of women veterinarians.

"The average client with a sick animal thinks a woman will be more gentle than a man with her pet," commented the dean.

A well-paying phase of this profession may be in boarding and caring for pets while owners are away from home. If you choose a good location for such a venture, there should be small danger of failure. Nevertheless, it might be advisable to try yourself out as an attendant or assistant in one of these hospitals before you open one yourself.

One young woman veterinarian we know combines this

boarding pets with her regular private practice. When we asked her how she happened to choose this profession, she replied that she had made her decision while still in high school, chiefly because she had learned to love all animals on the farm she had visited as a youngster. Later, she had helped in kennels—and always had pets of her own.

"I planned for college and veterinary school while I was still in high school," she said. "I got catalogues from four veterinary schools and took science courses and others that were listed as pre-requisites for entrance. Even so, I got stuck because I had used an old catalogue as my guide and missed a new requirement course. They let me take it during summer session, however."

After graduation from veterinary school, this young woman became a resident veterinarian in a hospital for two years. Although this was not required, she had the opportunity and felt that she learned a lot because there she came up against all the "tough stuff" that one would be likely to meet in the profession. Then she went into private practice in which she has been so successful that she is interested in finding a place in the country where she can expand her work.

"I can board only cats here," she said, "because they are quiet and my close neighbors do not object to them. I want to do more with dogs, though," she added as she looked proudly at two pets which she was preparing to enter in a dog show.

"Any job in kennels or in any phase of work directly with the animals has a lot of dirty work in it," she went on. "We have to mop up our own messes most of the time. It's not just 'walking a dog.' One girl wanted to know if she would have to look at blood. I told her she would not only look at blood but spill a lot herself if she did any surgery. We meet a lot of nice people, though—and some not so nice. It's amazing how often pets take after owners —nervous pets of nervous owners are hard to treat."

7. PHYSICAL AND OCCUPATIONAL THERAPISTS

IF YOU ARE INTERESTED in being a "Guardian of Health," take several looks at the growing fields of Physical and Occupational Therapy. Physical therapy includes hydrotherapy, electrotherapy, and massage. This work is helpful in correcting physical difficulties through the use of special massage, exercises, electricity, sun lamps, and underwater exercises.

Trained physical therapists are employed in hospitals and as private practitioners to carry out the prescriptions of physicians. Among the qualifications necessary are patience and perseverance, tact, sympathy, a desire to heal, and the ability to convince people of the value of the work. Thorough training is vitally important and to this end a certificate in physical therapy is required of every registered physical therapist. A number of universities give certificate courses in this field as part of four years' college work in connection with training in physical education.

Minimum requirements for entrance to a standard course in a school for training physical therapists—as approved by the American Medical Association—are: graduation from an accredited school of nursing, *or* graduation from an accredited school of physical education, *or* two years or sixty semester hours of college including courses in biology and other sciences.

According to the *American Registry of Physical Therapy Technicians*, the demand for physical therapists has always exceeded the supply. One reason for this is that many young graduates marry and retire from practice after only a few years of service. The rate of withdrawal due to age and death is also increasing. A third reason is the demand of the Armed Forces and veterans' hospitals where one technician to every 100 patients is employed in the general medical and T.B. hospitals and double that number in neuropsychiatric hospitals. In many of our veterans' hospitals, physical therapy treatments are given to out-patients to cut down on hospitalization.

Civilian needs are growing daily—chiefly because of industrial injuries. We are told that "insurance statistics have shown that adequate physical therapy reduces the period of disability and puts a man back to work without the handicap of stiff joints and weakened muscles, thereby not only rehabilitating the workman but saving industry the costs of compensation for longer or complete disability."

As improvements are made in methods and in equipment, more and more physicians supplement their treatments with physical therapy. Especially is this the case with orthopedic physicians. Expanding civilian rehabilitation and crippled-children programs, in which states are aided by Federal funds, also have encouraged the use of physical therapy in the rehabilitation of adults and children. The clinical and laboratory research of the National Foundation for Infantile Paralysis has found that prompt physical-therapy treatments are of great value in poliomyelitis. The demand for technicians to treat cases early and in epidemic areas accentuated the acute shortage of physical therapists during recent years.

These are the special influences that are tending to increase the need for physical therapists. They promise an interesting future for the young woman who is healthy, emotionally mature, interested in science (especially in biology and physics), and who has acquired or will acquire a college background in physical education or in the biological sciences as a basis for or combined with her physical-therapy courses in an approved school.

You will have strenuous work if you choose this field, but technicians who like it become so absorbed they scarcely realize how hard they are working. It is enough for them if, through their efforts, helpless arms, legs, or muscles anywhere in their patients' bodies, are restored to use again.

There are excellent opportunities as well in the field of occupational therapy. Here, you should have artistic ability, especially in handicrafts, and you must have the best possible training for this type of remedial work. This work is one of the "Guardians of Health" which is recognized by the medical profession "as a valuable adjunct in contributing to and hastening recovery from disease or injury."

In this field you must be trained to help patients in such creative arts as bookbinding, metalcrafts, pottery, weaving, and woodworking. Recreational activities which you will direct will include dramatics, gardening, music, and sports.

And you are likely to have patients who want to study shorthand, typing, radio assembling, and the like. There may likewise be reading and study groups under your supervision, lecture courses, and possibly correspondence courses.

Through any of these activities interest, courage, and confidence will be aroused in the patients, mind and body will be exercised in an effort to overcome disability and to re-establish their capacity for industrial and social usefulness. Muscle strength will be increased and general bodily health improved at the same time that the patients' mental attitudes are improved through pre-vocational studies and training, or through purely avocational projects.

Until World War I, comparatively little attention had been given to occupational therapy, but the splendid work of the occupational therapy aides in military and veterans' hospitals, in both world wars, proved its value. Particularly in mental hospitals has its worth been demonstrated. Almost invariably an improvement will be noticed if an apathetic patient or one who constantly listens to hallucinations becomes interested in making a basket, in weaving a scarf or rug, or perhaps in just hammering out his pent-up feelings on a piece of brass in the occupational therapy shop.

Training in social service, nursing, physical education, recreational and educational activities, and psychology are desirable in addition to the required study in arts and crafts. Considerable hospital practice training is demanded as well. Poise and common sense, diplomacy, and tact are essential, especially in mental institutions. You must know how to deal with an unbalanced mind firmly yet gently enough that you will not arouse antagonism. No weakling or timid person will be permitted to consider occu-

PHYSICAL AND OCCUPATIONAL THERAPISTS 55

pational therapy. Imagine such a person locked in a violent ward of an institution.

Employment may be in Armed Forces, or veterans' hospitals, in state and private hospitals, in public health departments, in schools for crippled children, blind and deaf, feebleminded, in homes for the aged, in community curative workshops, or with private patients. Salaries are rather small although they are improving as people realize the tremendous importance of this type of work in helping the handicapped, and particularly in assisting in the rehabilitation of mental patients. Beyond any monetary rewards will be the satisfaction of taking part in a splendid phase of health work.

"It is by no means a dull occupation," explained Professor Wanda A. Mistach of Ohio State University. "In my own experience I had the privilege of being 'imported' by the government hospital board of Venezuela to organize an occupational therapy department in their psychiatric hospital. It was a challenging two years' experience. Therapists are now going to Puerto Rico and Hawaii, and the Canadian association reports requests for trained workers in New Zealand and South Africa, so the possibilities are really international.

"The challenging aspect of this profession today is in its very infancy, and in the vast opportunity for expansion which it offers. As a direct aid in the rehabilitation of the war wounded it has a tremendous field to cover.

"In helping straighten the crooked bodies of little children, helping them develop into straight-thinking, capable and self-sufficient citizens who will be an asset rather than a liability in the world to come, the boundaries are still untouched."

II
Women Who Mean Business

8. CLERICAL WORKERS

WHAT DOES CLERICAL work offer as a possible career? Now, that is a question! We defy any human being to answer it satisfactorily. There's too much of the human element and, perhaps, a good deal of luck involved. Clerical work may be a blind alley or it may be the point from which you can climb to heights that would be out of reach in any other field. Frances Maule, in her book *The Road to Anywhere*, paints a rosy kind of picture as she describes the way an office job can lead you almost anywhere you want to go.

Miss Maule tells you how you can become a successful secretary or an office executive, make a success in high finance, or get a start in advertising, newspaper, magazine, and other publishing work, usually through stenography or other office work as an entering wedge. She recognizes the danger of entering a blind alley, but in her opinion office work is the field that probably holds the greatest number of possibilities for women, if not the *highest* possibilities.

But—wait a minute! How will you get on that "Road to Anywhere" to attain those highest possibilities? Ambition is of first importance. If your idea in seeking an office job is just to mark time until you marry, you may find yourself marooned in one of those dreaded blind alleys. You'll get nowhere in clerical work unless you are genuinely interested in the job itself and are willing to give full value to it, at least during working hours. Among the many qualifications required for success are: speed, tact, patience, application to duties, good hearing, understanding, memory, punctuality, neatness, cheerfulness and courtesy, ability to follow directions, a sense of responsibility, skill in operating business machines, intelligence, good health, and good mental training.

In some of the minor positions such as errand girl, receptionist, or mail clerk, you will need less education or specialized training than for other office work. That is, if you have the necessary qualifications and the ability to learn quickly on the job. These positions are occasionally filled by girls who have not even been to high school, but employers usually look with disfavor on anyone who is not a high school graduate. Such positions are likely to be blind alley jobs unless you go to night school for a high school or business course.

A few offices accept girls without high school diplomas for stenographic positions if they have ranked high in a business course and do exceptionally well on performance tests. It is generally conceded, however, that you can't go far in any business without at least a high school education.

In many high schools and vocational schools you may take a business course at the time you are acquiring that precious high school diploma. And in many cities you may take a co-operative business education program such as the one given in the Philadelphia Public High and Vocational-Technical Schools. Here's how that program works:

First the students learn. In the tenth and eleventh years, students take the fundamentals of business education, bookkeeping, typing, general clerical practice including filing, and a general introduction to clerical occupations. Some students take shorthand and, of course, they all take English and other general subjects required for graduation.

Then they apply their knowledge. In the senior year, students are placed in actual jobs where they can apply their knowledge and skill. Satisfactory work experience is then accepted for credit toward graduation, which means that diplomas given to students of Co-operative Business Education certify not only completion of certain courses, but also ability to apply successfully what has been learned.

The interesting feature about this program is the "alternating week plan." Students spend a full week at work, then a full week in school. Two "co-op" students working alternate weeks provide the employer with service equivalent to that of a full-time employee. And there is a teacher-co-ordinator who teaches and supervises these students. This person devotes four periods a day to the instruction of the in-school group and uses the remaining time for following up the out-of-school group at their places of employment. Teachers visit employers primarily to check the work progress of students and to secure comments and suggestions from employers which keep them up-to-date on business methods.

Down North Carolina way—in Greensboro's high school —we had an opportunity to watch such a program in action. Here carefully selected students are prepared for jobs in the city's business offices, stores, and factories, spending half of the day in school and the other half at work—about five hours of work per day. The purpose of these classes is to give students actual experience in the occupations of their choice while they are still in high school.

Nearly 100 per cent of these students keep their jobs when they graduate and are ready for permanent, full-time work. In fact, many Greensboro firms hold jobs open waiting for Diversified Occupations-Distributive Education students. Canny employment managers have discovered the superior quality of these young people. Moreover, surveys show that graduates of these classes have progressed to such jobs as private secretaries, personnel directors, skilled mechanics, store managers.

"Diversified" is indeed the right word for these classes. During the Greensboro visit, the writers talked to a number of girls who were doing their part-time work in a wide variety of places. One girl, for example, acts as general secretary for a firm of engineers—typing from dictation, operating the varityper and other office machines.

"I like my work," said this teen-ager, "even though dictation is difficult on account of the technical terms. I believe, though, that I'd like to have a civil service job after I graduate."

Another girl, working with the Merchants Association, does general office work—typing, filing, preparing credit reports for stores, and helping on a weekly bulletin issued by the Association.

"I have wanted to be a private secretary ever since I

was in the third grade," was the surprising statement of a bright-faced girl. "I know that will mean hard work, but the harder I have to work the better I like it. My part-time job is with Burlington Mills where I started in the purchasing department filing invoices and orders. After four months there, they sent me to the stenographic pool where I have learned all types of office work. Now I have a permanent job with the head of the department. One of the things I like best about the D.O.-D.E. classes is that they teach us how to get along with people. I'll need that if I become a private secretary."

"I do general office work for a motor finance company," said the next girl, "typing contracts for loans, posting daily payments and ledger sheets, and typing letters. I enjoy my work because of the variety in it and hope I can stay right there as long as I need to work."

There are many other ways of obtaining training which will help you get your start in an office. After graduation from high school, you might consider the possibility of two years in a junior college before taking a course in a private business school. There are many fine business schools which give one- or two-year courses for high school or junior college graduates—and for graduates of full four-year college courses too. There is also the possibility of taking a regular four-year course in business administration at a university. If you are aiming at an office management position or wish to become an executive secretary, you will be wise to secure all the education and business training your purse will stand. The trend is undoubtedly toward higher educational requirements for jobs in high places.

So many clerical occupations are open to the girl of today that we wondered how we could describe them all for you. Perhaps the best way to begin is by having a look at a girl who is entering office work in a large industry. Unless she is an exceptional person with years of experience and training, she may be assigned first to the company's central typing bureau or "pool." What a noisy and busy place this generally is! Everything that can be sent here for typing, mimeographing, or duplicating by other means, is likely to be in process at the same time. Typewriters clicking, office machines buzzing, and always the telephone ringing as one after another in the company pleads for a typist, a stenographer, a file clerk, or just a handy girl to help move things around in the office. A new girl may be sent to one office for a few hours, then to another, every day of her working week until a full-time vacancy occurs which she can fill.

Much depends on the impression a girl makes in the various places she works. Some girls stay in a pool weeks, months, or years while others pop right into good jobs with chances to climb to higher jobs. This happened to a girl we know. During her first three days with the company, she was just one of the "pool" girls—wearing out her shoes and feet going from office to office and building to building, hour after hour, until the gong sounded at the end of the day. Soon, though, it was discovered that she was a good enough typist to be kept at a typewriter in the pool. Then she had a chance to fill in for a girl who had been called away from her job in the office of the head of the firm. Luckily for our young lady, the regular girl did not return and, by that time, the "Big Boss" had discovered the substitute's ability and refused to let her go. WARNING —that sort of opportunity is RARE; but it *can* happen.

If you are not expert at the typewriter or office machines,

you will have a chance to become expert if you can endure the noise and confusion of the "pool" until you acquire the desired facility. The head of the "pool" is usually eager to have his girls transferred to other departments in the organization where they will have opportunities to win promotion.

Now—a look at several other types of jobs that you may secure when you are ready to step into the business world.

The receptionist is more important in business than many outsiders realize. She must be tactful, pleasant, and very resourceful as she sorts out all the individuals who approach her desk in a single day. She may also—in fact, usually does—act as switchboard operator as well.

The mail clerk has an exceedingly important task, even though it may be low in the wage scale. Accuracy is a first requisite for this work. How easily an inaccurate mail clerk could bring disaster to an organization by mixing up the mail or misdirecting an important letter that was vital at the moment! Ability to operate an addressograph and a thorough knowledge of postal regulations will be part of a mail clerk's equipment.

File clerks, too, play a significant part in the business office. Think how a busy executive will rave and tear his hair if an all-important document is lost through poor filing. Here, too, accuracy is a "must."

A stenographer's job is to take dictation and transcribe it accurately. Maybe you think that sounds easy, but it is not always as easy as it sounds. Suppose you are required to take dictation from an impatient person who mutters indistinctly or races like a fire engine. Will you dare interrupt if you miss a word? It may cost you your job if you do. You will need careful training to meet such emergencies.

Furthermore, you can't let your mind wander even for a moment. You'll be lost unless you pay strict attention.

In an office, the stenographer is constantly at the beck and call of her employer. Her only hope of getting out of that routine is in being promoted to the position of private secretary to an executive of the firm or in becoming an office manager. At this point we'd like to warn you that many large organizations are establishing central stenographic "pools," such as we described, instead of supplying private secretaries for each bigwig in the firm. This cuts down the number of openings and possibilities for promotion in the stenographic field and is likely to make the work less pleasant. Yet right there you may have a chance to become chief of this very group at almost an executive's rate of pay. There are compensations in every situation.

There is always the possibility of starting a business of your own and becoming a public stenographer in a hotel, office or apartment building, public library, or other public institution where emergency calls may come for stenographic work. A public stenographer has independence but may have to pay for it in lack of security and small chance for advancement. On the other hand, you may build up such a large clientele that you will need a corps of assistants and will not have to do any of the actual typing yourself.

In these days of mechanical appliances, the woman who is an excellent typist but not so clever at shorthand may be in demand. Think of the dictating machines, the mimeograph and multigraph machines, that require only expert typists or transcribers. Of course you must be quick, neat, and accurate to succeed in this work. Accuracy is equally important in the operation of machines such as the addressograph, graphotype, teletype, and the key punch machine which can, in a single operation, record the date, the salesman's number, the goods he has sold, and the price. The widespread use of these office machines has created a demand for trained operators which is likely to continue. Even though the machines seem almost human, they lack that prime necessity—a brain—which we hope you can supply if you want an office job. The increased number of reports required by the government during recent years have been one of the major causes of the demand for operators of these machines.

Among the important office openings are positions in accounting and bookkeeping. Don't turn up your nose at them, either, because they may lead to other good positions in the research or statistical phases of a large organization. Women have limited opportunity as Certified Public Accountants but they are fairly successful as bookkeepers and accountants in business offices.

If you want to be a successful accountant, you might start as a cashier, become a bookkeeper, and, while holding these jobs, train for the demanding job of accountant. Only a distinct type of woman, though, will find joy in these figuring jobs. She should have mathematical ability plus, an analytical mind and should love details, details and then more DETAILS.

For topflight jobs in accounting you will need college courses in such subjects as finance, commercial correspondence, business psychology, business law, statistics, mathematics, logic, economics, sales promotion and courses in accounting itself.

Here are some of the accounting jobs in a big industry: accountant, accounting clerk, auditor, cost analyst, billing clerk, operator of various machines, and statistician. In all

CLERICAL WORKERS

these fields there are positions in junior, intermediate, and senior grades. This will give you steps to climb from year to year. There are jobs, too, as billing clerk, billing-machine operator, bookkeeping-machine operator, cost clerk, key-card punch operator, payroll clerk, shop timekeeper, tabulating-machine operator, and statistical clerk.

The head of plant accounting in one large industry pointed out that there is a trend toward elimination of pure clerical operations by humans. At time of writing, huge machines make mechanical punch-card summaries of accounting information. One of these machines and ten people may be used instead of as many as 150 clerks and supervisors prior to installation of the machine. This trend indicates, in this man's opinion, that there will be a demand for more highly specialized accountants and fewer in the lower types of jobs.

This man also insists that women are not generally successful in this field. He admits, however, that when "one does find a competent woman accountant, she is often superior to most men. Such women are few and far between," he added ungraciously. This difference of opinion should warn you that if you aim at this type of work you'll have to be *good*. And your superiority will come from a knack with figures, a thorough knowledge of business law, and the techniques of the job. Moreover, you must have a super-head for business. Bookkeeping and accounting are occupations that require you to keep up-to-date almost as much as fashions, because here you will find constantly changing styles in machines. If you don't watch out, those machines will snatch your job away almost before you know what's happening. And yet there is a good demand for key-driven calculating machines, so you can learn to operate one of them if your job disappears.

Shorthand reporting may be a fine berth for a woman who has the right qualifications. These are, in addition to all the other qualifications we've mentioned in this chapter, exceptionally keen perception, prompt co-ordination of hand and brain, as well as an especially high degree of speed, accuracy, honesty, and integrity. In fact, one authority on this subject believes that no one can be a satisfactory shorthand reporter until she has had at least ten years' experience. In the old days, before there were so many conventions and meetings, the shorthand reporter had the title of court reporter because he was chiefly engaged in taking testimony of court proceedings. This worker has the difficult task of taking down a word-for-word report of discussions at conventions, board meetings, conferences, lawsuits, etc. This is one of the highest paid phases of stenographic work.

Women face keen competition in this field, particularly in reporting court proceedings. Many judges refuse to permit women court reporters to take testimony in their courts. But with the phenomenal increase in conventions and other meetings, more and more opportunities for women are likely to develop. Rapid reporters who can operate the stenotype machine are in constant demand and it is a demand that is more than likely to continue. At large public meetings, or even many of the smaller private ones, you will see the stenotypist busily pecking away at her little machine.

If a young stenographer does not follow the path of promotion to private or executive secretary, she may climb to the position of office manager. Here she will handle less actual detail work but she will have the responsibility of keeping all the office workers up to standard and seeing that the work is done quickly and efficiently. There must be a sympathetic understanding between the manager and her workers or the work will surely suffer. Certainly the ability to work with people and to get them to work with you is of primary importance in any office management position.

Today there are fine opportunities in civil service for well-trained office workers. Examinations are given at frequent intervals for federal, state, and city positions. But you will need to be expert to win out in them. These examinations are highly competitive and only the best prepared and best equipped workers are eventually appointed to civil service positions. Typing skill is exceedingly important and you must have a thorough knowledge of arithmetic, grammar, vocabulary, spelling, and filing. The kinds of positions available are: junior accountant, junior bookkeeper, senior bookkeeper, bookkeeping machine operator, calculating machine operator, general clerk, mimeograph operator, junior stenographer-clerk, senior stenographer-clerk, junior typist-clerk, and senior typist-clerk. Chapter 34 on Government Workers gives additional information on this type of work.

9. SECRETARIES

MOST OF US are willing to admit that the private secretary is the aristocrat of office workers. That is, if she happens to be the secretary of an important official of a large firm. She'll probably have an office of her own and chances to meet the great and the near-great who come to do business with "the boss." There's an even chance that some of these interesting visitors will realize that this young lady is the power behind the throne and will treat her with respect and deference.

However, don't waste your time training for secretarial work unless you are ambitious to go beyond that type of work. It can be almost as much a blind alley job as any other office position. Furthermore, if you lack ambition to get ahead, you'll probably not have a vital interest in what you are doing.

But ambition is far from being the only requisite for success in secetarial work. In their book, *Analysis of Secretarial Duties and Traits*, Dr. W. W. Charters and Miss Whitley list forty-six traits which a secretary needs. Although there are many such lists available, most of them shorter, we think this one is important enough to quote in full. Don't think we are doing it to scare you out of attempting to break into the field. Not at all! It's because you really should know what to shoot at in developing yourself for your career as a secretary.

The traits are arranged according to their relative importance in the opinion of the employers who answered a questionnaire sent out by Dr. Charters and Miss Whitley. Here they are: "accuracy, responsibility, dependability, intelligence, courtesy, initiative, judgment, tact, personal pleasantness, personal appearance, interest in work, speed, reticence, adaptability, businesslikeness, neatness, memory, good breeding, poise, self-confidence, graciousness, honesty, health, industriousness, executive ability, loyalty, a pleasant voice, orderliness, grooming, alertness, drive, ambition, curiosity, forcefulness, foresight, thoughtfulness, willingness, modesty, originality, patience, resourcefulness, self-control, versatility, fairness, self-respect, self-interest." If you can make a good grade on most of those points and can acquire the education, technical skill, and training that are necessary, we'll wager a large sum that you will be a great success in any secretarial job, or in any higher position beyond.

Suppose you are one of the rare girls who rates exceptionally high on this list of traits—what's the next step? Training and education. High school graduation will admit you to most of the good business schools but a college education will give you an advantage, particularly if you are aiming at an executive position. Often a college graduate will not be as successful in a business firm as the girl who has had only business training beyond high school, but that is usually due to the character and capacity of the individual.

One of the chief values which you may receive from college is learning how to get along well with others. Maybe you won't learn self-control in your classes, but wait until your classmates have finished with you. You'll learn how to get along with them, or else. And what girl wants to be shunned by her college mates?

If you're wise, you'll learn stenography and typewriting before you go to college or the university. There may be opportunities for part-time work while you are studying, and these skills will be most useful as well in your own academic work.

A careful examination of any secretary's manual or handbook will give you an inkling of the kind of work you will do. A successful woman secretary says: "The private secretary is one who knows as much about her employer's business as her chief does. She can shoulder responsibility; she must be able to transact the business without her chief and she must have good judgment. She needs a working knowledge of bookkeeping, filing, general office work. She must be more or less her chief's right-hand man; she must be able to dictate letters as well as write them so that they will be a credit to herself and her chief."

The book, *Analysis of Secretarial Duties and Traits*, lists 871 duties reported by secretaries who had actually performed these duties. We shall not attempt to quote the entire number—that list of traits was enough for one chapter—but the eleven main headings under which they were grouped will give you an excellent picture of a secretary's possible activities: mail; dictation; transcription; typewriting from copy or notes; filing, indexing, and cataloguing; telephone and telegram; editorial duties; duties involving meeting and handling people; financial; clerical; and miscellaneous.

There are many opportunities for the right kind of girl with good secretarial training and experience. Even when the field grows overcrowded, many employment managers insist that although there are many girls clamoring for jobs, there is really an inadequate supply of intelligent, well-educated, competent workers with attractive personalities. And here you won't meet much competition from men.

Take the advice of Frances Maule in her *Road to Anywhere* and be ready to advance into something better in advertising, high finance, publicity, publishing, newspaper or magazine work, or into a radio or an executive position. Above all, develop a specialty. Glance at the want ads in the daily paper and you'll discover the demands. Almost any day you will find calls for legal stenographers or secretaries trained in various other special lines.

Perhaps you think you'd like to be a social secretary. If you have a good cultural and social background, you may accomplish more as a social secretary than in regular office work. It all depends on the activities of the employer. If the lady is interested only in parties, balls, teas, and other social affairs, the secretary's job may become exceedingly monotonous and irksome. On the other hand, if the secretary is employed by a philanthropist or the wife of an important government official, there is no limit to the excitement and interest she may find. But there are chances of facing more exasperating situations here than in any other phase of secretarial work. Did you see or read the play *First Lady?* The secretary in that play worked all hours of the day and night. Furthermore, she had to be little less than a saint to keep her temper when her employer upset all the carefully laid plans for an official banquet or luncheon. If you want to be a social secretary, be sure to make the acquaintance of our guide and counselor, Emily Post. And then, use your head! Every minute you are on the job!

Another secretarial field is that of executive secretary. "She is essentially an American development," said Katherine Starbuck of Skidmore College, "an outgrowth of highly organized industry and business and the rapid growth of membership organizations in this country." Think of the various boards, clubs, and organizations that you know about! Most of the large ones employ paid secretaries to attend to the administrative problems of the organizations. And the salaries are usually good; occasionally they may even be called handsome. Of course the positions with the handsome salaries—and by that we mean upwards of ten thousand a year—are few and far between. For this work you will need tact in abundance, as well as executive ability, good judgment, and good health if a great deal of travel is involved in the job. Naturally you need most of the other traits listed by Dr. Charters, as well.

What does the executive secretary do? When she is secretary for a board of directors she must do all the work in preparation for meetings. Everything must be in readiness so that the board can have a complete picture of the business to be transacted and can make decisions without too much mental effort. Often the secretary is the real power behind the throne in settling important matters and it is therefore essential that she be both mature and wise.

"In membership organizations," Miss Starbuck said, "the executive secretary is the liaison officer between the directors and the members. She must interpret the one group to the other and make both groups realize that they are co-operating in the work of the organization. In industry this co-ordination is necessary between the directors and the workers and is no less important." The present trend toward less autocratic direction of both business and membership organizations demands that the executive secretary understand the new technique of conference, group discussion, and other methods for more general participation. When a firm has ten thousand stockholders and seven thousand employees, there is great need for a broad democratic board as a go-between. What a job for the executive secretary of such a business! Never would anyone begrudge him or her that handsome salary.

The secretary who trains herself in a special field will go places. For example: learn the vocabulary of science, medicine, law, real estate, insurance, or engineering and you'll increase your chances tremendously. Better still, learn the science itself, or at least the rudiments, and college professors or research workers will snap you up. You may then get a chance to work into the field itself. Ability to read, speak, or write a foreign language will have the same effect—especially in these days of American business expansion in countries "south of the border" and in other faraway places.

The chief advantages of secretarial work are opportunity for advancement, pleasant working conditions, and the chance of meeting interesting people. Another advantage —one that may not last, however—is the fact that you may find a position here straight from a high school business course. If you can't afford education beyond high school, you may earn a college degree with the aid of your secretarial training. And there are fine placement services for securing jobs in this field. Jobs there will always be as girls leave for homemaking and young men move on to the executive positions.

10. SALESWOMEN

"ONE OUT OF every five Philadelphians is employed in retailing" is a surprising statement in a pamphlet issued by the Philadelphia Board of Education. It is even more surprising to read that not enough students in the "Quaker City" are preparing seriously for this *one-out-of-five* occupation.

This is a field in which women can and do give men a run for their money. There are certain divisions where men predominate but, taken as a whole, women hold the major number of jobs; and the delightful feature is that approximately 50 per cent of the executives in most department stores are women.

Suppose we discuss first the opportunities in department stores and then take up the specialty stores such as: book shops, five-and-tens, women's apparel shops, gift shops, and the like. If working in a large department store looks attractive to you, consider that: "More people do more widely differing types of junior executive jobs than in any other businesses; any skill or talent you have may be used to advantage in some sort of store job, because of the many kinds of opportunities there; promotion for you may be a step-up in the same department, or to an entirely different type of work because of some particular ability you have shown; increased effort is rewarded by addition to one's salary in the form of commissions. Discounts on merchandise purchased by you add to your wages."

SALESWOMEN

At an occupational conference, the personnel director of New York's largest store told us that the major function of a department store is to act as a central purchasing agent for the community—securing a broad cross section of commodities, setting prices, and distributing to the customers. He gave a clear picture of department store organization by referring to a chart done in bright colors which presented the four major divisions in the organization. First was the merchandise division—colored bright green which gave the idea of fresh fields to conquer; then the finance division done, ironically enough, "in the red"; the publicity division was colored a drab gray; and finally came the all-important management division—colored brown. This is the division which co-ordinates all the others and is in charge of building maintenance and all personnel matters.

"Suppose we think of these divisions in terms of a theatrical organization," our speaker went on. "The people in the merchandise division are the ones out in front, the actors who speak the lines. Finance and publicity sell the tickets and bring in the audiences, while the management —well, we attend to the props and all that, then stand behind the scenes and get the glory."

In the merchandise division, girls and women are far in excess of men. Moreover, here is where they have opportunities to become executives more than in the other three divisions. They may rise to such positions as buyers, assistant-buyers, stylists, department managers, merchandise counselors, or might even become the head of all merchandise work. The reason for this was pointed out by our speaker—"Almost nine-tenths of a department store's customers are women and most of the commodities sold are used primarily by women; therefore the merchandising executives must understand women's viewpoints." He stressed this point because the department managers in merchandising act not only as purchasing agents for these women customers but they try to anticipate needs and create tastes for commodities that will actually raise the living standards of a community.

In the finance division there is less opportunity for women. Certainly the top position of store treasurer is not likely to be held by a woman except perhaps in an all-woman store. The store economist, an important individual, who acts as adviser on market trends, is usually a man, but women may find opportunities in the department of statistics and research or in the credit department.

The publicity division may offer many openings to women who have the right kind of training and ability. You may have to start in a clerical position, but you might easily step from that into proofreading or copywriting, and eventually work up to be advertising manager, promotion manager, or head of the advertising department. If you have art training and ability, you may do layout work or become a staff artist. It is a difficult but exciting phase of department store work.

The majority of positions in that all-important management division are usually pre-empted by men, although women have been found in practically all positions, except perhaps as truck drivers. Certainly they are playing an active part in the personnel departments. First of all, there is a general manager in charge of the entire store, then the assistant manager, and the sales service manager who supervises all adjustments, shifts clerks, is in charge of the packing service, etc. There is a manager of nonsales service which includes the receiving and stocking of goods, setting prices, and supervising the delivery fleet (unless a united parcel delivery service is used). And, of course, there is a manager in charge of store maintenance —the elevators, the electric plant, warehouse, etc. Mostly men's jobs, these, except in war years.

In the personnel department there is a department manager, a manager in charge of training, one who has general supervision of the personnel and another who supervises all non-executives. Women are particularly successful in the training and welfare phases of the personnel division, as we shall point out in a later chapter. (See Chapter 12.)

In any phase of department store work, there are certain personal qualifications necessary to success. The ideal saleswoman will quickly learn the stock in her department and will become vitally interested in everything and in every person connected with her work. Instead of dragging herself toward a customer with more interest in her hair and fingernails than in making a sale, she will move quickly and, with a pleasant welcoming look, will greet the prospective purchaser as cordially as a guest in her own home. Above all, this saleswoman will know where things are back of her counter, in order to save the time of her customer.

This model saleswoman must always be dressed exactly right for her job—in simple good taste. In a small city, especially, she will try to memorize bits of information about customers. Certainly a vital interest in people will help any aspiring saleswoman toward success and at the same time give her the satisfaction of being helpful to others.

Even in a large city store you can train yourself to discover people's needs by using all your intelligence and wit. A deep interest in people, interest in work, plus vigor which is based on perfect health will take you far in department store selling. And you must have that everlasting ability to get along with others to the *n*th degree.

A high school education is extremely important. If your own high school has classes in *distributive education* by all means enroll at the earliest possible moment. There you will get intensive training both in school and on the job and will be guided into the right kind of job and then carefully supervised by the teacher-co-ordinator and by the employer. It will be possible to earn several hundred dollars while in school and, as a graduate, you will be ready for a full-time job with a head start toward advancement in an organization that knows and likes you.

Suppose we see how one of our great states gives this type of training. We quote from *The Ohio Plan of Distributive Education:*

> For the most part, established programs in Ohio are using the plan of time distribution whereby the student attends classes for a half day, usually in the morning, and works a half day at his place of employment. The vocational classes are ordinarily organized for seniors, and vary from two to four subjects.
>
> A minimum of 15 hours' employment per calendar week is required of the co-operative part-time student in the distributive occupation for which he is being trained. Total employment time will, of course, not exceed the requirements of state law or educational policy.

Later in this publication we are told that "part-time employed students will receive for their working hours a monetary rate comparable to that paid other junior employees."

One of the excellent features of this Ohio plan is its promotion of Future Retailer Clubs for the Distributive Education students. These clubs have many advantages and benefits, such as: Developing student pride in his own organization, raising the level of students entering the program, promoting good relationships between employer and employee, providing opportunities for social life among students of like interests, developing civic consciousness and respect for the responsibilities of citizenship through community projects, increasing vocational knowledge through field trips to stores, factories, etc. Club members broaden their contacts, too, when they attend local, area, and national conventions of the Distributive Education Clubs of America.

At Georgia State College for Women in Milledgeville, there are Distributive Education courses on the college level that have become enormously popular with both students and employers. Although any student may choose this course she must be successful in a basic try-out course else she will be advised to select another major field.

According to the college catalogue: "This program is built primarily to satisfy the needs of those students who are interested in some phases of merchandising. It provides a background for employment in department stores and other merchandising establishments. It also provides for employment in the state office for distributive education and for teaching distributive education in high schools."

Some store experience is required of all students who major in distributive education at Georgia State College for Women. At least one quarter of such work should precede their senior year. Here are subjects these girls study as freshmen: English, social science, health, biology, art, education, distributive education (that basic try-out course previously mentioned), and physical education. Those who didn't fall by the wayside take English, humanities, social science, chemistry, physics, home economics, distributive education, and physical education in their sophomore year. As juniors, they study economics, education, art, secretarial training, mathematics, and take several courses in distributive education. This subject is emphasized again in the senior year, in addition to general business and art. In this final year students are allowed five elective courses.

Especially interesting in this college is a display laboratory where students learn how to prepare window, cabinet, and other displays of merchandise. For a display window there are standing and sitting figures of women and a small child. Glass cabinet counters and wall cabinets hold all kinds of merchandise arranged attractively by the students. Most interesting of all are blueprint plans which the girls draw for a mythical store. Merchandise for these displays is often borrowed from local merchants.

"All seniors were placed by May first, last year," was the pleased report of the head of the Business Administration Department. "Moreover, most of the girls had at least three positions to choose from. Thirty-five dollars a week was the minimum salary for those who became store employees. All of them were hired for a trial period or in a training squad and then received junior executive ratings as assistant buyers, personnel workers, or in advertising display work. Most of them, however, took straight selling jobs which they prefer for the per cent they receive on sales. Actually we could have placed five times more graduates than we supplied last year."

Many of the graduates from colleges like this take one- or two-year graduate courses in one of the excellent graduate retail training schools elsewhere.

Department stores offer fine opportunities to girls if they are willing to start at the bottom and are not too impatient for promotion. This is really a woman's world with not too much competition from men except for the highest executive positions. Even so, a large per cent of the executives in most department stores is women.

Successful experience in one store will equip you for finding a similar position in almost any part of the country —or a better one in your own city. Good saleswomen, buyers, and executives are always spotted by other stores.

Many of the largest department stores in our great cities are glad to take on bright young college graduates and put them through their own training schools with the idea of developing heads of departments and executives who can represent the firm creditably.

We have not said much about the particular duties of workers in all these divisions of department store work. However, most of them are so familiar to every consumer that it is hardly necessary to give details. We know that the salesclerk sells, the wrappers wrap, buyers buy goods for the others to sell, and the managers manage. On the other hand, there are some positions that may not be familiar— such as: telephone order clerk, stylist, comparison shopper, and some of the other non-selling work, such as educational director and personnel worker.

There is more to the job of telephone order clerk than merely answering calls of customers who wish to shop by telephone. This worker is often expected to phone customers and suggest merchandise that might appeal to them. And sometimes she takes complaints, makes adjustments, and acts as a general information clerk.

The stylist has an extremely responsible position in a department store. She must predict which of the newest fashions will catch the customers' fancy and for how long. Much of her work is with the publicity division in "pushing" the fashions she has advised the buyers to purchase. She must watch the best-dressed visitors at restaurants, the opera-goers, the women with the snappiest sports clothes at the fashionable horse-races, tennis matches, football games, or other sports events. And she will haunt teas and hotel lobbies before she is ready to appraise the buyers' selections or help them choose new merchandise. Hours of study must be given to magazines and newspapers, to gather the information she must pass on to the publicity and selling departments.

A comparison shopper is exactly what the name implies. She is employed by one department store to compare its prices with the prices and quality of goods in the stores of competitors. Each morning she is given a list of assignments and twenty-five to fifty dollars which she may spend on commodities which should be brought to the store for comparison. Out she goes, trying to be as inconspicuous as possible so that clerks in the other stores will not suspect her purpose and hide the day's choicest bargain. It takes a clever girl to get away with this job and all too frequently the position will be short-lived. Her usefulness is ended when her identity is discovered. A certain maturity is required for this work and with this must be an exceptionally strong physique. If a morning of shopping wears you out, don't fix your ambition on this kind of job. Selling experience is usually required, especially when the quality of goods is being compared. Certainly you are unlikely to achieve instant success such as that of the heroine in a short story, who not only did impossibly well with no experience but later married the boss.

Sometimes the comparison shopper may have the duty of shopping in her own store to check on the efficiency of the clerks. But here again the work may be short-lived because secrecy cannot be maintained long.

The personal shopper is another type of worker in the largest department stores. She assists individual customers in making selections for purchase. We might mention, in passing, that a comparison or personal shopper may build up an independent business accompanying inexperienced people on their shopping trips and assisting in the selection of clothes, household furnishings, and the like. Usually she charges the customer a small fee and may receive commissions from the stores.

The duties of educational directors and personnel workers will be described in the chapter on Personnel Workers in Business and Industry, Chapter 13.

Suppose we turn now to several other phases of retail store selling, particularly in the kinds of stores where girls find their greatest opportunities. One of the best fields outside a department store is in a women's apparel shop selling ready-to-wear clothes, hats, accessories, etc. Naturally women have the edge on men in these positions, even though ownership is rather evenly divided and the highest executive positions are frequently pre-empted by men except in the woman-owned shops.

High school education is desirable and college as well

—or at least a business course—if your aim is ownership. A person who likes independence may become the store owner of tomorrow. The choice is wide. You may use your talents to develop a store which specializes in sporting goods, or dresses, or you might like hardware, or books, or shoes. Then there is children's clothing, and photographers' supplies, and gifts, and a thousand and one other lines of merchandise that customers want. You are your own employer—you manage people, buy merchandise, and your job is as big as you choose to make it. Through store ownership you may become a leader in your community.

Although your aim may be to own a shop, you should start at the bottom and learn the business from the ground up. Begin as stock-girl or marker, then try selling, and go on to buying and managerial work. In this work a style-sense is absolutely essential and also the same kind of personality and ability we described as necessary for department store selling.

The president of a great New York women's store told, in a luncheon address, of her early poverty and how she longed for beautiful clothes. She attributes her success to the fact that this gave her the desire to see that other women got beautiful clothes of the kind that had been denied her. She has executive ability in large quantities, of course, and that keen business sense which is quite as essential as the other qualities we mentioned.

Modeling may offer you a chance in an exclusive dress shop, if you have a perfect figure, a good carriage, and know how to wear clothes. It's tiresome work and furthermore it may be seasonal unless you can fill in with employment as a part-time model in a commercial studio or for an artist who specializes in advertising women's wear.

Chain stores have increased rapidly in the women's apparel field, and you may find an opportunity for advancement in one of them. The successful saleswoman or buyer in one store will be in line for promotion to similar positions in larger stores of the chain and finally may become manager of a store. Or she may be made supervisor or district manager of a number of stores. There is always the possibility of reaching an executive position in the headquarters office.

Good saleswomen can usually find a place in the five-and-tens or in the variety chain stores. In the early days of these stores younger girls were hired as salesclerks but had jobs that were not much more than wrapping and packaging. Today, since this type of store handles a larger and more expensive type of merchandise women with experience in retail selling are preferred—with consequent increase in pay and in prospects for advancement. Although not many women become store managers, a woman who can operate office machines, type well, or is clever with pen or pencil may progress to an office position or work in the advertising department. In our local Woolworth store employees work 44 hours a week although 48 hours are permitted by law. Work here must be pleasant as openings are few and far between.

Book shop operation can be one of the most fascinating of all selling work. In some ways it is even more satisfying than library work because you'll have the feeling that you are getting "the right book and the right person together" permanently.

College training is almost essential in this field of selling. However, if a girl has grown up in an atmosphere of books, she'll probably be a success even though she never entered a college classroom. Certainly she'll do better than the college graduate who breezed through her courses with little or no appreciation of books and literature. Although you must know books in order to sell them, you must also have some retail selling training and experience, as well as all the other qualifications we've mentioned as requisites for success in department store selling.

Often a gift or art shop is combined with a book shop. Both appeal to the same kind of clientele, the person who loves literary and artistic things, and who usually has the means to satisfy his tastes. The person who sells gifts must be eternally on the lookout for unique and attractive objects which will appeal to the person who is looking for an unusual gift for a person "who has everything." In either a combined book and gift shop or a gift shop alone, the sales person must be unusually gracious and intelligent. Perhaps the day will pass with no sales at all and yet she must still be sweet and courteous to the person who ambles around, fingering everything, dipping into a book here and there, and then wanders out. A certain amount of dignity is exceedingly important. Sometimes the owner of an art shop will think it clever to be arty and may go too far. There are always the ultra-conservatives who may be offended by too much art atmosphere, or too much of the hail-fellow-well-met type of treatment.

Earnings are exceedingly variable in the book and gift shop phase of retail selling; so much depends upon location, amount of competition, the character of the community, etc.

A woman in "outside"—or "away from the counter"—selling must be a super saleswoman to meet strong competition not only from men but from other "Lady Drummers" as well. She must have boundless vitality and perfect health to stand up under the strain of constant travel. Attractive, well-groomed appearance, poise, and a never-failing courteous manner are musts for her. Mental alertness coupled with womanly intuition will enable her to beat her competitors in developing a paying list of customers for the line of goods she is selling. Force, interest in people, tact, initiative, industriousness, and just plain horse sense are other qualities that will help a traveling saleswoman to master her profession.

What education and training is needed for this type of selling? Fortunately for the girls who cannot afford college educations, this is a lucrative field where a great deal of academic training is not vitally important. That is, unless you expect to deal with such commodities as books, educational materials, or services such as life insurance and investments. Many of the great salesmen who have become powers in the business world have been self-made men. Often they had no more than a grade school education or a few years in high school. However, we are again insisting that if you can afford it you should go to college and study for your special vocation. Nowadays it is only the exceptional person who reaches the highest executive positions without a degree.

For a selling career, the best courses to pursue in college are: psychology, economics, commercial law, distribution, marketing, banking, sociology, finance, and special courses in salesmanship and sales management if they are available. If you have had only the liberal arts course in college, you may supplement it with a correspondence course or get the training in the organization for which you will be selling.

We are not surprised if you are perplexed about what phase of selling you want to invade; there are so many different branches. For convenience, suppose we divide them into the two large fields of selling: *services* and *commodities*. Under *services* there are three important subdivisions: insurance, securities and investments, and real estate.

Life insurance underwriting is a field of great promise for women. In a radio broadcast on the subject, a successful woman underwriter said, "At the end of each month and year, there is the feeling that estates have been created through your activity; that dependents will be comfortable because of your initiative; that people who meet adverse circumstances will have financial reserves because of your forethought; that people who reach retirement age will have guaranteed incomes which they never would have had if you had not shown them how, and urged them to action."

In addition to selling policies, the agent acts as an insurance counselor to her clients in recommending the best course of action in this important matter. The welfare of the client must always be uppermost in her mind and the amount of her commission should be a secondary consideration. There are opportunities for advancement from the position of insurance agent to supervising and executive positions, and of course there is always the possibility of opening an insurance agency of your own.

Another branch of service selling is investment securities. Especially in the large cities women have fine opportunities to sell investment securities to other women. Here a college course is almost a requirement, as well as a statistical turn of mind. The usual mode of entrance into this field is by doing clerical tasks in an office, taking the firm's special training course if there is one, and perhaps spending some time in the statistical division before stepping forth to persuade people to invest in the securities you are peddling. A great deal of study is necessary for the successful security saleswoman; study of the different securities, the laws, the effects of panics and just ordinary recessions.

The final phase of service selling which we shall discuss is real estate. First of all we'd like to quote a speaker at an Institute on Occupations. She said, "A woman has an easier time getting somewhere in the real estate business than in any other business, unless it is insurance. Sex is not a handicap in selling real estate. A woman who knows her business and has selling ability will be as successful as a man in that line of work. . . . Women understand values as well as men do; in renting and building and selling homes, a woman knows and understands what another woman wants and needs far better than a man does." That is why we frequently find women demonstrators in sample homes; often they are trained home economists who can speak the language of the feminine home buyer as they explain this and that new gadget which is designed to ease the homemaker's burden; the sort of thing that the average man might easily overlook.

It is important for the woman realtor to be familiar with real estate law, banking, and finance—in their relation to real estate. In this branch of selling you may have to enter through a clerical position in a large real estate office, then become a selling or renting agent, and finally you may be able to open your own office or buy a partnership in an established firm. If you have a car and can afford to work for some time without a regular salary, you may become an agent for an established realtor or for a building contractor who is constructing a large number of houses. Here you are likely to work only on commission unless the firm has a policy of allowing advances on commissions for future sales. Of course, there are many side lines such as the demonstrator mentioned above, renting in an apartment building, and the like.

The selling of *commodities* is a large subject for discussion. However, to avoid going too far afield, we are confining ourselves to what is termed outside selling.

In outside selling there is house-to-house canvassing as well as selling to dealers. You may not be thrilled by the idea of the house-to-house canvass because of the old prejudices which resulted from the actions of glib, aggressive young men who thought it was a smart trick to put a foot in the door while they forced the housewife to listen. But they belong to a disappearing school of selling. Generally speaking, this branch of selling may not be entirely agreeable but certain phases are not bad. For instance, the saleswoman may find she has something people really want when she starts out with one of the widely advertised custom-made girdles which are not obtainable in any stores. Few doors will be closed in the faces of these young women. In fact, they usually come by appointment and will find a hearty welcome. This is especially true if they are calling on satisfied customers for repeat orders.

The traveling saleswoman is likely to be most successful if she sticks to feminine articles such as: clothing, accessories, millinery, shoes, household appliances, foods, furnishings, and cosmetics. Even so, you can't expect unvarying success. There will always be anxious, nerve-racking moments until each deal has been actually closed.

In selling to dealers, there is no telling what additional duties you may have to perform besides plain selling. Suppose you are introducing a new substitute for lard. If you have had training in home economics you will probably have to run a cooking-school to demonstrate tested recipes which call for the use of your product. Or if you are selling flat silver, luncheons may be given to show the proper use of all pieces from tiny oyster forks to dainty after-dinner coffee spoons. Most of us have heard of, or perhaps attended, one of the famous church luncheons sponsored by firms to demonstrate anything from pots and pans to canned chicken à la king. The saleswoman may have the pleasant job of staging that show.

The traveling saleswoman must be on the alert to give other services, such as helpful hints that will move the goods from dealer's shelves. Women with bright ideas about displays, posters, arrangement of materials, and so on will win friends all along the line. Moreover, they will be assured of a cordial welcome and, best of all, repeat orders when they put in an appearance again.

The earnings of these outside saleswomen depend on the number of sales made. Sometimes they work solely on a commission basis with an advance to draw upon, or they may have a salary and expense account plus commissions. There is always the chance of being promoted to sales manager or to an executive position with the firm.

One of the outstanding advantages of selling is this commission payment plan. You can always increase your earnings—if you have the ability. You will have an opportunity to travel, rather than stay in one place. You can work up to a top-flight sales representative. Saleswomen are really in business for themselves because they are working on their own responsibility and are independent of office hours. The work is usually full of new and interesting experiences and you will have the satisfaction of rendering valuable service to the community. You run no risk caused by investing your own money; that risk is taken by your employer.

On the other hand, you may become discouraged and want to quit before you have built up a paying clientele. There are no nine-to-five shifts in this field and the work may be very hard. Furthermore, if your digestion is weak, selling is no place for you. Irregular and frequently poor meals will surely send you on the way of the dyspeptic.

11. GIRLS AT MACHINES

IF YOU LIKE to work with your hands, you may find just the opening you want in one of the factories that employ chiefly girls. Because the garment industry employs the largest percentage of women, we'll discuss it in considerable detail and give less attention to the other types of factories.

New York is still the center of the garment industry in spite of the number of mills and factories that have moved to the cotton fields of the South and to the Southwest. The power machine operator is in greater demand in the South, however, and further expansion is expected. Girls who have learned to operate power machines might find better openings in the southern factories, or in the Southwest.

Good health is the first essential for the power machine operator because illness usually means loss of pay. When she is paid on a piecework basis, even slight illness will lower her output and that of all the other workers in the progressive line system. In some of the higher positions sick leave with pay may be allowed, but continued absence will result in discharge. Strong, nimble fingers, with no hang-nails to snag the materials, and good eyesight are necessary for this work, as well as good co-ordination. Steady nerves and a good disposition are decided assets.

There are no special educational requirements. A certain degree of intelligence is demanded, but girls with elementary school training may do quite as well as the high school graduate; everything depends upon speed, accuracy, and the other traits required for the work. However, when there are opportunities for advancement to higher positions in this industry or in related fields, the amount of education may be the factor determining how far one may go. In many cities, trade schools and vocational high schools train for the garment industry and other factory positions but the usual method is to learn on the job.

Suppose we tell you what the power machine operator in the garment industry actually does. Each operator sits at a machine built into a movable table. She works on either a number of like pieces, which is called the bundle system, or one set of matched pieces at a time, passing them on to another worker for the next step. This is called the progressive line system and it is extremely important for all workers to co-operate closely. One laggard will slow up the entire process. If anyone is injured or forced to leave her machine, she is replaced by a member of the "flying squadron" which will be described later.

The work of the power machine operator is determined by the kind of machine used and the type of material. There are many kinds of machines such as: stitcher, serger, hemstitcher, taping machine, ruffler, embroidery machine, Zig-Zag machine, shirring machine, buttonhole machine, binding machine, button sewing machine, snap machine, sleeve setter, etc.

There are four types of industries employing power machine operators: manufacturers of boys' and men's clothing, women's and children's clothing, flat work (sheets, bedspreads, pillow cases, etc.), and knit goods (hosiery, sweaters, dresses, suits, underwear, etc.). In the manufacturing of women's and children's clothing there are six divisions: coats and suits, dresses, underwear and negligees, corsets and brassières, cotton garments, infants' and children's wear.

The power machine operator who develops a high degree of skill and who wants to climb may be promoted to the position of assistant forelady, then to forelady, and finally to be superintendent. An operator who has learned how to operate several different machines may be promoted to the position of forelady and be a "pinch hitter" in taking over a machine when the operator is forced to stop work. Or she may become a member of the "flying squadron" which consists of girls who can take over any machine at a moment's notice. The next step in advancement is to become forelady. She must be an exceptionally fine operator and have executive ability and a thorough knowledge of every phase of the work. Her chief duty is to keep the work going at maximum efficiency, to adjust complaints, and supervise the work of her assistants. She is the mediator between the employer and employees and therefore must have tact and intelligence of a high order. Although women are rarely appointed to the position of superintendent of a plant, one who is well-educated and has unusual ability may be appointed. In addition to the plant management, the superintendent orders all the stock materials, makes up payrolls, and employs and dismisses personnel—unless there is a personnel department.

It is by no means true that you are forever bound to your power machine, even though you may not win promotion to one of these supervisory positions. There's always the chance of being transferred into a related field. For instance, there is the pattern grader, the worker who cuts out dress patterns from an original model and alters them for varying sizes. This, however, is a job that is frequently given to men. Or you might be a pattern maker, which is a more difficult job because it involves making the model pattern from an original design. Here the operator with a talent for drawing may cash in on her ability. She may then aim even higher; to a position as designer, which is the highest position in the garment industry. If this girl is a really talented artist and can acquire a thorough knowledge of fashions, the job may eventually be hers. However, special training is almost essential, especially if she aspires to the position of designer for a smart Fifth Avenue shop. This training can be secured in evening schools and extension courses. The designer not only prepares the original design but she must supervise the pattern makers and sample makers, as well as check the cost of the sample garment.

A relatively small number of positions are available for

trained power machine operators as hotel linen-room supervisors, who will be in charge of repairing and altering the hotel linens. Another possibility open to the well-educated girl who is skilled in the use of many types of machines is as an instructor of sewing machine operators in factories, shops, sewing schools, and vocational schools.

The alteration departments of large stores may also offer opportunities to the girl skilled in the use of many kinds of machines. Certainly the increase of ready-made garment buying has developed this phase of garment work, since many women cannot wear the standard sizes without alterations.

This work may be pleasanter than that in a large factory. Maybe there will only be four or five workers in the alteration room—small stores have even fewer—and probably not more than a machine or two will be in constant operation. That would not be as hard on sensitive nerves as a busy stenographic office of a large firm. There is opportunity for promotion here, too. In the larger stores there is usually a forelady or supervisor of the alteration department who is responsible for turning out work as rapidly as possible, who passes on finished garments before they are sent out, and sees that they are properly packed. The power machine operator may also become a fitter if she is properly qualified. Only one drawback may be found—the hours may be longer than in the unionized factories and in rush seasons overtime may be required. Some of the special machines used in the alteration room are: fur sewing, monogramming, hosiery repair, elastic stitcher.

Working conditions are steadily improving in all phases of the garment industry, although there are still far too many instances of unsanitary, uncomfortable, and unhealthy factories. But air conditioning in the modern factory no longer elicits astonished exclamations, any more than it does in movies, restaurants, and department stores. Many of the newer factories have excellent lighting and all the conveniences that add to the comfort of the workers. In plants large enough to have a staff of trained personnel workers to look after the health and well-being of the employees, the working conditions are usually as up-to-date as the newest streamlined train. They will have good lighting, comfortable posture chairs, adequate ventilation, cafeterias, first-aid equipment, and recreational facilities. Happily, the old days of sweat shop factories are rapidly fading away.

Hours in the garment industry are now regulated by law throughout the nation. The forty-hour week is generally in force with Saturday and Sunday free. Work is not always steady in some highly seasonal phases of this industry. Nevertheless, in the higher priced ladies' apparel industry with an average of thirty-five to forty weeks of work a year, earnings of power machine operators are usually much higher than in some factories which have year round employment. The alteration department of department stores and certain types of garment factories do not have a slack season. Legal restrictions in the matter of age limits and health certification are also improving factory working conditions.

There are two ways of starting to work in a garment factory. You may go in as a beginner or apprentice for six or eight weeks and learn on the job, or you may take a training course in power machine operation where you may learn to operate many different types of machines. These courses, which vary in length, may be taken in trade or vocational schools.

In Philadelphia's vocational schools, as in such schools in many large cities, there is a course in power machine operation which offers instruction in the quantity production of women's and children's clothing as it is made in factories. Training is given on all types of machines commonly used in industrial establishments, such as the single-needle, two-needle, Zig-Zag, hemstitching, merrow, buttonhole, shirring and tucking machines. There are also some special attachments for the single-needle machines which are used for specialized processes on garments.

The course includes the making of complete garments such as boys' wash suits, aprons, women's and children's dresses, cooking uniforms, and knit goods. School workrooms are organized, as far as possible, in typical shop manner and work is done according to trade standards. Various materials and their handling and good workroom habits are parts of the course.

In order to qualify for the course, which is planned for a period of one year, an applicant must be over sixteen years of age and must have completed the 8B grade. She must be quick in taking and following directions, since accuracy combined with speed is essential. Manual dexterity is also an important requisite in the trade. Girls with special aptitude for the work often acquire enough skill and experience to be able to qualify for jobs in a shorter period of time.

There are hundreds of manufacturing establishments carrying on a wide variety of work, in which the services of the power machine operator are necessary. There are also custom workrooms which require operators for the more speedy processes on custom-made garments. The operator either works on separate parts of the garment, or, in the better quality garments, she may be responsible for making the entire garment. For most operators, advancement comes with increases in pay resulting from increased efficiency. A few of them may become sample makers or foreladies.

Since wage payment in most factories is on a piece-work basis, earnings depend upon speed and accuracy. However, since the industries in which power machine operators are employed are in large measure engaged in interstate commerce, a fair minimum wage is assured. A five-day week is common in a great many factories.

Among the disadvantages of this work are the minor injuries that are possible, such as needle punctures, blisters and burns, cuts from knives and shears. Eyestrain and nervousness, the confining nature of the work, poor posture due to working in one position, add to the health risks. The seasonal nature of the work in many phases of the industry is also a drawback unless compensated for by higher wage scales while working.

But the industry has advantages too. It is a growing one, particularly in the South and Southwest. Working conditions are generally pleasant, hours are short and wages usually good.

In Dallas, Texas, we had an enlightening interview with an employee of a small blouse-making factory with from thirty to thirty-five girls on its payroll. This girl works from eight until four-thirty five days a week as a special machine operator. She has been trained to operate several different machines, such as tucking, pinking, serging, and covering buttons.

"Guess I'm lucky," she replied to our question about layoffs. "My firm makes blouses from samples and only for orders, so we have no lay-offs. No stock is kept on hand except the samples."

"I like my work," she went on enthusiastically, "because we usually have nice materials and that means more money. Of course, as a special operator, I am on straight time but maybe some day I'll be good enough to go on piece work. Then I'll make the whole blouse and will be paid according to the number I turn out. Our best operators on piece work make $50 to $55 a week, depending on the value of the blouse and the type of work required in manufacturing it."

Other industries which employ women more than men are the textile factories, where conditions are rather similar to those in the garment factories, and the millinery and candy manufactories. The millinery field is one of the very large industries, including millinery factories, stores and wholesale establishments. Four basic kinds of hats are produced and sold—wool, straw, fur, and fabric. The small retail shops produce one-third of the hats in the country.

Jobs in the millinery factories consist of making hats—designing, cutting, sewing, blocking; in straw hats—sewing, shape-blocking, finish blocking; and for all kinds—finishing, trimming, inspection, and shipping. No particular education is required. This is another case of learning on the job, although some preliminary training may be secured in private trade schools or public, technical, or vocational schools—particularly in the larger cities. Typical of such training facilities is the millinery course given in the vocational schools of Philadelphia. Here, we were told,

The object of this course, which is two years in length, is to give the student the fundamental requisites of making hats, irrespective of the particular styles in vogue. School workrooms are arranged in a manner similar to the regular workrooms found in the trade, with steamers, crown blocks, sewing machines, and other necessary equipment.

The student is taught every process necessary to produce a finished hat—cutting, blocking, sewing, and trimming. She learns how to manipulate all kinds of millinery fabrics, to understand their uses and adaptability, and to drape, stitch, and trim the various types. She also learns how to design hats from fashion illustrations in newspapers and magazines, and to copy hats. Hats are made to individual order as well as to stock size.

For the millinery course, girls should have good health and eyesight, aptitude for sewing, and skillful and active hands.

Girls with millinery training work in custom retail shops, drape shops, and factories. They begin work as makers and trimmers. With increased skill they are advanced to the position of draper or copyist. A girl with executive ability may be put in charge of the workroom, while one with artistic ability, originality, and style sense may become a designer. Others, after working as milliners, may open their own shops and go into business for themselves. There are also selling positions for girls with millinery training.

The fact that millinery is a fashion trade may affect employment regularity. However, competent workers are usually steadily employed. Because of the diversity of their training, they may be able to secure employment in the making of novelties or lampshades when the millinery season is slow. Work in the millinery trade is carried on in pleasant surroundings. As in some other trades, earning capacity depends largely upon the ability and initiative of the worker.

Throughout the garment industry, and the needle trades, emphasis is being placed increasingly on training in the operation of various types of machines. There are always jobs for skilled power machine operators and it is therefore highly important to acquire all the skill you can get before you go to work, while you are on the job, and climbing to higher places.

In the confectionery industry there is a fairly bright prospect. This is today one of the nation's greatest industries. There are many flourishing branches of this business in all parts of the country. New improved machinery and low cost of sugar has been responsible for this phenomenal growth. Moreover, dietitians are now pointing out that candy produces energy, if eaten at the proper time and in proper amounts.

Girls have a good chance of securing the ordinary jobs in this industry. Here, as in most factory jobs, you must have finger and manual dexterity. Perfect health is required, as in all food production work. The work may be seasonal and there may be considerable nervous strain during Christmas, Easter, and other rush times. Here men usually hold the supervisory positions, leaving the girls to perform the duties of dippers, wrappers, packers, etc. Occasionally a girl may become a forewoman in a plant—if she is very good. The demand for workers is seasonal here to some extent and there are usually more applicants than openings.

The qualifications required are: good health, cleanliness, neatness, freedom from skin diseases, dexterity. Dippers, particularly, must have a fine sense of touch and nimble fingers. No special education or training is required and the work may be learned on the job very quickly and easily. However, if you want to forge ahead and reach the higher supervisory positions or go into the business or selling end, high school graduation or its equivalent and some business school training are essential. College education will be a great asset for promotion.

In large candy-manufacturing plants there are various

departments such as: gumdrop and marshmallow, cream-center, lozenge, fudge, bonbon, panning, caramel, hard-candy, chocolate-dipping (both machine and hand dipping), and packing departments. Some of the smaller plants may specialize in one branch; this is particularly true of chocolate-dipping.

The forty-hour week with the eight-hour day prevails in most parts of the country. Overtime is usually necessary before Christmas and Easter. Good employees are reasonably sure of steady employment and there are few menaces to health and safety in this industry.

12. THE LADY BOSS

Now, suppose we look at the work of women who become the bosses of the girls at machines—and of other workers in various lines of work. Every ambitious girl wants to attain independence or reach a top post in her occupation. In our chapters on the individual occupations we are pointing out the positions at the top to which you may climb, and are trying to indicate certain specific qualities that will get you there. Always barring misfortune, of course.

"But," you are likely to protest, "everyone can't be boss."

We admit that—but only to a certain point. Suppose you marry—you'll more than likely employ someone at some time to help you in your job of homemaking. Or if you're one of the 25 per cent who don't marry, you're just as likely to become someone's boss. We are mentioning in many chapters the possibility of owning a business of your own, such as a tearoom, beauty shop, an advertising agency, a real estate business, a woman's apparel shop, an insurance agency, a book shop, and so on.

Because conditions are rather discouraging to small businesses, it is difficult for women to make a success of owning their own business. And yet increasing numbers are becoming owners and managers. Ownership and management require a fine personality, a good business head, knowledge of financial matters, and a good reputation. This is one of the situations in which your time is your own, but it's a twenty-four-hour job.

We have described the administrative and executive positions in dozens of occupations and professions. If you reach one of them you'll certainly be in charge of others. If you are a forelady in a factory, a section manager in a department store, or a supervisor for a telephone company you should make yourself the best boss you can possibly be, particularly because you're a woman competing with men in their own domain.

"But *why* because you're a woman?" the feminists will storm.

If for no better reason than to keep people from saying —and men are not the only ones who say it—that women are not good executives. They do say it. Unfortunately it is too frequently true. Not long ago, the head of a big organization was heard to exclaim in a disgusted tone:

"What in time gets into women, anyway? Give 'em a

little power and they start riding rough-shod over every other woman who gets in their way."

Another frank man said that women were not good fellows on their jobs. They are afraid some man is going to take advantage of them and they demand every pound of flesh.

We refuse to admit that women get power-drunk any more than men when they're given authority, but how quickly people pounce on the few women who do become tyrannical, condescending, or just plain high hat. "Isn't that just like a woman?" they shout, gleefully. That's one of the reasons why it's important for you to start right now to train yourself for being a good executive.

But it's not alone to add to the good repute of your sex in business that we hope you'll be the right kind of boss. Think of the people who will be under you and what you can do to or for them. This is not a sermon on how to be your sister's keeper, although there is something to be said for that point of view in business. But we'll stick strictly to the practical end of the matter. It is really good sound common sense to do your best for the workers under you. Cracking a whip is not the way to get efficient work out of people. Far from it. Treating them as human beings is by far the best way to speed up production and quality of work. We could quote you dozens of statements to prove that point.

Although you may now be a long, long way from the goal of the "Lady Boss," you should think about the subject very earnestly. What kind of executive will you be— if and when you get there? Suppose we describe the two distinct types of executives one is sure to encounter in the business and professional world. There are many who possess qualities of both the best and the worst executives, but for our purpose let's contrast the extreme cases.

First of all, we'll describe the power-drunk lady—the autocratic, tyrannical type. Egotism and selfishness are generally her outstanding characteristics. Never will this person willingly share the limelight or privileges of her high office with any of her associates. And she'll be ruthless in riding rough-shod over anyone who gets in her way. She will be intolerant of weakness in others, impatient with minor offenses or errors, and she will probably harbor grudges against individuals who have incurred her displeasure.

Sometimes it seems as if this woman delights in discouraging new employees and in breaking the morale of others. Of if she isn't quite as bad as that, she is likely to stifle the initiative and crush the enthusiasm of youthful workers by nagging or sarcastic reprimands. Rarely will a word of praise come from this type of executive. Perhaps she has driven herself relentlessly to win her position and she attempts to drive others at the same pace. Unfair discrimination in the matter of promotions and salary increases may be expected and she will distrust everyone. Whim and caprice too frequently influence her decisions; her orders are likely to be issued impulsively with no thought of the consequences to others. And she may be moody and emotionally unstable. Rarely will this self-sufficient, all-powerful woman discuss her problems with her associates. In short, this type of executive thinks of her employees only as means to winning glory for her organization and, incidentally, for herself.

At the opposite pole we see the woman executive who thinks of her employees first and foremost as human beings.

She will not be chummy with them in order to discover their troubles, their secret longings, and ambitions. But she'll find out in some way and will do all in her power to help. She will be thoughtful, kind, tolerant, and considerate. But don't think that she'll be an easy mark! She'll be gentle but firm in matters of discipline and simply because she is fair and treats everyone with consideration they'll be constantly on their toes to do their best for her. Tact and good judgment in handling personnel problems will accomplish more in developing efficient, happy workers than carping criticism, fault-finding, and severe disciplinary action.

Let's see how this ideal "lady boss" got that way. Because she had vision, initiative, a generous nature, a real understanding of "why we behave like human beings," insight into the minds of others, and, that most important of all administrative gifts, the ability to induce her employees to work with her and *with each other*. Always the workers will realize that this woman considers them trustworthy and that they can count on her to be loyal to their best interests—perhaps to the point of risking her own position in a crusade against injustice. If at all possible, she will work out a definite program of educational and professional advancement for each individual under her; a program that will make them better workers in their present jobs, that may prepare them for more profitable lines, or will help them toward promotion.

"That's a lady with a halo!" you exclaim, with skepticism written all over your face.

"Sounds like it," we agree. "But we'll wager there are more like her than the unhaloed kind. At any rate we can introduce you to several any time you like."

Our argument is this: it is wise for you to begin this very day to think about the personality you must develop if you want to be a "lady with a halo" boss. If you're still in high school, there will be innumerable opportunities to set yourself on the right path. Form good habits in your relationships with your fellow students and then practice them every day; habits of kindness, thoughtfulness, consideration for others, unselfishness, and so on. If you keep on with these habits, we predict little trouble for you in getting on well with your schoolmates and, later, with your business and professional associates. Then if you ever become a lady boss, you will certainly be the right kind.

Above all, though, try to keep yourself sensitive. The minute you become hardened and insensitive in your dealings with others—off will go that halo! If you allow yourself, perhaps heedlessly, to hurt the feelings of that homely little girl whose clothes are not as nice as the other girls', you may get more and more callous and end up as a dictatorial, hard taskmistress.

When you get to be the owner of a fine shop or become a highly-trained business executive, what are your duties likely to be? First of all, you'll be responsible for everything that is done by the workers under you. It will be your task to see that they perform their duties properly. Whether or not you own the business, you'll be required to look after the maintenance of the property; you'll probably hire and fire the workers under you (a heartbreaking job that can turn your hair gray) and you're likely to be the one to recommend or decide upon promotions (another big headache—or shall we say heartache—for you); working out schedules or, at least, approving the hours of service, the assignment of duties, and the like make up the daily work of the executive.

That's not all. In most occupations, there is at least one organization whose meetings must be attended by the executive and, when feasible, by some of her assistants. This is one of the most important points in the program of professional advancement. She must always be on the watch for new mechanical devices, new ideas, or new techniques that will increase the efficiency of her business or profession. And it is usually at these professional gatherings that she runs across the latest improvements. At the same time, she must keep in mind the duty of training employees in the use of these new machines or techniques, so that they will not lose their jobs because of them.

13. PERSONNEL WORKERS

ONE OF THE leading books on the subject of personnel work tells us that: "Major personnel policies may be defined as that body of principles and rules of conduct that governs the enterprise in its relations with its employees." This indicates that a business establishment, although run primarily for the sake of producing goods such as shoes, or services such as dental work, is not operating efficiently unless it pays attention to the welfare of the persons whom it employs—its *personnel*, a term that has been borrowed from the French.

In order to carry out its personnel objectives, a large firm usually organizes a Department or Division of Personnel. This department is headed by a Personnel Manager, or Director of Personnel. Members of his staff perform the following duties: interviewing and selection of workers; effecting promotions, transfers, discharges and separations; maintaining records on employees; conducting a training program; formulation of policies regarding wages, benefits, etc.; health and safety; employee-service activities; research on all these matters.

These activities have become so complicated and technical that they warrant calling personnel work a profession which requires specific training.

Despite this consideration, we must confess that many persons are doing personnel work in industry without adequate training; they fell into their jobs by accident. At this writing the Bureau of Labor Statistics advises that the immediate outlook for employment in this field is not good. One reason why the field is overcrowded, says the Bureau of Labor Statistics, "is that during World War II many inadequately prepared people gained some experience in personnel work in civilian industries and the armed forces. The number of these partly qualified workers who are seeking jobs now greatly exceeds the number of available openings."

Many owners of businesses do not realize that personnel techniques are specialized and so they think that any pleasant person who has a "knack of handling people" can do the work. It is true that a worker in a personnel department should be one who likes to deal with people, who has what is known as "the human touch." But he needs more.

Since personnel work is recognized as a profession, the aspirant should first be a college graduate who has taken postgraduate training in personnel work, though not many universities give this training. The courses offered in one institution, on a graduate level, are as follows: Principles of Personnel Management; Techniques of Personnel Work; The Psychology of Adjustment; Work Analysis; Vocational Testing; Statistics; Job Evaluation; Motion and Time Study; Safety Work; Industrial Relations.

Pre-professional courses on the undergraduate level should be chosen in psychology (general, experimental, and abnormal), economics, sociology.

One further essential for entrance into the field is work experience. The personnel specialist should at some time have been a worker herself so that she can understand from first-hand contact the problems workers will bring to her. One large manufacturing firm requires everyone who enters its personnel department to first serve a tour of duty in a production job.

The old adage that "a rolling stone gathers no moss" is all wrong for the young woman who would like to become a personnel worker. Roll from job to job as much as you can but try to find a different experience in each one. You have no idea how that will help you when you deal with people who have worked in many phases of business and industry. A variety of experience in your work past will be a decided asset, too, if you want to do research in the personnel field—and a great deal of research needs to be done, especially if a company decides to change its training or educational program, or start new insurance, pension, or sick leave plans. The researchers are likely to be the ones who turn the trick in selling to "top management" any new ideas that will benefit employees.

In addition to the preparation already advised, a woman might prepare herself as a secretary, and through this avenue, begin work in a personnel department. After the manager comes to appreciate her good qualities and learns that she also is trained in personnel techniques, he might place her in a technical position when an opening occurs.

It is estimated that at the present writing about 30,000 persons are employed as personnel workers. About 5,000 of these work in governmental agencies, for almost every large unit of government has a personnel division. Only about 25 per cent of the members of the profession are women. While women have little chance at present of getting top positions in this field, many are employed in interviewing, selection of applicants, testing and research.

The duties of a personnel director may include the employment of workers, attention to their health, development, and general welfare. In a very large concern she may act in an administrative capacity, directing assistants who will divide these duties.

The employment manager, under the personnel director, selects new employees and keeps track of all the old ones. After the person has been employed, someone must see to it that she learns the work thoroughly and speedily; not only that, but keeps on studying and training for higher jobs until the limit of promotional possibilities has been reached. An educational director is usually employed in large organizations to direct this phase of personnel work, unless there are qualified supervisors or section managers who can carry out the program under the direction of the personnel director. There are interviewers, too, who greet applicants and take their application blanks, also file clerks.

Health and safety in business and industry have become so important that safety campaigns are carried on frequently by trained workers under the direction of the personnel manager or by a supervisor who is a specialist in this field. This person may be in charge of insurance plans sponsored by the business, as well as looking after any of the employees who are ill or injured. Psychometrists are often employed to administer and score tests.

If you are the sort of person who does not care to work with people but is interested in fact-finding research, there may be a fine opportunity for you in the personnel department of a large business. Research is playing an increasingly important part in the management of business.

In a large business it is possible to start with a small job, possibly as an interviewer or file clerk, and work into any one of these assistantships; you may even be promoted later on to the position of personnel director.

This work may bring you satisfaction because you are helping others to find more happiness in their work and in their play. In addition to this, your work will probably be in pleasant surroundings and your contacts will be stimulating and agreeable. On the other hand, there may be considerable nervous strain. If your employer happens to be the old-fashioned driver type, the job of acting as mediator between him and the employees may be a difficult one. Furthermore, this is one of those fields in business that is likely to go out the window at the first indication of a depression. When paring begins, the good of the employee may not seem as important as making the wheels turn at the lowest possible cost. Overtime work may occur if the specific duties of the personnel worker have not been clearly defined. She may be called upon to help in almost any activity in the interest of employee welfare. However, this is still a new and growing field where satisfaction in the work may counteract any disadvantages. If you feel that you are fitted for this kind of work, by all means go ahead.

Experience in personnel work in business or industry will give you an excellent background for a job as employment, rehabilitation, or personal counselor with a State Employment Service, with a community agency, or in a private employment agency. Ever since Federal employment service was turned over to the individual states, Uncle Sam has had relatively few openings of this sort—the chief ones now being as vocational adviser or personal counselor with the Veterans Administration, in the personnel divisions of the various government agencies, or in a clerical or administrative type of job in the U. S. Employment Service.

In large cities, you might find the kind of opportunity one young woman of our acquaintance made for herself. During the early days of the war she was assistant employment manager in a large war plant—her duties chiefly with women workers. This experience won for her a position as administrative assistant to the executive director of her city's employment center. After this center closed, the young woman joined two of her masculine co-workers in opening a private employment agency—her job in charge of the women's department.

"I feel that the private employment agency is one of the most effective, established sources for supplying qualified personnel to local business," she told us. "It is also of real service to job seekers because it knows of available job opportunities, knows working conditions and job potentialities of local businesses, and eliminates the frustration of 'cold canvassing' routine—especially for young women who come to large cities in search of jobs. We do not claim that we do more than schools, public or community services in placing girls in jobs—but we do offer another avenue, not only for the job seekers but for employers as well. Through our careful screening process we present a minimum of applicants to employers and thus save the time of busy employment officers. It is really fascinating work."

14. ADVERTISERS

IT IS A GREAT enterprise, this business of helping in the distribution of the world's goods to the world's buyers, and there is good money, as well as plenty of fun and satisfaction for a great many types of workers. Although it is far from true that huge salaries and immense wealth are here merely for the asking, you may well find an excellent means of livelihood in one or another phase of advertising. Think of the amounts annually appropriated by large firms for their magazine, newspaper, radio and television advertising alone—amounts which may range from several hundred thousands up to millions. Why shouldn't you earn a share of that by becoming an advertising manager or his assistant, a copy writer, an art director, research worker, solicitor, space seller, or perhaps by having your own advertising agency? That is, IF you have the necessary qualifications.

Here is a list of those qualifications which was prepared by a group of advertisers who had themselves reached high places: organizing ability, executive ability, knowledge of human nature, originality, mental alertness, facility in expression, imagination, artistic judgment, selling ability, intuition as to human relations, and business sense. Tact, honesty, enthusiasm, and persistence are also essential; persistence is of special importance in the early days when you are trying to break into the work.

"Must I have a college education to get into advertising?" you inquire.

There is less "must" on that point in this profession than in medicine, teaching, librarianship, and the like. A gift for writing effective copy based on original ideas is more important than academic training; but, as we have hinted a few times before, all the education you can afford is the best old age security you can have for any line of work. Some girls have become successful advertising workers with no more than secretarial training. You will hear about one such woman later in this chapter. Others entered by writing a bit of catchy copy for a department store's advertising department. Experience in selling and use of a product has been a starting point for others. However, the special courses in advertising which are given in various schools and colleges will be the best preparation if you are aiming for higher administrative positions. Training in art is required for the person with artistic ability who wants to become an advertising art director, as expensive art jobs cannot be entrusted to novices. The high cost of advertising is the reason why experts are in demand—and why training counts.

If you haven't artistic talent or a flair for writing and you still want to enter advertising, you should take courses in merchandising methods. The business aspects of advertising are chiefly concerned with selling, as you will discover in courses which include such subjects as: psychology of advertising and selling, advertising as a business force, advertising procedures, campaigns, retail and department store advertising, direct mail advertising, the agency, radio, television, and motion picture advertising. Typography, copy writing, and layout work will also be in your training course.

Some advertising techniques can be learned successfully by mail, but you must be exceedingly careful in your choice of a school. As one of the best correspondence schools states in its announcement: "Anyone who has common sense, the power to observe, and the ambition to study, can learn this art of salesmanship-in-print by mail." The method is to teach students to observe correctly from the ad-writer's point of view and to analyze articles and propositions so as to bring out the selling points. Students are trained to write convincingly; to plan advertisements, catalogues, booklets, folders, and other kinds of advertising; to draw up sales plans and campaigns. The significant point in learning any occupation by mail is "ambition to study," for you must be your own taskmaster.

Suppose we survey the advertising field and consider its ramifications. There are several large divisions such as: advertising work with large industrial firms, department store advertising, agency, radio and television, newspaper and magazine advertising, direct mail, and window display. The person who finds a position as advertising manager for a large firm will be on the way to excellent financial rewards.

The duties of an advertising manager in a large manufacturing plant include: conferences with the sales manager, with the head of the agency handling the firm's advertising; making decisions on type, sketches, radio scripts; planning the direct mail advertising; checking on the effectiveness of present methods; and planning work for assistants. The copy writing, layout work, correspondence, and other detailed work will usually be handled by assistants.

In department stores, the work of advertising manager will be similar to that of the manager with a large manufacturer, although here she may be called upon to do more of the copy writing and layout work. It will be her job to decide on effective methods for selling certain items of merchandise, securing illustrations of them, laying out the pages, and seeing that the advertisements appear in the best newspapers and magazines. In the larger cities, department stores frequently send out weekly sheets of special bargains, which is another small chore for the advertising manager in the matter of preparation and distribution. She may be in charge of interior and window displays or fashion shows as well.

A modern advertising agency is one of the most exciting places in the entire world of work. Through the work of this agency, a small business which employs only a few persons may be developed into a national organization with thousands of employees.

Agencies vary in size from those with a mere handful of workers to firms with hundreds of employees—some scattered all over the world as foreign representatives. Work in an advertising agency will be in pleasant surroundings since it must have up-to-date offices and equipment as its means of silent advertising. Here you may start at the bottom and work up, beginning in a clerical or even in an unskilled position and studying in evening classes to prepare for higher positions in one of the varied departments in a large agency. You may be in the copy department, the art department, the research, the mechanical production, or the purchase department.

In advertising agencies professional workers plan and arrange the details of advertising campaigns, estimate appropriations, secure space in the proper media, prepare advertisements and send them to the publisher at the proper time. New accounts are solicited by account executives who also supervise the advertising prepared for established accounts.

If you have an idea of one day starting an agency of your own, it would be wise to try for a position in one of the smaller advertising agencies where you can learn all phases of the business quicker; how newspaper, magazine, mail, radio and television advertising are handled. In a small agency with a small staff you would have a better chance to gain an over-all picture of the business, and to secure training and experience as copywriter, layout worker, salesman, and research worker.

Radio and television, newspaper, and magazine advertising are large fields that provide an ever increasing number of opportunities—radio and television especially. Most of the radio and television programs are for advertising purposes, which means big business to advertising managers who arrange for those programs, to the salesman or contact man who sells the time, and to all others involved. Count these programs in your own newspaper and think of the bill for talent alone and of the total bill for network advertising programs. Chapter 29 on Radio and Television Workers will give you information concerning work in the advertising phase of these fields.

Newspaper and magazine advertising offer possibilities in copy writing, art work, or selling. The advertising sellers call on all types of advertisers and agencies to sell advertising space, or they may concentrate on certain kinds of accounts such as automobile retailers, department stores, or places of entertainment. They prepare data on their publication, such as the number and educational or income level of their readers. They also map campaigns, suggest ideas to advertisers, and write copy.

Direct mail advertising includes all sorts of jobs from getting out huge catalogues of well-known mail order houses down to short sales and follow-up letters, small folders, and brochures. Here the person will succeed who can condense information that would fill two sheets of typewriter paper to fit a penny postcard.

Window display advertising is another important phase that has openings for many types of workers, particularly in connection with displays of large manufacturers that are sent out to merchants. Artists design the cutouts and other items necessary to fill a large store window; lithographers reproduce the work of the artist. The person who installs the display may be the store owner himself or the employee of a window display agency which has taken the contract to install the displays for a large campaign. This latter phase of advertising can be a good business of one's own, although it can be quite hazardous at a time when business lags. Here, too, are jobs for the artistic person who can secure a position in a large store as window-dresser or who can work up a business of dressing windows for small store owners.

Now let's consider some of the specific jobs in advertising. The account executive is the person who plans and carries out an advertising campaign. She must have good judgment and the ability to think through a complicated problem to its solution. The planner selects the advertising materials, decides on the media to be used, figures out the most attractive opening, the most effective development of each piece of advertising copy, and settles all the other problems concerned with division of space, the market to be aimed at, and so on. Good judgment is vital as well as good business sense, artistic taste, and many of the other traits in our long list.

The planner would have a serious time indeed without the services of investigators who dig up all the information about the commodity or service which is to be advertised, the most likely market, the ways of reaching that market effectively, and so on. These investigators must be trained research workers with a fondness for facts and figures; they must have the detective sense that keeps them digging and digging until they unearth all that is required and they must be accurate to the last degree.

Copywriters and art directors are highly specialized experts in the advertising field and require special skills and training. Don't think you can be a successful copywriter simply because your daily compositions were praised by your teachers. Imagination, conciseness, and force in your writing are far more important than a fine literary style.

An art director is of course a well trained and experienced artist, capable of supervising the layout and preparation of art work for an ad, or of performing these functions, if the department is a small one. Advising the advertising manager on all artistic points is also an important phase of an art director's work.

Make-up, or layout work, is the business of arranging an advertisement—text, illustrations, decorations, designs, and so on—in the most effective form for the space allotted. To be successful in this phase, you should have some artistic training in order to use the right principles of balance, contrast, and proportion; knowledge of type and experience as a copywriter will be important—and you must have unerring taste.

Production is the job of actually getting each piece of advertising into the newspaper, magazine, booklet, or whatever form it is to be issued in, as well as making arrangement for distribution to the consumers who are to be reached. Training as a proofreader is a valuable asset here; and you must be exceedingly accurate, have will-power, perseverance, and force. If you say a piece of work is to be finished by a specified time, you must make it understood that you mean it; and yet you must be tactful, or you will not be able to get along well with your fellow-workers.

Many a woman with good selling ability may become successful in selling space for newspapers, magazines, or other publications. She must know a good deal about advertising and also how to convince possible advertisers that the readers of the publication she represents will be interested in their goods.

As we have suggested, there are plenty of opportunities for advancement in advertising. If you begin as clerk, you may be promoted to copywriter or layout person; you may be sent out as a solicitor, or you may become assistant to the manager and eventually manager.

ADVERTISERS 123

"Go West, young woman!" might be good advice to a girl who is interested in a career in advertising. In San Francisco in 1949, we found that women predominated in the advertising field, especially in retail stores—possibly because the longtime executive director of the Advertising Club chanced to be a woman. This is her story.

Shortly before the up-and-down twenties, Florence Gardner took a temporary job with this organization to help raise money for a convention. When the regular secretary left, Miss Gardner stayed on and, in a few years, was given the executive position that she holds today.

One of her major jobs is running an efficient employment service for advertising people. This is on a service basis without fees. The club office acts also as a clearing house for advertising information, always promoting "Truth in Advertising."

"Ours is no knife and fork club," insisted this energetic woman. "In addition to this clearing house and employment service, the club backs all worthy community projects, helps advance civic enterprises, and influences legislation affecting advertising. I like most of all, however, our educational program. This includes arranging vocational conferences to help young people discover what they will need for an advertising job. The club, in co-operation with the Golden Gate College, sponsors a School of Advertising which has an excellent curriculum outlined for beginners and advanced students. A scholarship is given annually to assist some worthy student in our field and we run a creative writing contest on some advertising subject in our high schools. More girls than boys entered essays the past year.

"You see," she went on, with a twinkle in her eye, "this club has always believed that there is no sex in brains. Since its beginning in 1903, women have been members on an equal basis with men. There is no Women's Advertising Club here, as in your eastern cities."

Don't be misled by all this into thinking that you can fly West from any point in the U. S. A. and pick up a big-time job in advertising, like the "forty-niners" of the past century with their golden nuggets. At the time of our visit there was a definite oversupply in this field. For that reason you might find it advisable to take a job in a less crowded occupation and enter one or more of those evening courses for beginners in the Golden Gate College School of Advertising—or take similar courses in one of the city's universities.

If you have your own agency, you may have trouble keeping your head above water in lean years. The business is usually done on a commission basis, so that you may do very well indeed during a large campaign and then have to wait—and possibly keep an office staff going—for another large account. But in any phase of advertising you will have pleasant, stimulating work with congenial associates and an outlet for creative imagination.

Although advertising is fascinating work, it has drawbacks for the person who dislikes overtime or working under high pressure and extreme nervous tension. A heavy expenditure of energy is demanded, especially in the creative positions. It is not easy to be under daily pressure to create ideas—the hardest kind of mental work. The possibility of temporary, uncertain employment just for the duration of an advertising campaign may be a disadvantage as well. Moreover, the advertising manager or agency owner must be constantly on the alert to avoid legal entanglements caused by misstatements or misrepresentation of goods.

There have been many changes in this field during recent years and it is now admitted that women have a very fair chance in advertising. In certain fields, especially, possibilities for women have been steadily increasing as men have recognized the fact that women have the advantage—in foods, fashions, child care, personal hygiene, and labor-saving devices for the home. Manufacturers may spend huge sums for scientific research on these matters but it takes a woman, every time, to translate the findings into the vocabulary that will appeal to the feminine consumer. Because of her peculiar understanding of the needs and desires of other women, the advertising woman has an even chance with men for success. BUT she must have all the traits—listed at the beginning of this chapter—which are required of men.

15. LADY BANKERS

IS THERE A PLACE for girls in the great world of finance? Of course there is! A leader in this field says, "I believe the financial world offers a great opportunity and secure field for the more mature woman in business on account of her experience and good judgment. Investment business demands people in whom confidence can be placed; integrity and capacity for detail, as well as dignity and tact."

Take stock of yourself before you decide to try this career. Do you have that good judgment mentioned above? Do you confide all you know into any willing ear? The financial world will have none of you if you do. Caution and discretion are watchwords among the wary on Wall Street and in the lesser Wall Streets scattered all over the country.

Furthermore, you must almost be a seventh daughter of several seventh daughters in the matter of foresight and vision if you would succeed in this business. Women's traditional intuition is exceedingly important in helping you understand your clients' needs and their points of view. Imagination and tact will help you at this point, too, and again we must insist on sympathy, integrity, ability to get along well with others, and a good disposition.

A broad educational background is required before you should think of specialized training for work in the banking and investment field. The college subjects that will be most useful to you are: statistics, economics, psychology, all the English courses you can carry, business law, commercial geography, and foreign languages. The languages will come in handy if you have a chance to go abroad in the interests of your firm.

In many of the large banking and investment houses, there are special training schools to which well-equipped women college graduates may be admitted for a period of intensive training in the methods of that particular organization.

Many bank officials advise young people to get experience in the smaller cities or towns before attempting a career in Wall Street.

"But how can a girl get a chance to be a banker—even in a small town?" you are likely to inquire.

Here, as in many business jobs, you may enter through a clerical opening and learn the business from A to Z right on the job. "Start low and aim high" is good advice to any girl who would go places in banking. In Frances Maule's *Road to Anywhere*, she points out the value of stenography and clerical ability to the girl who is "sneaking up on high finance." It would be fun to discover how many of the women officials in our nation's banks climbed from obscure office jobs.

Don't turn up your nose at a humble clerical job if that is the only way you can move toward high finance. Get your start that way and you may go far if the right opportunities present themselves and you are not too impatient about advancement. This is a field where the climbing is slow and sometimes painful.

Perhaps you can never go beyond the position of bank teller, cashier, or financial adviser to women. Don't be too sad about that; it is interesting work with the possibility of a good income that can be depended upon.

In banks that have special women's departments, there may be a fine chance for you to become manager. These departments are organized to help women clients with financial problems, budgeting incomes, the wise investment of money, and learning how to take care of their checking and savings accounts. Women with sound judgment, first-hand knowledge of family needs, and skill in reading human nature are sure to succeed in this special field. They will understand women's needs and those of their children better than men, and they can more quickly win the confidence of their clients. The women's department of a bank generally handles trust funds or estates of widows and orphans. The woman in charge of that work must keep herself informed regarding inheritance, tax, and trust laws.

In addition to the various positions open to women in commercial and investment banking, there are possibilities with building and loan associations, in income tax work, and as statisticians, librarians, or in advertising and publicity work. In any of these fields you will have an equal chance with the men for advancement.

For the girl who has sales ability, the business of selling securities is an outlet for her talents. However, we might warn you that there are stiff examinations for the would-be stockbroker and saleswoman, and you might be wiser to choose less precarious phases such as: advertising, if you have a flair for writing; statistics, if playing with figures doesn't give you a headache; or you might try your hand at running the library if the institution is large enough to have one for its employees. Here, however, you will need special library training to give the most efficient service. But clever college girls have been known to carry on this kind of work successfully after taking only one or two library courses such as: special library administration, reference work, and cataloguing. It is sound common sense, however, to secure the very best training you can for the particular job you are planning to undertake.

In the financial world income tax work is becoming an extremely promising field for women. It requires expert knowledge of tax laws, accounting, corporate law, and investments in addition to all the other qualifications we've stressed in this chapter. Bureau of Internal Revenue positions are open to women and there are opportunities as private advisers on tax problems. If you can gain a reputation as a tax expert, your future will be secure and your income may go beyond your wildest dreams.

It is interesting to read what the Institute for Research has to say about the openings for women in *Banking as a Career*. We quote:

> From the discussion of individual jobs, it is clear that women have about the same opportunities for employment in banks as have men. Practically all of the clerical work can be done equally well by men or women, while in some special activities women excel. They are usually preferred for filing, typing, and secretarial work. Progressive banks are finding it desirable to have some women meeting the public at the tellers' windows and at information desks. Special Women's departments are being opened, managed by women to serve the women customers. Bankers find carefully selected, capable women very satisfactory and especially trustworthy. Women have excellent opportunities for a career in banking, especially since it is a fact that the majority of the wealth of the United States is passing by inheritance into the possession of women.

Women may succeed in banking and in any other phase of high finance but it is likely to take long years of hard, routine work to get there. In the lower clerical positions, there will be little excitement in the daily grind unless the stick-up men put in an appearance. And safety glass, electric wiring, and other devices for protection are being used to discourage such breaks in the monotony. Furthermore, it is another of those indoor jobs that may make you pasty-faced and, as your responsibility increases, give you lines of care. Salaries may be discouragingly low in the minor positions, except perhaps in smaller communities.

On the other hand, banking is clean, agreeable work in

pleasant surroundings with congenial associates. Experience in high finance will give you prestige that may help you find a good position elsewhere; that is, if you get weary waiting for a promotion. Work with the public can be very stimulating. The hours are fairly good, although they are not what the general public usually believes. Most of the employees in a bank work from 8:30 to 4:30 or 5, except during the visits of the bank examiners when night work may be necessary.

This is the way one young woman reached a position as junior officer in a banking institution. She graduated from Mount Holyoke College where she had trained to become a language teacher. Instead of teaching, however, she entered a business college to learn typing. Her new skill won her a job in one of the largest investment houses in the country. To prepare for the new work, she was given an intensive two-month course in a bond school where she was the only girl in the class. Most important in this school was training in how to sell securities. After completion of the course, this young would-be high financier became assistant to the sales manager in one of the branch offices of the firm. Here she gained experience in statistical work and in selling securities which is invaluable in her present position.

Later, this young woman became assistant to the president of a small manufacturing company but, during the three years on that job, she wanted to return to the investment business, and finally offered herself for any opening in the company in which she is now an officer. "My first job was as a 'floater,'" she explained, "to substitute for any woman employee in the company, although I was taken on chiefly with the idea that I would be available as a secretary to a trust officer when an opening came. The floating was marvelous for my later job as I became acquainted with everyone in the company. My chance came when the secretary to the Executive Vice-President left because of ill health. In a month after I began to pinch hit for her, I was given the job, and, when my boss became President, my duties broadened as his assistant. Now, as Assistant-Secretary of the company, I am one of three women junior officers in the institution."

16. TRANSPORTATION AND COMMUNICATION WORKERS

WOULD YOU BELIEVE that the prosaic terms transportation and communication could offer fascinating opportunities for women? Well, it's true. When you think that telephone operators are classed under communication and that aviation comes under the dull-sounding transportation you will sit up and take notice.

Let's discuss the older, more established jobs in transportation first. Are there opportunities for girls in railroading and bus service? Indeed there are, although women are rarely employed in the operative phases. Before the first World War, women boilermakers, welders, and other shop workers were practically unheard of; but while the men were overseas, the trains had to run—more of them than ever before—and the women saw to it that they did. Later on most of the women in the mechanical end of transportation had to step out and give the men their former jobs.

During the second World War, girls and women again took over many operating jobs and, this time, a considerable number have remained on the job—mostly, however, as hostesses rather than operating vehicles.

Where, then, are the opportunities for girls? Go into any of the offices and you'll find out. The clerical positions in transportation, as in most other businesses, are largely held by women. Even a few of the higher executive positions have been given to women, but don't let that lead you astray! You have practically no chance of jumping from a stenographer's job to the presidency of a great line with a private car at your beck and call. There has been only one such lady in the land—that inevitable exception that proves the rule. In the transportation area you will have your best chance in the following jobs: stenographers, typists, multigraph and comptometer operators, clerks, bookkeepers, switchboard operators, and possibly in selling tickets or as passenger representative.

For these clerical positions you will need at least a high school education, although some have been successful without it, and the special business training required for the particular job. Examinations and stenographic tests are usually given to applicants for positions.

First among personal qualifications is good health, particularly if your job includes travel. You must be able to get along well with patrons of the road as well as with your fellow-workers. No snappy answers will be tolerated. Courtesy, honesty, accuracy, dependability, punctuality, and unwavering loyalty are essential to success. We hope you'll use your head as well as an information clerk we talked to recently. Not only was she prompt and accurate in answering our query about a train but she volunteered several sensible suggestions that would never have occurred to us. Think of keeping your wits like that all day with phone calls coming in as fast as they can be answered.

There is not much chance for advancement in this field. Of course an unusually fine stenographer may become chief clerk of a department or secretary to an official, and there are various other supervisory positions to which she may aspire. Or, if she can write good copy, she may find a place in the publicity and public relations departments, or may become editor of a railroad magazine.

Although only a small proportion of the station agents are women, you might be fortunate enough to capture one of those positions. Here again, there is little chance for advancement. On the other hand, the work is light, working conditions are usually good, and you will be more or less your own boss.

The wages of all railroad workers, as the newspapers remind us from time to time, are regulated by labor agreements. One of the recognized advantages for women in the railroad business is the fact that they receive the same rate of pay as men workers in similar positions. Possibilities for travel with free transportation and old age pensions are attractions for women who like to rove and yet want a sense of security.

Bus and trucking services are growing rapidly and there may be unexpected opportunities for women even though they are denied positions in operating the vehicles. However, there are executive and administrative positions to aspire to as well as the possibility of ownership. A lurid novel written many years ago told of a dauntless and daring woman who successfully ran an overnight trucking service between New York and Philadelphia. It was a wild tale of competition with racketeering rival companies but it showed very clearly the possibilities for a clever business woman who could hold her own in a man's field.

That is one of the chief disadvantages in this business. Except in the clerical jobs, there is keen competition from men with the odds against you. When women win good jobs in bus transportation, however, they are more than likely to find the pay substantial and opportunities for promotion.

So at last we come to the opportunities for women in aviation, and that's a moot question. Does a woman really have a chance in the air? As air hostess, or stewardess, naturally, there is slight competition from men. All that is required is the right height, the correct weight, good looks, intelligence, and a personality that will appeal to the guests of the airline. Here again, woman's intuition is important and poise is absolutely essential. Problems may arise which will require all the tact and resourcefulness of the air hostess to settle without arousing anatagonism. Good health is of prime importance too.

The duty of the air hostess is to make the passengers happy and comfortable with the small attentions that mean so much to travelers. She serves meals and refreshments, answers questions, furnishes treatment for minor ills or for major ones such as a heart attack or stroke. She helps mothers traveling with babies or young children. She arranges recreational diversions for long trips.

Although there are no special educational requirements

TRANSPORTATION AND COMMUNICATION 135

for the position of air hostess, she should have sufficient education to pass the training course which is given to new employees to prepare them for all these duties and emergencies. As in all work in which there is contact with the public, especially if it involves giving information, a college education will give you precedence over other applicants and will make your work more satisfying.

Have women a chance as civilion air pilots? Here's where the great doubt appears. Many feminists will dispute our contention that there is small chance for women in this branch of the air service. "Look at the women flyers who have won trophies," they will shout, "and what about ones who made fine records with the WAF during World War II?"

Take a look at the record—just how many female air pilots are there?

Possibly your imagination has been fired by novels about daring women pilots but, if these stories were based on fact, it was indeed the exceptional person who was the original of each heroine. You will not have much chance to pilot a great transport plane across the country—unless, of course, all our civilian pilots are flying war planes.

Suppose we let one of the exceptional women transport pilots tell us about it:

"The first thing you must do in taking up flying is to find out whether or not you are physically and mentally qualified to fly. An appointed Department of Commerce Flight Physician very thoroughly checks your personal history as follows: infantile period; environmental factors; education, schools and college; disciplinary period; trend of thought; occupation; amusements; use of tobacco and alcohol; athletic training in school and after; drugs, medicines (reasons for use); financial, family or social difficulties; temperament.

"To be fit temperamentally, you must be cheerful, stable, self-reliant, aggressive, modest, frank, fond of people, satisfied, serious, co-operative in work and in examination, sportsmanlike, moderate, enthusiastic, and adaptable."

In view of all this, it might be wiser to try some other phase of aviation work, such as radio operator, control tower operator, meteorologist, navigator, or operative in an aircraft factory. And there will always be many opportunities in office positions. A reservations clerk will have especially interesting contacts in her job with an airline. Moreover, this type of experience will prepare her for good positions in travel bureaus or to start in business for herself as a travel agent. Aeronautical research may offer good opportunities for qualified women. In the route-mapping phase of the work, in teaching, and in design, women may play a very important part and, of course, statistics can be furnished by a woman with a good head for figures just as well as by any man.

Of course there are many attractive features about all branches of aviation, or the field would not be so crowded. For pilots and stewardesses, the hours are short, salaries are higher than elsewhere, the work is highly exciting and dramatic, and the training period is comparatively short. On the other hand, the work is dangerous and sometimes there are harrowing experiences or accidents that permanently incapacitate flyers.

How would you like to be a telephone operator? This type of work will appeal to a girl who has the spirit of service—who wants to be ready to serve in time of need. We have heard again and again of heroic girls who stuck to the switchboard, risking their lives—or even losing them—in their efforts to warn others of danger in fire, flood, storm, and earthquake. In recognition of such service, medals are awarded every year to heroic employees of the American Telephone and Telegraph Company.

The everyday business of linking voices together has its rewards, also. Important, as well as merely pleasant personal affairs are carried on by phone. Big business that affects thousands, or even millions of lives is often transacted by telephone—over connections put through by girls at the switchboard.

This gives us a hint of what you will need in the way of personal equipment if you want to enter this line of work. Loyalty, speed, efficiency, and, above all, dependability are vitally important. A "cut-off" in that business deal, when seconds may be precious, might be disastrous to the deal. Naturally, too, you will need a clear, pleasing voice. Even temper, nimble wits, and tact will go a long way toward success. And a good memory is a prime requisite.

"Any chance for a girl who couldn't go to high school?" is a frequent question.

Well, it all depends upon the local situation and the demand. High school graduates will usually be given preference. On the other hand, lack of such education will not rule you out if you are well-qualified otherwise. To find out, go to the nearest telephone company employment office, fill out an application blank as neatly as possible, answer all questions in your interview as intelligently as possible. Then, hope for the best. Be sure to dress carefully in simple, neat clothes and, most important of all, be certain of your grooming, which includes cleanliness and daintiness.

If you are accepted, you will discover that wages are likely to be good. It is a policy of telephone companies to attract high-type operators with good pay—the sort of girls who are needed, they say, "to give the most telephone service and the best at the least cost to the public."

Many other advantages will be found here, such as: job security, accident and sickness benefits, health care, insurance and pension plans, and the like. Saving is encouraged by arrangements whereby regular amounts will be deducted from salaries for government bonds or deposited in the bank according to the wishes of the employee.

Here, too, you will discover fine opportunities for advancement. We quote what the Bell Telephone of Pennsylvania has to say about that all-important matter:

> Promotion in this business is on merit. Pull doesn't count! You don't have to worry about Somebody's daughter or niece getting all the breaks. The women who do good telephone jobs get along. All our Chief Operators and all the women in supervisory positions in this company started at the bottom. So did our executives.
>
> Yes, the opportunity to get along in this business is better than good. And the reason is simply this. The company always needs capable, ambitious women for supervisory positions. And the women for these jobs come up from the ranks, every one of them.
>
> You'll find right through your telephone career that you will be given every chance to fit yourself for the next job up. You will get plenty of on-the-job instruction. The first thing to do is to lick the job you have. Then you are set for the next step up.
>
> Of course, it takes time to acquire the experience and knowledge needed to fill up-the-line jobs. It is no overnight proposition. And everyone doesn't have what it takes. But the opportunity is here.

TRANSPORTATION AND COMMUNICATION

Send to the Bell Telephone Company of Pennsylvania for their booklet *A Friendly Place to Work* which tells about the experience in the business world of a girl called Ann . . . how she found interesting, enjoyable work . . . met sincere, friendly co-workers . . . earned a good salary . . . provided herself with a secure future with the Bell Telephone Company.

Here are advantages that you will enjoy as a telephone operator: Good pay from the start, regular increases at frequent intervals, on-the-job training, experienced supervisors, ample opportunity to advance, excellent working conditions, pleasant lounges, company cafeterias and kitchenettes for a meal or snack, co-workers of your own age, vacations and holidays with pay, recreational activities, self-development courses, a liberal employee benefit plan at no personal cost, steady employment and security, interesting work of essential nature.

Outside the regular telephone companies are the switchboards of hotels, clubs, schools, colleges, stores, and all kinds of business organizations. The position of switchboard operator may be extremely interesting in a large firm if it includes service as receptionist or information clerk.

We'll turn now to jobs in the telegraph industry which was launched by Samuel F. B. Morse. You might enjoy reading the story of his work in Kaempffert's *A Popular History of American Invention*. In this field, jobs have not been so plentiful for women. Men have always had the inside track here so that, even today, a very small per cent of the women working in communications are telegraph operators.

In telegraphy the jobs are: telegraph clerk, telegraph operator, telegrapher, and the usual clerical jobs that are found in all large organizations. In these clerical jobs there will be opportunities for advancement to supervisory positions.

The jobs of telegraph clerk, telegrapher, and telegraph operator sound a good deal alike, but there is a decided difference, not only in duties but in the amount that is in the pay envelopes. Experienced telegraphers are much better paid than clerk or operator; a reason why men predominate in this job.

A telegraph clerk is the girl who takes your message at a counter, checks it for length, figures the cost, and hands it to the operator who sends it out. This woman may have charge of the delivery of messages as well. Usually she will do several types of clerical work, which means that she must have training in business or commercial courses in high school, in a trade school, or have taken a short business course.

A telegraph operator usually operates only an automatic type of machine in sending and receiving messages and, therefore, does not have to learn the Morse code. Her machine will take care of that. Girls slightly older than eighteen are preferred for this work. They will have a chance of promotion to a supervisory position as head of a division in a large office or as branch manager. Telegraph companies maintain training schools in which new recruits are taught the operation of these automatic machines. The course lasts from six weeks to three months with a pay envelope passed out to you at the end of the first week of training.

The telegrapher is a hand key operator who uses the Morse code to transmit by the old dot and dash method. Although automatic teleprinters are rapidly replacing this

TRANSPORTATION AND COMMUNICATION 141

old system, the job is one of importance where it is used and, consequently, commands a higher rate of pay. This worker can look for promotion to assistant chief operator or chief operator.

High school training, or its equivalent, is required for most of these jobs. Most important of all, you must be able to spell correctly and speak our language well. Here, too, will be a physical examination with special attention to eyes and hearing. They must be GOOD. Accuracy is as necessary here as in telephone jobs. It may be just as much a life-and-death matter to the individuals who use this means of communication. That's why you will find this a decidedly worthwhile line of work.

III

People Are Their Business

17. TEACHERS

"I'M GOING TO BE a 'fidgical' education teacher when I grow up," announced a youngster of our acquaintance a number of years ago. We laughed at her then and thought no more about it. Lately we discovered that the child was as determined as ever and something would have to be done about it. What we did was exactly what we'll try to do here. We gave her as clear a picture as we could of teaching: its pitfalls and possibilities, the personality and training required of the ones who would succeed in this largest of all "Ladies First" professions, and the duties in typical teaching positions.

Let's see what goes into the making of a successful teacher. First is *personality*. Think of all the teachers you've had, and you'll realize the importance of developing the right sort of personality. Here are a few of the traits you'll need: common sense in very large quantities, patience, intelligence, persistence, courtesy and politeness, consideration for others, sympathy, and ability to get along with all kinds and conditions of children or young people and, naturally, with your associates. You must be healthy with not a sign of nerves, else you may turn into one of those fussy, cranky "schoolmarms" shown in cartoons which make the whole world chuckle. You will need will power, but never stubbornness. Honesty, courage, and high ideals of service are essential, and you should be attractive and have a cheerful disposition.

If you have all these personality traits and are really eager to teach, go right ahead. But be sure to give all the time you can possibly afford to the acquisition of knowledge and skills that will make you just a little better than the average graduate of a teacher-training institution. All the brains and personality imaginable won't make you successful unless you have the best training obtainable.

Choose a college where you can be sure of gaining a thorough foundation of general education as well as specialized training for teaching. If you expect to develop desirable attitudes in your pupils, it is essential for you to take part in all the activities that will help you become a well-rounded individual. Attend a college where you will be given apprentice training of the kind that is better than the old-fashioned and frequently ineffectual "practice teaching" courses. If you want to teach your students how to do something in the world, you must certainly learn how to teach in the most effective way.

There are few places today where you can teach unless you have a degree from a four-year college course with a specified number of credits in educational subjects, which are required for certification. If you want to teach in high schools you should have a Master's degree and, if you want to have your turn when a man leaves a top job, a Ph.D. degree will usually be necessary.

You'll have to learn how to live in a community and to realize the vital part a teacher should play in that life. Otherwise how can you expect to help your future pupils understand the complex world they live in? Teaching is a very serious business. It is one of the strongest social forces in the world today. One writer has said that the teacher is the "producer of trained and informed intelligence to keep civilization from crumbling." Think what that means to you who may one day be such a producer!

In the following pages we are quoting, in part, from *Teaching as a Profession* by Agnes Snyder and Thomas Alexander.

Teaching in the kindergarten-primary grades appeals especially to girls who get along well with very small children. The kindergarten-primary teacher is first of all responsible for the personal and physical care of children. She—the kindergarten-primary teacher in the United States is generally a woman—must busy herself constantly with detail. Habit formation and the building of right attitudes are her particular responsibility. She must have a fund of general information about the world around her and she must be on the alert to add to that information; otherwise, she will not be able to keep alive in children that inquiring attitude which they lose all too soon if their questions meet with no satisfaction.

Teachers in the middle or intermediate grades bear the chief burden of equipping each generation with those elements of the social heritage that should be the common possession of all. The foundation in the skills has been laid in the primary grades. The teacher in the intermediate grades is concerned with rendering these skills more effective, and with opening new intellectual and social horizons to the children. This means going along with the children farther and farther afield—on actual excursions and, vicariously, through books.

The junior high school teacher is, in turn, a teacher, a counselor, and a citizen in a school community. Her classroom teaching is confined to one subject or group of related subjects. In her teaching she is particularly concerned with the interest her subject holds for each pupil, since the main function of the junior high school is the guidance of children toward their right vocation. As counselor to a small group, she keeps many kinds of records in order that their study may yield the knowledge necessary to the true guidance of the children intrusted to her, and she must be sensitive to the needs for counsel and always ready to listen and help. As a citizen in a school community she is a participant in student government, in assemblies, and in the clubs which form so potent a factor in the life of the early adolescent.

The work of the senior high school teacher is similar to that of the junior high school teacher in its specialization of subject matter, its counseling, and its participation in school activities. The students are carrying groups of subjects preparing them, in a broad sense, for some general vocational field. The high school teacher must be watchful to see whether decisions have been made wisely and, when mistakes have been made, to be ready to steer in other directions. It is of particular importance, at this age, that right moral standards be developed.

Here are some of the subjects in which you might specialize if you want to teach in high school: English, social science, mathematics, physical sciences, biological sciences, foreign languages, commercial subjects, arts, music, physical education, and home economics.

There is a growing field in special education—that is, the education of the mentally and physically handicapped. The teacher of any of these groups carries the responsibilities of the teaching of normal children of the same age and, at the same time, must meet the particular needs of these handicapped groups and be ready for all kinds of physical and emotional emergencies.

Dr. Lois Mossman insists that the school principal must "lead teachers in their growth into ability to live fully in order that they may, in turn, bring richness of living to boys and girls." In doing this, the principal teaches, works co-operatively with her group in the plans for the whole school, and co-operatively with the parents in the whole education of the children. She is immediately responsible to the superintendent for the management and control of her unit in accordance with the larger lines of policy of the school system.

The supervising teacher works co-operatively with the principal and the superintendent. While the principal has a particular school for her responsibility, the supervising teacher covers a larger school area, integrating the work of the several schools in that area as the principal integrates the work in one school. Like the principal, she is responsible to the superintendent for carrying forward her work in accordance with the policies of the school system.

The superintendent is an executive and a professional leader. She must see that unity is achieved. She is responsible for all the children of the school system of which she is in charge. She is the co-ordinator of the work of the various schools of the system. She is the liaison officer between the schools and the public.

There are many types of jobs for the college teacher. First she is an instructor in some particular field. She may be the head of a department, in which case she will organize as well as teach. She may be a research professor with teaching limited to a small group of graduate students. She may be a special investigator lent to a government commission for consultation or administrative work. She may be a dean or other administrative officer.

What about research in teaching which is the scientific approach to the study of a problem? Every teacher can be, and should be, a research worker, for teaching and investigation go hand in hand. There has been more research, experimentation, and planning to adjust schools to modern needs during the past three decades than there was during the previous century. The main fields of specific educational research are:

1. Bureaus of research connected with state or city school systems.
2. Graduate research and research of professors in departments of education in universities.
3. Institutes of research financed by educational foundations.
4. Surveys financed by foundations.

Teaching is an occupation that is hedged around with certain restrictions called certificates. For instance, if you want to teach in an elementary school in Ohio, you must have an elementary teachers' certificate issued by the state; for teaching in a high school you will need the high school teachers' certificate. Moreover, each certificate calls for the completion of a specific program of training. These vary from state to state. Accordingly in making your plans you should inform yourself of the requirements in your state.

Certification is a protection both to the children and to the teacher. The children will be taught only by those who have reached a certain educational level; the teacher will belong to a group recognized as representative of certain intellectual attainments.

Now, we'd like to give some details on several of the most promising fields of the future—the teaching of agricultural subjects, physical and health education, and vocational counseling.

Agriculture has been taught in all grades of the public schools and in extension and vocational agriculture schools, ever since the passage of the Smith-Hughes Act in 1917. Teachers must have had a four-year course which includes agricultural subjects as well as methods of teaching. Practical farming experience will be invaluable to you as there may be keen competition with men in this field.

Here a young woman may start her teaching career on the elementary, junior or senior high school level and, later on, arrive at the college level. In all the Land-Grant Colleges scattered throughout the country considerable emphasis has been given to the teaching of agricultural subjects, in the training of teachers to train farm youngsters in ways of better farm living. And there are exciting openings in agricultural experiment stations connected with many colleges and universities.

The physical and health education teacher may have the following duties in addition to regular class work, or work in corrective teaching and with restricted groups: Teaching hygiene and kindred subjects; organizing hiking parties; coaching games in the various sports; supervising the equipment; interpreting the program to students, faculty, parents, school administrators and the general public; carrying many business responsibilities in connection with the purchase of equipment, inventories, student records, etc.

Teaching of health and physical education has become a vital part of the teaching program from the elementary grades into college and university. There are interesting and worthwhile teaching positions on all these levels and supervisory positions as well. The supervisor in this field co-ordinates the work of all the physical education teachers throughout the school system.

The prospective "Phys.-ed" teacher must have a strong physique with no serious handicaps. Leadership ability, youth, enthusiasm and a good voice that carries are needed, as well. Better specialize in the health education phase if you want to carry on into later years as youth counts in the active phases.

In preparation for this kind of teaching there should be special courses in physical and health education which will include principles of physical education, its relation to health problems, the nature and function of play, theory of corrective gymnastics, tests, etc., as well as practice which will develop your own skills in gymnastics, sports, and the like. Graduate work is required for supervisory positions and for teaching on the college level; indeed, a doctorate may be necessary for the larger colleges and universities.

One of society's most pressing needs is a service which will help people in choosing their vocation and in planning their work-life. This service is rendered by the vocational counselor. The scope of her task is indicated by the definition of vocational guidance as: "the process of assisting the individual to choose an occupation, prepare for, enter upon, and progress in it."

In the performance of this task the vocational counselor helps individuals to obtain facts about occupations, to appraise their vocational possibilities, and decide on a field of work. She helps them to choose educational and vocational courses that will prepare them for work, assists them in finding a job and follows them after they have entered the occupational world in order to render any post-counseling assistance needed.

Tools which the vocational counselor works with are books and pamphlets on occupations, records showing the individual's accomplishments in school and in jobs, records giving his social and economic background, his medical history—anything that may have a bearing on his vocational adjustment.

The counselor trained in psychometrics may give tests; at any rate she considers test scores as a part of the individual's record.

The vocational counselor may preside over groups discussing vocational problems, particularly the problems connected with choosing a vocation and finding a job and behaving effectively on the job.

She makes contact with members of the community who can assist her: teachers, social workers, employers, physicians, ministers, etc.

Vocational counselors are employed in schools—chiefly high schools and vocational schools. Here the counselor is likely to have some teaching duties as well. Some colleges maintain vocational counseling, often in the Placement

Office. Many social agencies have a vocational guidance department, among them Y organizations, settlement houses, community centers. Agencies devoted to the welfare of the handicapped engage in vocational guidance as do the State Departments of Rehabilitation. The Veterans Administration employs a good many vocational counselors, women as well as men.

The State Employment Services, while organized to help people find jobs, do a good deal of vocational guidance and many of the "interviewers" in these offices are trained as vocational counselors. Likewise many persons employed in fee-charging employment agencies.

Finally, a good deal of vocational guidance is done in industrial establishments, though it does not go under that name. It is generally centered in the Personnel Department (see Chapter 13).

Vocational counseling is classed as a profession; hence the training for it is on the graduate level. Recommended courses include: Introduction to Vocational Counseling, Personality Adjustments, Measurement for Vocational Counselors (statistics), Rehabilitation of the Handicapped, Educational and Occupational Training Opportunities, Occupational Information, Labor Market Analysis in Vocational Counseling, Labor Problems, Personnel Administration in Business and Industry, Community Organizations and Vocational Counseling, Public Personnel Administration, Techniques of Vocational Counseling, Supervised Counseling Practice.

This entire sequence is offered in only a few graduate schools of the country, among them, Teachers College, Columbia University, New York University, University of

Minnesota. It ordinarily leads to the Master's degree; post Master's study is desirable.

Appropriate undergraduate courses that should precede these professional courses are: general and experimental psychology, educational psychology, abnormal psychology, social psychology, economics, sociology.

Experience in the working world is also a prerequisite, for it is obvious that you cannot give much realistic help to persons in solving vocational problems if you have never worked yourself.

As we have intimated, a large fraction of the vocational counselor's work is in schools. Here the vocational counselor may counsel about many problems that are not strictly vocational in nature—about failure in academic subjects, health, home conditions, etc. Many persons are appointed to deal with all the personal problems that arise among pupils. They may bear the title counselor and they may or may not be trained vocational counselors. When they encounter problems with which their training does not permit them to cope, they are expected to refer cases to appropriate specialists such as psychologists, physicians, social workers, psychiatrists, etc. It is recommended that a person receiving such an appointment secure training in vocational guidance, for surveys of youth's problems have shown that the vocational problems are their greatest perplexities.

Another thing—most of these counselors devote only a part of their time to counseling; the rest of the time they teach. Accordingly, to serve as a counselor in a high school you need to be certified to teach some curricular subject. Salaries are on a par with those paid to teachers.

The route of promotion for a vocational counselor in high school leads to Director of Vocational Guidance or

TEACHERS

Guidance in a city school system where one is on the administrative staff of the Superintendent of Schools and receives a salary equal to that paid to city supervisors of various curricular fields. There are only about 100 such posts at the present writing, many of them filled by women.

As we intimated earlier in this section, vocational counselors serve in various social agencies, where their salaries are on a par with those of case workers. In the State Employment Services they receive the salaries paid to "interviewers."

Closely allied to vocational counseling is the job of psychologist. A school psychologist aids the schools in the task of trying to find out "why we behave like human beings" and what the schools can do in helping individuals to make better adjustments in their home, school, social and working lives.

Training beyond the Bachelor's degree is usually required and often a Ph.D. degree may be necessary. If you have only a B.S. or A.B. you will be eligible for a few trainee positions as junior psychologist in the Federal Government, or as a psychologist's assistant. You may find yourself in a blind alley in such positions, however, unless you are willing to work for a higher degree.

Prospects for clinical psychologists, vocational counselors, and for applied psychologists in general are considered very bright. Write for more information to The Director, Office of Psychological Personnel, 2101 Constitution Ave., Washington 25, D. C.

What about financial rewards in the various fields of teaching? "The average salary of those in the teaching profession is well below the average of all gainfully occupied persons in the United States," Professors Snyder and Alexander point out in *Teaching as a Profession;* "a little higher than that of routine clerical workers, and a little lower than that of workers in manufacturing industries. On the other hand, while the average salary in the country at large is low, the salary of the well-trained, experienced teacher in the larger centers is not low."

The importance of fixed salary schedules which protect teachers from the whims of individuals should not be minimized, nor should we overlook the fact that many states now have tenure laws which make it impossible to remove teachers without just cause. Usually these tenure laws are not effective until after the teacher has been in the service for several years. Immorality, inefficiency, and neglect of duty are some of the causes for dismissal. There are pensions and retirement systems which add to the security of teachers.

We shall quote again from *Teaching as a Profession* in pointing out the social satisfactions and restraints:

As the standards of the profession are raised, teachers generally are accorded respect by the desirable elements of a community. A teacher who participates in the life of a community —shares in its work, its play, its worship—finds himself in a position of leadership. Such leadership cannot fail to bring a high form of social satisfaction.

A teacher must, however, be prepared to be held to high standards of conduct. He is in the public eye and must expect his own personal affairs to be of considerable interest to the community. Often it will be necessary for him, out of deference to the prejudices of a community, to forego forms of amusement, innocent in themselves. The important thing for him is his ability to work effectively with the people. Therefore, he may sometimes be called upon to make sacrifices in his own inclinations.

The greatest social satisfaction of the teacher comes in his contact with youth. His own spirit draws refreshment from the spring of youth. The trust and confidence of devoted students strengthen the faith of the teacher in himself and in all humanity. From these he draws continuous urge to look forward and to go forward. He cannot lay down his work while youth looks to him for guidance.

The student looks to the teacher, the community looks to the teacher, and society looks to the teacher. If governments are turning to education as the chief means for national progress, heavy obligations are imposed upon the teacher. The school and the community in which he lives are his field for work. His wider contacts must be made from these, and he can hope for effectiveness in the larger relationships only as he is able to assume leadership on his own ground.

The biggest job ahead for all teachers is related to bringing about a change of spirit in the people themselves. This is a recognized need of today with which every prospective teacher should be vitally concerned.

"Thoughtful men, as well as military leaders," says one writer, "realize that all discoveries, all of the advances of science are of little avail in human progress unless a corresponding advance is made in the spirit of men. If such an advance can be made now, it is possible that we shall enter into one of the great periods of human history. Medicine, the physical sciences, knowledge of geography and other peoples, have all made tremendous advances. But none of these developments will bring about human happiness unless there is a corresponding development in the souls of men."

"But what can one lone teacher do?" may be your despairing question in dark hours.

Exactly what one lone Quaker lady from Philadelphia

did for some time in Tokyo. Betty Vining—known as Elizabeth Janet Gray to young readers who enjoy her lives of William Penn and Sir Walter Scott, her stories of girls and boys of the past and present—has helped to turn Japan into a peace-loving nation.

Mrs. Vining tutored Crown Prince Akihito, taught English to the Empress and other members of the royal family, and endeavored to instill her liberal ideas into seventy-five future leaders of the Land of the Rising Sun who were her pupils in the School of Peers. Through talks to educational organizations Mrs. Vining helped to influence the teachers of our former enemy country to teach democratic principles and ideals of peace and co-operation. Now, her successor will carry on the work she began, a work which teachers of the future should try to emulate.

18. SOCIAL WORKERS

IF YOU ARE INTERESTED in being a social worker we advise you to read Jane Addams' *Twenty Years at Hull House*. The book tells how Miss Addams became aware of the miserable condition of the poverty-stricken inhabitants in the Chicago slums and describes what she did about it. After a visit to Toynbee Hall, a famous settlement in London, she established her own Hull House Settlement in 1889, in a rented mansion which was later donated to her work. It is hard to believe that the great settlement of today could spring from such small beginnings. Yet its growth is typical of the entire field of social service; a growing profession that will go far beyond anyone's dreams for it. The Hull House development may be small in comparison with what the future will bring in social work.

That is why we suggest that you consider this as a life work. Helping other people will be your opportunity and your challenge in this field. Never in all the years of history have there been such opportunities and so great a challenge. The needs are great and social work is undoubtedly a well-established profession for all time.

In the old days, women who entered this type of work not only frowned on the idea of pay for their services but frequently gave most of their private means to the philanthropic ventures in which they were interested. Of course, that was a bad professional attitude and has resulted in sadly inadequate salaries for trained workers who are dependent on their earnings for a living. Nevertheless, salaries have improved during recent years and will probably continue to improve until they reach a reasonable figure.

Why do you think you want to be a social worker? Is it because your heart aches for the pitiful, unhappy millions still "ill-fed, ill-clad, and ill-housed"? If that is your only reason for undertaking this work, we advise you to get rid of your emotions on the skating rink, golf course, or tennis court. Deep sympathy and a desire to aid your fellow men are certainly desirable prerequisites for social service, but not if they make you go sentimental at the sight of a shrunken, undernourished ragamuffin. You must like people and want to help them, but you will not be a success in this profession if you allow your feelings to rule your better judgment and common sense. In addition to the urge to help people, you must have a sympathetic and realistic understanding of another's point of view, of the strength and weakness in human characters.

This is another of the professions for which you *must* have adequate preparation. First you should be a graduate of a four-year college. Then you need to attend a school for social work and take a two-year course leading to a Master's degree. Many jobs are open, however, to persons who have completed but one full year in such a school.

The usual requirement for entrance to accredited schools of social work is twenty or more semester hours of pre-professional curriculum. This includes courses in psychology, history, economics, anthropology, political sciences, and English. Many students will also take, as electives or as additional courses, such subjects as home economics, art and music to broaden their cultural background.

In the professional course itself, the subjects taught fall into three large divisions: theory, field work, and research. In field work you will spend perhaps half your time in a social agency working under the supervision of experienced and understanding social workers. Research methods are taught in all of these professional schools with the aim of developing a group of workers who will devote their time to the study of social conditions and the work of the social agencies to determine the adequacy of existing services. Students who specialize in research will do statistical and research work for government departments, private social agencies, and foundations.

Administrative ability is of vital importance to young women who consider entering this profession. Although the distaff side will always predominate in social work, this take the responsibility of looking after the child while he is on probation or she will help him over the trying period which follows discharge from a reform school. Often this worker will co-ordinate all the agencies that can be used to benefit a delinquent child and his family.

Group and community work may be in many different phases. Recreational workers are employed in recreation centers, clubs for boys and girls as well as for men and women. And there are positions in settlements, community centers, with Girl Scouts, and in the Y.W.C.A. Social programs must be planned so that community needs may be adequately met through the development of necessary services.

In public health work there will always be opportunities for trained social workers, especially those who have had nursing experience or home economics training. Nutrition classes for children will be given as part of the health information and educational services of city, state, or government public health departments. Education for the prevention of tuberculosis and other diseases is a phase of public health work that is open to social workers, and public health nursing is the most important and promising field of all. Most of these positions are under civil service in established public welfare departments and the requirements are being steadily increased to raise professional standards so that they will equal the requirements for admission to the American Association for Social Workers.

The woman trained in social work may turn to the position of policewoman—a field which is constantly growing in importance. Many large cities now have a well-trained, nattily dressed corps of policewomen whose work is concerned more with the preventive and protective side than with apprehending criminals. Especially is this the case in dealing with women and children. Civil service examinations are required for these jobs.

For full details concerning all opportunities in social work, we suggest that you consult catalogues from various schools of social work and visit various community agencies to see the workers in action. Here you are likely to find someone who has the duty of explaining the work to prospective recruits. Their contagious enthusiasm for their work will probably help you make up your mind at once to join their ranks—if you can qualify.

19. LADIES OF THE LAW

IT IS PROBABLY a safe guess that many a girl is in law school because of the thrill she had on first hearing the famous words:

>The quality of mercy is not strained,
>It droppeth as the gentle rain from heaven
>Upon the place beneath. . . .

Actually women are less acceptable as trial lawyers than in any other phase of the legal profession. In most instances a woman's connection with a case will be almost entirely behind the scenes. One woman attorney-at-law states: "Opportunity for women in the legal profession is changing rapidly, and for the better. I know of no profession where the opportunity has advanced more than it has in this profession. In the recent past a woman lawyer was practically unheard of and unthought of, and especially was this true in trial work, or in any phase of work in the courtroom . . . [but] it is not now a rare thing to see a woman lawyer thoroughly preparing the case before it is carried to the courtroom."

Men will cling tenaciously to their dominance of the regular courts even though they are willing to admit you elsewhere. Of course the competition you face is heavy—but the proportion of women in this profession, though still small, has risen steadily since 1910. On the other hand, if you are not afraid of that sort of competition and are convinced that no other work will suit you quite as well as the law, we'd better see how you will suit it.

First, and most important of all, do you have a clear, logical mind? You may be on the right track if you were once the star of your high school debating club or if you have always been told that you should be an actress or public speaker because you express yourself so well before an audience. Your scholastic record should be above the average, too. You must be tactful, healthy, even-tempered, and able to get along well with other people. Sympathy and a sense of responsibility are exceedingly important and you must have plenty of push, without being unpleasantly aggressive.

After you have satisfied yourself that you are the right kind of girl to undertake a law course, check up carefully on your financial resources. Training for a profession runs into money. You will need to maintain a high record even in your pre-law courses if you hope for admission to a first-class law school. That will keep you busy, so there will be little time to earn any money to help yourself along. Although in some places it will be possible to work your way through on a part-time basis, it will be far from easy; and certainly cannot be done as easily as in training to be a teacher.

You will have at least two years in law school after you have finished your college course, and then comes the preparation for bar examinations. After that you're supposed to be ready for a job. Maybe you'll get one if our optimistic lady is right in her statement concerning the opportunities, but the chances are against it. Judges and juries may like women lawyers because they are likely to be more painstaking and conscientious than their brothers at the bar, but clients have not yet acquired real confidence in the ability of women in the legal profession. And clients *are* important. However, you may have a chance to take care of cases in juvenile or domestic relations courts. There are opportunities in the legal departments of large businesses, such as advertising agencies, or on legal magazines and journals, and various Federal Government agencies, particularly the Department of Justice, employ women lawyers.

"But look at the women judges," you remark.

"Of course," we admit willingly, "and you may turn out to be the first woman Justice of the Supreme Court!"

Indeed, a legal education may lead to a judgeship for a woman; it has happened in a number of cases. Moreover, women have been appointed to other high legal offices. But these are the rare exceptions who almost prove that the law is not a promising field of work for women.

Why do we say that? Well, she must be exceptional in

all the subjects that are considered essential for the profession or she cannot secure admission to law school. After she is admitted she has the strenuous task of holding her own in the class work. In law schools much of the teaching is based on the case-book method which means long hours of concentrated study of cases which were previously tried in court. Furthermore, the procedure of the courts is used in the classroom which is sometimes hard on the girl student—even though it may be very good for her. After she has hurdled all these obstacles, she must pass the difficult bar examination and then build up her practice. The college vocational counselor is not far wrong who warns a girl against expectations of making a fortune in law. She's more likely to find herself acting as a clerk in a law office where she is little more than a page boy.

We have had a good deal to say about the drawbacks of law as a career for women—the long, expensive training period with discouraging prospects ahead—but we have failed to mention the overcrowded condition of the profession—even for men—except in time of war. Furthermore, the lawyer will have heavy expenses for books unless she is fortunate in being near a really good law library which she is permitted to use.

On the other hand, there are new opportunities developing in the administration of women's business affairs. A tactful woman may be chosen to handle the legal affairs of a large estate, or she may take care of the property problems of women clients of a law firm more satisfactorily than a man, simply because she understands a woman's needs better. Salaried positions of this sort or in the legal departments of large industrial firms are really the safest bets for the girls who have followed the call of Portia.

What is more important, it gives them a chance to learn the routines of the courts which will be invaluable if they decide to establish independent law practices.

If she does not mind being at the beck and call of a dozen or more women, the woman lawyer may find a fairly lucrative field in serving the legal needs of various civic and charitable associations which are made up chiefly of women, or are devoted to the welfare of women and children. Justine Wise Polier, daughter of famous Rabbi Wise, made children's welfare her business in her job as Justice of New York Domestic Relations Court. Justice Polier, author of *Everyone's Children* and *Nobody's Child*, is an outstanding example of a woman trained in law who reached top places and does work of tremendous social value to her city and to the world. And in such work a woman lawyer has a chance to make a name for herself which will count heavily if she ever decides to go into politics.

The woman who has studied law will be wise to avoid criminal law, the field of property and personal damage technically called Torts, or corporation law. But she may be successful as a tax lawyer or she can safely specialize in real estate law, perhaps in connection with a flourishing real estate business of her own.

The income is more than likely to be meager, especially if you try to start a general practice immediately after admission to the Bar. On the other hand, there is the possibility that in ten or fifteen years you can develop a practice that will provide a higher income than you would ever earn in a salaried position. After the first small-income years have been weathered, you may find success that means far more than anything money can give you in the respect of your fellows, the feeling that you are giving real service to the world, and in the friendly contacts with a fine group of people who accept you as one of themselves.

20. RELIGIOUS WORKERS AND MINISTERS

CLOSELY ALLIED to the field of social service and often overlapping it is religious work. The same general qualifications are required, but it is believed that the girl who elects religion as her field should have, in addition to these qualities, strong faith, deep spiritual insight, courage, and the ability to speak forcefully and effectively in public. The finest youth of the church is needed for its leadership.

Vocational opportunities through the church are unlimited. There is need here for every talent you possess. The call comes for workers in agriculture, architecture, business administration, Christian education, education, engineering, evangelism, home economics, journalism, medicine, nursing and medical technicians, music, preaching ministry, recreational leadership, rural community work, public relations, and social work.

It is estimated that the Methodist Church alone will need in the next four years (from time of writing): 5,000 ministers, 10,800 physicians, nurses and technicians, 1,100 in overseas mission service, 1,000 in home mission service, 1,600 Christian educators. You can serve the church through your vocation wherever you choose and wherever your talents meet human need. In a local parish, in a mission station at home or abroad, in a large industrial center or a small rural community, in a hospital or clinic, in a home for children or for the aged, in a church school or college; in fact, wherever human need calls or wherever people wait to be led to a more abundant life.

Except for social work sponsored by religious organizations, special training in schools for social service is not required, although it will be helpful. Frequently girls who wish to work in the religious field will secure their training in a theological school which admits women or they may major in religious education in college. Stenographic or secretarial training will be a decided asset, particularly to the girl who wishes to be a pastor's secretary, or to work with one of the larger youth organizations.

Types of positions in the religious field are: director of religious education, assistant pastor, pastor's assistant, church secretary, pastor's secretary, teachers in church schools or of religious education in colleges and universities, religious social work, work with young people in the churches, work with the Y.W.C.A., editorial work, or missionary service at home or abroad.

The director of religious education in a church has a rather inclusive type of position in her administration of the educational program of the church. This person should have executive ability and understand young people thoroughly. If she doesn't she is lost. All the teachers in the various phases of the church work will be under her direction, as well as the leaders of the young people's organizations. And in many places she is taking increasing responsibility for adult activities as well.

"You will find that this is largely a woman's field," we have been told, "as most of the men go on for ordination."

Teachers are frequently paid for their work in the church schools, particularly in the vacation Bible schools which have become so popular during recent years. The Sisters in the parochial schools of the Roman Catholic Church perform a highly important service in religious as well as secular education. These teachers are needed for all grades from the elementary to college and university level.

Occasionally there is an opening for a girl with the right qualifications to act as pastor's assistant. The duties here are slightly different from those of the assistant pastor which are given later in this chapter. She is the one who relieves the pastor from many personal calls, discusses minor personal problems with members of the congregation, and attends to many of the business and social affairs of the church. Tact and the ability to handle people are prime requisites.

The pastor's secretary performs all the duties of a private secretary and also takes care of all the church records and files. Sometimes she serves as the church secretary as well, when the church is not large enough to employ both kinds of workers. The duties of a church secretary are more in the nature of an executive secretary of a board for any large organization.

An exceedingly important center for religious work is the Y.W.C.A. Some of the best group work in the country is being done in this association. Many outstanding teachers of group work in the social service field were once

Y.W.C.A. workers. Because this work is so important and offers such splendid opportunities for the woman who is interested in religious work, we are describing in some detail several types of professional positions in the organization: Executive Directors, Program Directors, and their assistants.

Educational requirements for these workers are: a Bachelor's degree from an accredited college, preferably study in social sciences, religion, education and the arts (or a major in health and physical education, if that is your interest). Professional education at the graduate level is desirable for staff holding responsible administrative positions and program directorships.

Personal qualifications desired are: sincere desire to apply Christian ideals to daily living; positive and progressively developing attitudes on the social implications of international, interracial and economic affairs; sensitivity to people and demonstrated ability to work with them in a democratic way; belief that individuals grow and develop through group relationships.

Experiences that are particularly valuable are: teaching, group work in social agencies and in recreation; personnel administration and community organization. Such experience should include an understanding of group work philosophy and practice of its techniques, program planning and work with adult volunteers.

For the recent college graduate, experience as a leader in college activities, in volunteer work in the community, in camp counseling or in summer playground work is desirable. Participation in student summer projects is helpful.

Now, the jobs themselves. First, Executive Directors—for community, college and university associations. These

RELIGIOUS WORKERS AND MINISTERS

positions involve administrative responsibilities in a worldwide membership organization—entailing democratic group leadership in work with boards of directors, volunteer committees, staff and membership, and with community agencies—to plan the program and to secure the leadership, budget and facilities to carry it out.

Program Directors for community associations use sound group methods in developing educational and recreational programs to meet the needs of the community and of individuals. This Director has responsibility for the training and supervision of volunteers and paid workers; development of leadership; promotion and publicity; work with other agencies.

Program Directors for teen-age groups develop a program where fun, fellowship and thoughtful discussion develop mature attitudes toward personal and family relationships, work, religion and social responsibility. The Directors for young adult groups (business, professional and industrial women and homemakers) plan programs which provide opportunities for creative leisure-time activities; for growth in the understanding and assuming of citizenship responsibilities, and for study and action on the social and economic problems which affect young women.

Program Directors for health and physical education use sound group methods in a positive program to raise the level of community health and to develop, in individuals, increased vitality and emotional well-being and the capacity to find creative uses for leisure time. Responsibilities include administration, teaching, health counseling and maintenance of facilities.

Jobs as Assistant Program Directors offer an opportunity

to work under the supervision of a program director in any of these phases of Y.W.C.A. work.

Do these workers like their jobs? In the leaflet from which most of this information has been taken are published seven letters from directors in various fields all over the U. S. A. under the heading "I'm Glad I Chose the Y.W.C.A." One—a director for a teen-age program in a midwestern city—writes:

"I like people! They may be unpredictable, changeable, temperamental, but they are exciting, diverting, challenging! If you have convictions about a new way of life there is every opportunity to help others achieve it. These are the Y.W.C.A. attributes that make my job satisfying and meaningful: (1) Its Christian purpose—the motivating force; (2) Methods of work which give freedom of planning and creativity; (3) Its cross-section membership-inclusiveness; (4) Its national and international scope and strength; (5) Its breadth of program which means opportunity for ongoing experience in a fellowship of women and girls."

An Executive Director ends her letter with the words: "To me the Y.W.C.A. is not just a career—not just a profession. It is a life—a life with an integrating purpose. Through it I can use my talents and be a whole person." And an Oriental Associate Teen-Age Director writes: "I feel the Y.W.C.A. will accept me, whatever my race, color or creed, because I believe in its Christian principles. I share in the development of appreciation for all people."

Similar in satisfactions is the work of the woman minister. Read Anna Howard Shaw's autobiography, *The Story of a Pioneer*, if you feel that you would like to become a minister. When Anna was fourteen she first began to feel the call of her career—that career which eventually made her one of the greatest women of her time. She was then living in the wilderness of Michigan. In her life story she wrote: "For some reason I wanted to preach—to talk to people, to tell them things. Just why, just what, I did not yet know—but I had begun to preach in the silent woods, to stand up on stumps and address the unresponsive trees, to feel the stir of aspiration within me."

A few years later she broke her family ties—it was many years before her father was reconciled to her action—and went to college to prepare herself for this great adventure. She endured almost unbelievable hardships and privations as she earned her way through a small western college and Boston University theological school. Everywhere she met almost as violent opposition as in her own family circle, but there was always someone who encouraged her to go on—and on she went until she won her degree from the University and was ordained for the ministry. It was in a small parish—East Dennis on Cape Cod—that Anna Shaw had her first experiences as the pastor of a church of her own. *Shepherd of a Divided Flock*, which is the title of the chapter in her book that describes her seven years on Cape Cod, tells its own story of long years of fighting and bickering in the young minister's congregation. Only a strong, determined person, man or woman, could have ended that strife—and Anna Shaw did it.

The early experiences of this most noted American woman minister may not be duplicated today, but you should not undertake a career in the ministry unless you have an equally forceful character and a comparable zeal to serve. Dr. Shaw's story of her life gives an excellent idea of the scope of a minister's duties which include far more than two sermons on Sunday and occasional calls on members of the congregation. Birth, marriage, and death require ministration. Pastoral visits, guiding the work of the Sunday School and various church societies, as well as handling social affairs, publicity, and business matters may fall to the lot of the minister of a small church. Larger churches frequently have assistant pastors, church secretaries, or student assistants to share these duties so that the pastor is released for more important work.

"Where can I serve after I am trained for the ministry?" may be your question.

Although women are admitted as ministers in a number of denominations, they are not welcomed cordially in conservative areas. Limited opportunities without ordination or regular charges are granted in some sects, but women are still excluded and probably will be from the ministry of the Roman Catholic and the Protestant Episcopal churches.

If you belong to one of the sects that admit women and you are convinced that you possess the necessary qualifications, get all the training you can afford. Like Anna Shaw, you must go on until you are thoroughly equipped with the scholarship which will stand the test of competition. After four years of college you will have three years of professional training leading to the degree of Bachelor of Divinity. And it is wise to seek advanced degrees as well. Study will never end for you—all your life you will need to study the Bible, read volumes of religious history and criticism, as well as keep abreast of trends of thought in both secular and religious matters.

Listen to this story of a woman minister in a remote section of New England. What a background of fine training she has for this work. First she was graduated with a

B.S. degree in Chemistry from a high-grade technical school, then she earned an M.A. degree in Religious Education at Union Theological Seminary and prepared for work in foreign missions at General Theological Seminary. Later she was graduated from the New York Training School for Deaconesses and took a position in religious education in the middle west. After that came personal religious counsel work in a large hospital in New England.

During World War II, this patriotic woman used her scientific training in technical work in a war plant. It was there that she conceived the idea of entering the ministry.

"It was a revolutionary decision I had to make," she said, "but there had been something in my life years before which helped me to follow God's will. I spent a winter with a creative Christian group—an experience I never forgot. It was this that helped me decide to become a minister. I went back to the mill and told my associates that I was not only becoming a Methodist but a Methodist parson! —because God wanted it that way."

Those associates followed her work as she progressed in this new field and were delighted when she was assigned to a "yoked charge" of two churches—the first woman minister to serve these two churches in the hundred and ten years of their history.

If the young woman graduate of a theological school cannot secure a pastorate, she may become an assistant pastor, a director of religious education, or a religious social worker. Many women study theology with the object of going to foreign lands as missionaries. There are executive positions on the staff of various denominations or, if she has literary ability, a young woman may do editorial work on a religious publication.

The income of the woman minister is not likely to be very large. However, ministers usually care less about financial rewards than about the opportunities to carry a message of faith to their fellow men.

Advantages in this field are never tangible. There are the close ties with members of the congregation that become almost like family relationships, and many other spiritual satisfactions to reward a minister. Our New England woman minister summed up her experiences in the words: "Life is certainly opening into wide beauty." On the material side there is the comparative comfort and freedom in the life of a minister as well as the position of respect in the community.

Missionary work has long had an appeal for the serious-minded, religious young woman. Nowadays the mission field needs more than just evangelistic workers; there are splendid opportunities for teachers, physicians, nurses, social workers, home economists, and others who may or may not have trained for the ministry. Women physicians render useful service in the foreign mission field as we have pointed out in the chapter on Physicians. Nutrition and child welfare specialists do equally splendid and helpful work.

Although the hazards and privations of the past in this field are rarely present now (except when bandits or war machines are on the prowl), the separation from home and family, as well as the difficulty of adjusting to foreign situations and strange people, may become almost unbearable. For a moving and authentic account of this drawback, read Pearl Buck's *The Exile* and its sequel *The Fighting Angel.*

21. LIBRARIANS

EIGHTEEN THOUSAND trained librarians are needed! These are encouraging words for any girl who considers librarianship as a career. What a change from the warning, back in 1931, to "Beware of libraries, except for information!" because there had been a 50 per cent cut in opportunities during that year. The library profession has had many ups and downs but, through the years, this field has never been overcrowded like many other service professions in which women outnumber men.

Suppose we see how library work happened to turn into a vocation for women. It didn't begin that way. In days of long ago, scholarly old gentlemen were the guardians of book collections. Then came the time when a maiden sister or indigent widow whose husband had died in the war between the states needed an occupation. What could be better for her than sitting at a desk in the little town library a few hours a day handing out books to friends and neighbors? Thus library work often became the refuge of ladies who could not find suitable work anywhere else.

But Melvil Dewey, inventor of the Dewey Classification which is used in the majority of libraries, soon put a stop to that sort of thing. After he opened the library school at Columbia University in 1887 and sent out trained workers to show how books and people should be brought together, the frail ladies began to fade out of the picture. Other library schools sprang up over the country and now there are many accredited schools besides innumerable short courses in universities and teachers' colleges.

At first these graduate librarians were in such great demand that they were offered positions long before graduation day. Naturally this delightful condition could not last, as more and more girls flocked to the schools or entered training classes of large public libraries. Matters were not helped, either, by the depression which brought that 50 per cent cut in opportunities.

During World War II, however, many new types of library positions were created. These, in addition to vacancies caused by resignations of librarians to enter better-paid war jobs or the Armed Services, created that 18,000 shortage. For many years ahead, there will be no reason to "beware of libraries," if you can qualify as a good librarian.

What kind of girl should become a librarian? Certainly she should have more than a fond parent's idea that "Ruthie would make such a fine librarian; she just wants to sit around and read all day." Poor Ruthie! What would happen to her in a hospital library where she would have about as much chance to sit around as the nurses? Or if she were driving a book truck all over the countryside for a county library? Take the following description of a typical day in an industrial library. After such a day, and all the other days that might be even busier, the librarian might be too weary to do even necessary reading at home.

The telephone is likely to start ringing in the morning before the door is unlocked, and the librarian will be lucky if, within the next two hours, she has a chance to draw a full breath. Most of the early calls are apt to be for book renewals, to ask that certain magazines or reports be sent in a great rush, to request that a special book be borrowed from a nearby library, or to order a photostat. In the midst of this may be one or more "long-search" questions which may occupy spare moments for weeks or which may demand trips to several outside libraries, long-distance calls to the Library of Congress or the National Bureau of Standards in Washington or to other helpful library sleuths in nearby large cities. Without such friends strategically placed, the librarian is lost. The day goes on with such duties as circulating hundreds of magazines, helping visitors who come to the library, purchasing books and other materials, and preparing them for use. The person is right who said, "Almost anything can happen in a library." Librarians have been called upon to advise on such matters as naming the new baby and when to set out frail seedlings in the spring.

At the moment of writing, libraries in the business and technical field—known as special libraries—offer excellent opportunities. If you are eager for excellent training and experience and are not afraid of uncertainty, you will do well to try special librarianship.

"Why uncertainty?" is a question you may ask. Because business has been known to sweep service groups (such as libraries) out the door when budgets shrink and profits approach the vanishing point. For this reason it is wise to investigate pretty carefully the business with which you plan to cast your lot. Ascertain the rating of the company. If it has several plants or large offices scattered about the country, chances may be bright for promotion, and you will have more security than with a smaller organization.

Among other prospects in the special libraries field are hospital libraries of the Army, Navy, and Veterans Administration. Salaries may not be high here, but you will have satisfactions that far outweigh cash rewards. Here will be the task of selecting the best books for the particular type of patients you serve; of preparing them for use; and that most important job of all—getting them used. This will involve regular trips to all the wards—and we hope you will not undertake such work unless your arches are pluperfect; that is about equal in importance to your ability to prescribe books so that they will have therapeutic value.

"What do you mean by that?" asks the young person who knows the word "therapeutic" but who has not considered it in connection with books. Well, in a mental hospital, it means that you must suggest books or magazines that will divert disordered minds from their delusions for brief intervals but which contain nothing that will cause a disturbance. This requires judgment of high order. Or, this type of work may mean securing textbooks for disabled men who want to prepare for new lines of work. If, later on, you find that your books have helped a neurotic patient make an adjustment to life outside hospital walls or that a disabled person has become a normal earning individual through the use of books you will not worry about the amount you were paid in the doing.

All this does not mean that industrial and hospital libraries are the only promising phases of the special libraries field. In all sorts of associations (commercial, trade, professional, civic, labor, and the like) you will find challenging opportunities. Likewise there are interesting openings in museums, foundations, newspapers and publishing houses; with boards of education and other municipal bureaus; in our thousands of federal and state agencies; with public utilities, advertising firms, and so on—and on. Librarians of special subject departments in large public and university libraries are regarded as special librarians as well.

A noted librarian once defined the qualifications for any librarian as "90 per cent common sense and 10 per cent genius." Nowhere in the wide field of librarianship are these traits needed more than in library service for children, whether it be in a public library or in a school library. Publishers may issue the finest children's books of all time but there must be someone to stimulate use of the books. What a job is ahead for children's and school librarians in helping to prepare today's children for their heavy responsibilities in the changing world of tomorrow. Each school library carries a heavy schedule of classes, as well as constant work with individual students and teachers. The children's room in every public library must supplement the work of the schools not only in education of boys and girls who come to the library but of their parents as well. It also offers unlimited opportunities for reading for pleasure.

Let's see what goes on each day in the life of a children's librarian as described by the busy and successful head of the children's room in an industrial town where the library serves children from widely varying national backgrounds. Many are of Dutch descent, although the largest group is Polish; then come the Greeks followed in numbers by Russians, Hungarians, Austrians, and Czechs. Here are some of the two dozen activities listed by this children's librarian: helping children select books; answering many reference questions; conducting a story hour every Saturday morning all year round and one in the Y.W.C.A. every Monday afternoon during July of each year; visiting schools (giving book talks and telling stories in lower grades); book talks to parents' and teachers' associations; lessons to teen-age groups at the Y.W.C.A. on how to tell stories to children in camps, parks, and elsewhere; guiding *Bookworms*, a teen-age book discussion group which meets in the library. In addition to all this work directly with children, parents, and teachers, there are such jobs as mending torn books; keeping the picture collection up to date; selecting, ordering, and cataloguing new books; preparing books for the bindery, and so on. And, of course, there are reports (monthly and yearly), inventory, registration of new borrowers, etc. This young woman insists that "to me being a children's librarian is lots more fun than doing any other kind of work. No two days are ever alike as you never know what the day is going to bring. If you like people—if you like books—what could be a better combination in a career, especially when you work with children?"

Perhaps your school library had a library club in which you saw a little of the work your school librarian did in supplying you and your classmates with materials for your lessons. But you could not know how hard she worked to make sure that the books you needed were there when you wanted them. How many lists of titles she checked! She had to secure the interest and co-operation of the teachers, and the principal probably needed occasional prodding about the book funds. There was much more to her work than you saw. Going into the classes and explaining the use of the library or having classes come into the library for instruction was only part of her duties. Working with the teachers and keeping up with new books for children and young people and with professional literature took hours of her time.

A young college student had this to say about the importance of such a librarian's work: "I often wonder if librarians have any idea how much their sympathy with a boy's interests means to him, especially if he meets with none at home. I wish I could make them understand what it is they are doing for the children who go to the library."

Another fascinating phase of librarianship is work with grownups—called *adult education*. Here the library's function is to provide sources of learning for adults who come to the librarian for help. This is the work such a librarian does: selection of books and pamphlets especially suited to informal, popular education; counseling individuals with a serious educational purpose; associating reading with programs of groups and organizations having educational purposes; stimulating interest in continued learning through reading for more effective living. Adult education work is usually carried on by public libraries.

"Every population group in a city large enough to be serviced by a neighborhood branch library is also large enough to warrant the services of at least one general adult education specialist," insists a noted librarian.

By this time you probably realize that you'll have to prepare as carefully for this profession as for medicine, law, or the ministry. This is especially true if you think you'd like to be an adult education specialist or a librarian in a college or university. You must have a college degree plus specialized technical training in an accredited library school. In states which have certification laws, in city, state and federal libraries which operate under Civil Service plans, you must have such training or its equivalent in experience. The usual plan is to take a four-year college course and then enter a library school for a one-year course. At the end of this graduate course, some library schools now give a Master's degree in Library Science. In some universities you may combine a college course with library training and may finish in four years. It is a stiff course but a good one, because you study the subjects in the arts, sciences, and languages which will be most useful in your library work.

Among the library subjects which you will take are: bibliography and reference; history of books and printing; book selection; fundamentals of library science; administration of every kind of library; cataloguing and classification; publicity service in public, special, school, or college libraries; principles of library organization. A Ph.D. degree will be desirable if you expect to reach the top in college or university library work. A college librarian is not likely to be given the rank of full professor unless he has this degree.

Another type of preparation for librarianship is the apprentice class in a large public library, where technical training is combined with paid practice work. During recent years many large libraries have dropped their training classes, but there are still a few remaining. This is a way for the girl who cannot afford more than a college education to secure a position in one of the lower grades of the large public library. It is also an excellent way of gaining practical experience, but the ambitious girl will not be satisfied to remain in a lower grade. Sooner or later she is likely to break away and take a library course so that she can reach one of the positions open only to graduate librarians.

Now you'll want to know what kind of work you will do after you have had all this training.

Reference work in a library can be a most satisfying type of work. One of the most amusing detective stories we have read describes a man who tried to discover who actually killed Christopher Marlowe. His difficulties, until he finally digs out the truth after tracing clue after clue through old library and legal files, make an absorbing tale. Finding elusive information for people, however, is not the only satisfaction in reference work. It is equally gratifying to help students learn how to use indexes and various reference books so that they can dig up their own answers.

If you have a particular interest in science, art, business, or a similar subject, you will be wise to specialize in it. Many large public libraries have special subject departments and are often in need of assistants in the field. The Library of Congress and other government libraries have positions with excellent salaries for specialists in various subjects. The Army Medical Library, for example, is the largest medical library in the United States. The library of the Department of Agriculture is the largest agricultural library in the world. Write to the U. S. Civil Service Commission for the pamphlet, *The Librarian in the Federal Civil Service*. This publication gives information concerning methods of securing government library positions and describes a number of selected government libraries—including the Department of Labor Library, the United States Patent Office Library, the Treasury Department Library.

If you are bookish but don't care much about dealing with people, there is a good spot for you in the library world. It is called preparation work, which includes ordering, classifying, and cataloguing the books—in fact, all that happens to them before they are ready to be borrowed from the library. Cataloguers need exceedingly careful training in detail and sometimes they are given larger salaries and have shorter hours because of the difficulties and technicalities in their work, particularly if they are familiar with many different languages.

The readers' adviser is a relatively recent service in large public and college libraries. You might aim at this kind of work if you have an understanding of human psychology, which you will need in trying to discover what can be done to aid readers in undertaking a systematic course of reading, in selecting books that will help solve their particular problems, or in developing their reading interests. The readers' adviser keeps in touch with local adult education agencies, and frequently is a leader in this movement. There are limitless possibilities in this fascinating phase of the profession.

A flair for writing is an asset in library work. Publicity is important as a means of enticing new readers into the library as well as luring cash from the wallets of wealthy citizens for the support of the library. There are book lists and pamphlets to be prepared, perhaps a column for the local paper, or a monthly publication issued from the library. Some libraries have a special publicity department which will give you all the outlet you wish for your imagination.

Are you too restless to consider being shut up for long hours in a library? Then you might prefer county library work, or extension work for a large public library or state library commission, taking books to the people instead of waiting for them to come to the library. This work can give you greater returns in personal satisfaction than any other because of the close personal contacts with your readers and their dependence upon you. Driving a bookmobile through lovely farming country may sound delightful, as well, but you must also think of the snowdrifts of winter and the danger of icy roads. It will take courage, resourcefulness, and devotion for you to be a success in this kind of work.

What does the small library have to offer? Usually not much in the way of pay or easy hours, but the work may be great fun. There is never any monotony, especially if you must do everything yourself. Not only will you be librarian, cataloguer, reference librarian, but also administrator of business matters and loan desk worker. The librarian of a small town has to control herself almost as carefully as the school principal or the Methodist minister. But she will also mean as much in the social and intellectual life of the people.

College and university libraries offer opportunities in reference, research, circulation, administrative and teaching positions. Here one may have a stimulating campus life, usually on a faculty basis, although salaries and vacations are sometimes on the clerical level.

Large public libraries may make you feel at times as though you are just a cog, but many of them have excellent provisions for promotion. You may enter in a low grade at a small salary, possibly through the training class, but additional study, experience, and personal development will help you pass an examination for a higher grade, with increased salary. Thus you may climb to an administrative position that would rarely come in a smaller library.

This brings us to a question that has caused a great flurry among the women of the library profession. Are too many of the well-paid administrative positions going to men? Figures show that 90 per cent of the library workers are women, and yet young and often inexperienced men are replacing women as heads of university and large public libraries. Many people fear this will discourage ambitious young women from considering library work as a profession, but they aren't likely to get anywhere in any profession if they are as timid as that. Perhaps men can accomplish more as heads of university libraries where men predominate on the faculties. Certainly any woman who can handle the affairs of a large public library as well as did Linda Eastman of Cleveland, Althea Warren of Los Angeles, or Beatrice Winsor of Newark, has nothing to fear from men. There are places in the highest ranks for women who have the right training and ability.

You may not like the dull routine of clerical jobs which everyone is almost sure to have to do; many a brilliant person has been lost to the library profession because of the irksome detail. The higher you climb in the profession, however, the less routine work you will have to do, as a rule. In public libraries, unreasonable taxpayers who demand their rights may irritate you; students in high school or college libraries may be ultra-demanding. On the whole, however, people are pleasant to deal with and very grateful for the help given them. Among other disadvantages of the library profession are low salaries, strenuous work which often means being on duty two to four evenings a week, and the consequent sacrifices that one must make. Salary scales are being raised, however, and hours are improving.

On the opposite side of the ledger are: stimulating contacts with books and people; the opportunity to use everything you have ever learned; opportunity to be of service to all classes of people and an important part of community life; work in pleasant surroundings with congenial associates; and good opportunities for promotion and for personal growth.

One of our topnotch university librarians has pointed out that "the librarian of the future will be rich in opportunity, ideas and enthusiasm. He will also be blessed with the human capacity to dream dreams and the good fortune to see many of them realized. He will be measured by the degree to which his library provides intellectual understanding of life's problems and joys. His most important duty will be to live helpfully. In that activity he will rejoice exceedingly in his calling." That goes for both men and women of this profession.

22. HOME ECONOMISTS

DID YOU EVER hear of Ellen H. Richards? You'd do well to make her acquaintance if you are interested in becoming a home economist because she's the person who first brought science into the home economics movement. At the beginning of her career, Ellen Richards vowed she would never marry because matrimony might interfere with her work. In the 1870's when she was safely launched as the first woman sanitary chemist, she wrote to a college friend: "I can now change the query, 'Will it pay to sacrifice love for fame?' into the declaration, 'It has paid so far.'"

Although she later changed her mind and married a fellow-scientist, she continued her career as long as she lived. And it is fortunate for all domestically inclined women that she did, for from Ellen Richards' pioneer efforts in scientific homemaking have sprung most of the developments in home economics. Her experimental work in Boston "launched a thousand ships" in this field and paved the way for countless jobs for women. Before her time practically the only opportunities for home service were in teaching, sewing, and cooking; now we have experts in food and nutrition, in child development and family relations, in clothing and shelter. There are commercial demonstrators, research workers, journalists, dietitians, institution managers, experts in business, and, of course, scientifically trained homemakers who carry on within the home, as well as the skilled teachers of home economics.

Before Mrs. Richards and her friend, Mrs. Abel, another pioneer home economist, started their cooking demonstrations at the New England Kitchen in Boston and in the Rumford Kitchen at the Chicago World's Fair of 1893, there had been little or no interest in the scientific preparation of food. Gradually the efforts of these women attracted a group of workers who branched out in all directions to develop new ideas for better living; one chose to work with farmers' wives, while others spread happiness and health through their cooking schools and recipe books which quickly became the guides of many young brides.

Being domestically inclined is not all you need to become a successful home economist. You need to feel keenly all that makes for good home living; such as a working knowledge of child development and family relationships, an understanding of the importance of good nutrition for the family, and of mental hygiene.

"I don't like economics," you say. "And I hated messing

around with test tubes in the high school chemistry lab."

Then stay out of the food and demonstration aspects of home economics. You'll be a total loss unless you like science, and economics is vitally important, too. There are many other branches of home economics in which to specialize.

In almost every phase of this profession you will need to get along well with others, and, what's more important, you must have a sincere interest in them and their welfare —an interest so deep that everyone you meet will recognize it. This is particularly true if you decide to do any form of extension work, which will mean organizing programs and inspiring others to carry on the work during your absence.

If you enter commercial demonstration work, you will need poise, adaptability, sales sense, a forceful personality, good voice, a pleasant manner, trim appearance, charm, and tact. For institutional work you will need most of these personality traits plus the capacity for hard work, executive ability, and expert knowledge of the special field. The teacher of home economics needs all the qualities of any teacher: good judgment, ability to advise, sympathy, tact, accuracy, and progressiveness. In addition she must have certain mechanical skills and a large fund of adaptability, because she has such varied material to present.

"That's a large order," remarks the aspiring home economist. "But suppose I do have all the necessary personality traits, what's next?"

"Education," we reply, "and plenty of it." Of course you might find some kind of work after taking only the home economics courses offered in high school or vocational school, but most of the good positions call for four years of high school and four years of college work. And for teaching in college or research work, graduate study will be necessary. There are short courses in tearoom management, candy making, and the like, but if you can afford it attend a good college and get all the training you can. Without a college degree, as we mentioned before, you cannot get a good teaching position nor a job in government service. If you aspire to college teaching, you will need a doctor's degree if you really want to reach the top.

The college course in home economics includes most of the usual liberal arts subjects necessary for a cultural background. In addition are courses in household sciences and arts: the scientific study of food, nutrition, textiles, and appliances, the arts of home decoration, sewing, costume design, dressmaking, and millinery. There are also special courses for students who wish to become experts in such fields as dietetics, research, teaching, child development, demonstration, or institutional work.

Teaching home economics in the public schools may be much more fun than pushing a lot of unwilling youngsters through algebra and English. Assisting in the management of a model home, usually with a real baby to mother, will appeal to girl pupils so that it will seem like play school to them. There is need, however, for mastering all household skills so that one is able to teach them efficiently. There are many opportunities for promotion in this field, particularly into supervisory positions.

Here is the story of one young woman who has been very successful in this field. After graduation from college, Frances Urban taught in a rural school. Then she took a degree in home economics education and taught in high school where she had several adult education classes. Study in Iowa State College for an advanced degree came next in her career. After various teaching and supervisory positions, Miss Urban became the Field Secretary of the American Home Economics Association.

"In this position," she explained, "I represent more than 20,000 college-trained women. I am in close touch with all projects which aim to advance the professional welfare of home economists in homes, schools, laboratories, offices, or wherever they are practicing their profession. I am in close touch, too, with programs of consumer education and those devoted to the promotion of international understanding through study grants to foreign students. Any legislation that is likely to affect families throughout the nation is of deep concern to me in this position."

Although most of this young woman's experience has been in teaching, she urges young would-be home economists to take a serious look at all the varied phases in this profession before choosing their special fields. We suggest that you write to the American Home Economics Association, 1600 20th Street, N.W., Washington 9, D. C., for a copy of the leaflet *Reach for a Star* which describes briefly jobs in research, extension work, textiles and clothing, in teaching and homemaking, in public welfare and child care, in business and with institution foods.

Among the most promising fields today are: county or home demonstration work; commercial demonstration of foods, textiles, public utilities; sales promotion work for various products used in the home; institutional management; budgeting services in banks; advice on costume; department store buying, especially in materials for the home; research work in experiment stations, agricultural colleges, or with the Federal Government.

County and home demonstration work is one of the most rewarding branches of this profession. The demonstration agent travels around the country doing things for people that will make life more livable. It is sad, however, to think that it took four acts of Congress to launch this demonstration work and to promote the development of a profession which is offering increasing opportunities to specialists in home economics.

The chief task of the home demonstration agent in government or state extension service is to help housewives improve the health and happiness of their families. The best means of accomplishing this is through local meetings. First of all, the agent plans a careful program with a few local people, forms a committee to arrange for a big get-together, then puts on the kind of show they request. This may be a lecture demonstration on food and nutrition or new kitchen equipment; a group discussion on economical ways of keeping the children looking neat and respectable; how to make a successful household budget; or any other home problem. In addition, the home demonstration agent goes into homes and helps individuals to solve their personal difficulties.

In the social service field there are similar positions with charitable organizations that are aiding the "ill-clad, ill-fed, and ill-housed." The problem of diet for undernourished children, diabetics, or people suffering from other diseases calls for attention, as well as aid in budget-making, housekeeping efficiency, and the like.

If you are fond of tinkering with appliances, you might train for commercial demonstration work. In the early days, demonstrators for commercial firms were forced to wear gaudy, bespangled costumes and bake biscuits to waltz time to attract attention. Not so today! A trim, businesslike young woman in a crisp white uniform will demonstrate new recipes for the refrigerator or the newest kind of electric stove with all the poise and dignity of a judge on the bench. There are countless opportunities for you to demonstrate household goods and services for commercial firms and public service companies—positions filled with daily thrills that come from meeting and helping all sorts and conditions of women. As an afterthought we might mention that this is usually a very well-paid field, although there are no fixed salary standards.

In this work you may be sent out to give lecture demonstrations to adult groups, or to schools, colleges, 4-H clubs, Girl Scouts, Camp Fire Girls, etc. In an industrial establishment you may serve as a kitchen-laboratory hostess, serving meals to company officials, visitors, a "tasting squad," etc., or you may prepare products for photography and act as a model in action pictures.

If you like teaching and are successful in demonstration work, you may be asked to train crews of demonstrators or conduct classes in training for this type of work. As we have pointed out, there are many other possibilities for the home economist in the business world.

The institutional field offers you the chance to be a dietitian, manager, or housekeeper of educational, charitable, or state institutions, clubs, or camps, manager of a cafeteria, school lunchroom, tearoom, restaurant. In this type of work you'll use all the business and executive ability you possess in addition to your thorough training in food and nutrition. Buying supplies, food, and equipment, directing assistants, and complying with public health requirements will keep you on your toes. The most exacting task, however, is planning varied menus with proper food values and an appetizing appearance that will please the clientele or keep the inmates of an institution from complaining about the food.

The hospital dietitian has many more duties. She helps to plan therapeutic diets, serves special diets and test meals, keeps in touch with reports from the laboratories, makes case studies based on the effect of diets, teaches dietetics to nurses, and works with the doctors. She must of course be able to adapt herself to the limitations of institutional life.

In food service there may be more possibilities for you than in dietetics, or owning and managing a tearoom or restaurant. You may start a bake shop, sell foods ready to heat and serve, or conduct a home canning kitchen. If you open a food shop, be sure you have sufficient capital. You'll have to build up a reputation and that takes time. A keen business sense is important in such an undertaking and, above all, a strong physique, because the work is hard and your hours may be from dawn until midnight.

Research in foods, textiles, and clothing is an interesting field for the girl who enjoyed laboratory work in high school. All the experiment stations of state agricultural colleges, as well as the great Bureau of Home Economics of the U. S. Department of Agriculture, have openings in their laboratories. Hospitals, advertising agencies, and commercial firms may need your research services if you have had the necessary scientific training.

For the woman who writes there are three possibilities—first, as a free lance writer on home economics subjects; second, editorial work; and third, as a writer of advertising copy or as director of other writers. The free lance writer in this field must work up a reputation in one or more phases of the subject and, even then, she will probably need to combine writing with teaching or some other work. On the other hand, an editorial position may provide a very good living. Almost all the newspapers and magazines have a section addressed to the homemaker, and there is usually a home economist as editor. The editorship of one page in the Sunday paper which describes new household appliances constitutes a lucrative full-time job, especially if the editor is a specialist in testing appliances. But the chief job of the home economics editor is reading and accepting manuscripts for her magazine or newspaper, as well as writing some articles and editorials herself. The third branch of writing—advertising copy for agencies, stores, magazines, or newspapers—may be exceedingly worth while. Here you will be driven as in no other field of home economics, and there will be that terrific strain of striving for the unique and original. The writer of advertising copy must know all about homemakers and about what will appeal to them.

Today there are many radio and television opportunities in this field. How often does a trained home economist tell you the latest news about kitchen equipment, time-saving devices, laundry soaps, and other household aids and hints and, often too, demonstrate these gadgets and products on television? One of the most fascinating jobs of this sort is held by a woman who goes from city to city all over this country—first broadcasting the good news about the product she is advertising and then demonstrating its use and its fine points in one of the local department stores. She secured that position in a radio voice contest. That's a hint to take speech courses if you want this kind of a job.

Like all fields of work, some positions in home economics may have drawbacks. The hospital dietitian may find institutional life monotonous and sick people may be trying. On the other hand, some people have a gift for working happily with sick people. There may be small chance for experimental work. And the commercial dietitian faces constant criticism and the uncertainty of business. This also affects the commercial demonstrator whose job may be the first to be dropped if her firm starts going "into the red." The work day is often long. And there are some women who will object to working almost exclusively with other women. It is too narrowing, they say, but we are not convinced of that.

On the other hand, the advantages far outnumber the drawbacks. The chief advantage is the lack of competition from men except in the hotel and restaurant fields. The fact that this profession is "woman's natural sphere" will cause fewer mental conflicts and will prepare her for matrimony as a career. You must not overlook the point that marriage will not diminish your ability to earn your living again in this profession, if that should be necessary. You will be even better prepared to step into a good position and make a success of it after you have run your own home.

No one knows in what direction home economics will evolve. Think of the developments since the day of Ellen Richards and Mary Abel! It is undoubtedly the most promising field that is open almost exclusively to women. Moreover, there are certain inner satisfactions which will mean everything to the socially minded woman; satisfactions that come through the human contacts and the sense of adding to the welfare of mankind by increasing health and happiness. In a period when many changes are taking place in the home, there is a great challenge to home economists and to welfare workers to help in stabilizing and strengthening the ties which hold families together.

23. RECREATION LEADERS

"WHEW—THAT TOUGH job's done," exclaimed a researcher friend wearily. "And I'm too tired to do anything but play tennis."

How strange that would have sounded a decade ago! But we're wiser today. People have discovered that the only way to keep well in this period of high pressure working is to have a certain proportion of one's time spent in some form of play or recreation. And what a fine field of work this need for play has opened up to girls. There are few fields more in need of workers and the delightful point is that the demand will probably exceed the supply for some time.

In the field of physical education it has been estimated that there are many more positions for men and women in the United States than there are adequately trained workers.

Don't think of going into any phase of physical education or recreation work unless you are physically strong. Appearance means almost everything in this business. You may be expert in all the tricks of the trade but you'll get nowhere unless you have a well-built body and fresh, wholesome-looking skin. Good health, good humor, and general attractiveness are prime requisites for success. Athletic excellence is desirable although one does not necessarily need to be a champion in any field. Alertness, poise, strong, pleasing voice that has a ring of authority, and a real zest for life are other important traits you should have, as well as a fine social attitude, ability to lead others, some creative ability (particularly in the specialized fields such as arts and crafts, the drama, music, etc.), and moral habits that are above reproach. You must like people sincerely and be liked by them and be willing to sacrifice your personal interests to the needs of the job.

College education is required for most of the positions in this field and you should prepare for college in high school by taking social studies, natural sciences, physics, English, and public speaking. Your four-year college course will include advanced work in all these subjects as well as training in soccer, tennis, the dance, swimming, volley ball, field hockey, softball, golf, archery, and the theory of these sports. There will be much of value in the sciences such as chemistry, anatomy, physiology, biology, bacteriology, and psychology. There may be a chance for you to have a minor position without a college degree, but you can find nothing worth while with less than two years of college training in physical education. For the higher administrative positions in both teaching and recreation leadership, you must have additional graduate courses. A Ph.D. is desirable for college teaching, although chiefly for the head of a department.

The recreation leader plans, schedules, and supervises playground activities; organizes classes in dramatics, the

RECREATION LEADERS

dance, sports, and other activities; oversees the organization of athletic teams and leagues; administers first aid when necessary; keeps records and prepares reports; stimulates interest in recreational development and community work; supervises equipment; assists in planning training classes for assistants. The recreation assistant performs the following duties: keeps playground in good condition; takes charge of the distribution, placing, and collection of equipment; sees that the equipment used is in good condition; gives instruction in various types of games, such as basketball, baseball, etc., on the playgrounds; assists in supervising and refereeing athletic games; assists in supervision of swimming pools and in teaching the rudiments of swimming; conducts classes in handicraft, manual arts, and dramatics; maintains order on the playground; gives first aid when necessary; prepares programs and attendance reports.

Advancement in this work usually depends upon the amount of training and successful experience acquired. In a well-organized community recreation program of a large city, there are six types of positions available. The top administrative position is as superintendent of the entire program, in charge of the department and its personnel. The superintendent must be more than twenty-five years old and well-trained in all phases of community organization and should have taken graduate work in city planning, personnel management, educational administration, etc. The position calls for the hail-fellow-well-met promoter, organizer type of personality and pays a good salary. These jobs are usually held by men.

The general supervisors of playgrounds and community centers are in the division just below the superintendent and must be almost as well-trained and experienced. They must be able to organize people in all sorts of recreational activities and must be able to train subordinates who will carry out the program of special activities. Special courses in adult education, group discussion and forums, will add to this person's effectiveness in dealing with adult groups.

Just below the general supervisor of the community center are all the supervisors of special activities, and these positions offer many opportunities for women. In large cities there may be six or seven of these supervisors, although in smaller places one person may be required to supervise all these activities. These special supervisors must be well-trained in their fields and must be able to inspire interest in recreation. First is the supervisor of athletics who should have experience as a director of a playground or experience in teaching physical education, and who must have some personal skills in athletics, high ideals of sportsmanship, etc. The supervisors of music, drama, and the dance must be capable performers and have experience in teaching or directing in these phases of the work. Their aim should not be to show off their own skills or even to put on a good show just for the show's sake. That's far from the purpose of their work, which is to use the dance, the drama, and music for social and cultural ends and not primarily for public display. After all, the object is to give the people who come to the center what they need in the form of recreation and individual satisfaction. Never mind if Susie Jones can't sing well, let her sing regardless of what happens.

There is frequently a special supervisor for activities in arts and crafts, who should have personal skill as well as ability to teach such crafts as basketry, weaving, batik, sewing, household arts and embroidery, metal craft and jewelry, bookbinding, wood carving, leather craft, drawing, painting, etc. There may be a supervisor of nature activities who will be specially trained in the natural sciences and able to make them interesting to others. This person should have wide experience in outdoor activities and in science teaching. Camp work is a decided asset to this supervisor.

In some of the largest community centers there may be a supervisor of girls' and women's activities, who will adapt the program to their special needs, capacities, and interests. This work, however, is usually part of the duties of an assistant superintendent or the general supervisor.

Community recreation work is by no means the only field open to you. Industrial recreation has become a promising phase since employers have realized that organized play will increase the efficiency and production in large industrial plants. Some industrial organizations believe in the idea so firmly that they are willing to finance a recreation program for the entire community where the factories are located. The Goodyear Company, for example, has a two-million-dollar recreation building. Buick, Chevrolet, and others divide their recreation activities into four fields —amusements, social, cultural, athletics.

On the other hand, there are instances where the industrial recreation leader must work without adequate equipment. Perhaps there will be little more than a vacant lot. Yet a great deal can be done even there in the way of baseball, basketball, outdoor dancing, sings, etc. Bad conditions may be just the opportunity for the recreation leader to show what her work can do to promote better feeling on the part of the employees toward their employer.

A position as recreation leader in industry may not pay

very well in one of the less progressive plants. However, this may be an entering wedge for a better position in the personnel department or may even lead to the position of head of that department at a salary which will be worth all the waiting and effort.

Summer camp work is another important phase of recreation leadership either in private camps or in those sponsored by various clubs or charitable organizations. There is usually a recreation director in a camp of any size. Students in physical education or teachers of education find this a happy and profitable way of spending their vacations. For the girl who is a good sailor and likes to see different countries, there is an occasional chance to act as recreation leader or swimming teacher on a cruise ship or transatlantic liner. Better not get too excited about that possibility, though, for you would be eligible only for an American ship and that places decided limitations on your chance of landing such a job. Another phase of travel that is offering new opportunities in our country is as recreation leader in the youth hostels. The worker has the task of organizing a community for the hostels. She must have a college degree, love the outdoors, be a good public speaker, a good executive, and be satisfied with simple living.

Recreation for the physically handicapped and in penal institutions or hospitals offers fine possibilities for the specialist in arts and crafts, music, dramatics, and some of the simpler sports. Usually the inmates of hospitals or penal institutions are required to take part in some of these activities and the recreation leader is charged with the responsibility of seeing that they actually do participate. The work may be very taxing in mental hospitals but it may be decidedly satisfying if the patients are responsive and improve as a result of their activities. Here, physical therapy is exceedingly important.

This is a specialized field, very closely allied to the work of the recreation leader, and has been discussed in an earlier chapter.

Nearly every phase of recreational leadership includes the task of promoting the program, of interpreting your work to the people you are serving (the community, industry, or elsewhere), and of arousing enthusiasm for participation in the activities that are offered. Usually, you will have to be constantly striving to increase enrollment of participants in order to sell the program to those who make the allowances for space and equipment. There are many angles to this job, also, that are concerned with safety, meeting strict regulations, checking equipment, and being prepared to administer first aid in any emergencies.

In this entire field of recreation leadership there is the drawback of long irregular hours. The hardest work is usually done on Saturdays, Sundays, and holidays. There are always heavy demands on the health, and it is a relatively short-lived occupation. Youth is essential here more than in any other field. On the other hand, health education is absorbing a few of the workers who have reached the maximum of their effectiveness in recreation work.

Although you will not make a fortune, in many places your salary will be entirely adequate and may be even more than that. And there are rich rewards in helping the people in a community live happier, healthier lives. You will have a position of respect and importance in the community and will feel that you are doing constructive work in developing the physical and moral standards of the people.

24. BEAUTICIANS

"COSMETOLOGY"—OFFICIAL TITLE of the beautifier's job —is a high-sounding word but it denotes a familiar and important profession for women.

As you have suspected, cosmetology is the ancient and honorable art of beauty culture, an art which has been practiced since before the dawn of history. But never before on such a large scale as in our own beauty-mad America. Here cosmetics has become one of our largest industries. It is a constantly growing business with almost limitless possibilities.

Would you like to know how cosmetology gave rise to jobs for women? Back in the twenties, when the bobbed-hair craze was set off by lovely Irene Castle, men barbers snipped off most of the long hair and kept it trimmed to the Castle specifications. Even today, men in beauty shops are usually the specialists with scissors and clippers. In those days, women beauty workers constituted only a small per cent of the total in the field. That situation was quickly changed, however, as ladies started to crowd into beauty parlors for hair waving, facial packs, and other types of beauty treatment.

Before the rush of the twenties, women had a very small part in this beauty business; slightly more than 1,500 were in the beauty parlors of the nation in the seventies. Their number more than doubled, however, in the eighties, remained nearly the same in the nineties (when a depression hit this luxury business), and reached 7,284 by the turn of the century. By 1910, on the other hand, women more than tripled that figure, then zoomed right along—hitting well over 100,000 by 1930 and, despite the most disastrous depression of all, reached more than 200,000 by 1940, and have been increasing in number ever since.

Suppose we quote from a government publication (*Women's Occupations Through Seven Decades*) on the way this job grew up:

Following World War I a tremendous development took place in the field of beauty culture work. The ranks of women barbers, beauticians, and manicurists were swelled by nearly 80,000 additional women from 1920 to 1930 and by nearly 105,000 from 1930 to 1940. These occupations had a total of 218,132 women in 1940, over 140 times the mere 1,548 women in the same fields in 1870.

What kind of women are found among those 218,132 and the ones who have joined their ranks during the past decade? You will be sure to notice their attractive personalities and good grooming. Beauty isn't necessary because a woman who makes the best of irregular features and other beauty handicaps will be a fine advertisement for her own work or that of her co-workers. One New York operator insists on 90 per cent personality and 10 per cent ability in his operators.

In addition to that personality plus and good grooming, a beautician should be intelligent, pleasant, self-possessed, sympathetic, tactful, and physically strong. She needs strong arches plus a supple back to endure long hours of bending over customers.

Good taste is also important and an artistic eye to see all the possibilities of your client. It will be your job to give her a make-up or style in hairdress that will make her more attractive than she would be without your magic touch. If she is determined on gay coloring that would ruin her appearance, you must stop her—by fair means or foul. This requires tact. You can't say, "See here, you'll look perfectly terrible in that shade of rouge and lipstick." Instead you'll have to drop a subtle suggestion here and there until you turn the trick. In other words, you'll have to be an expert diplomat in this line.

When it comes to styles for the hair, you'll need super-tact, especially as fads for ups-and-downs, bunches of curls, page-boy effects, feather and other types of short cuts come and go. You will need to be an artist to bring out the best points of your clients, but what fun it is! Suppose your deft fingers are the means of helping to change a colorless individual into a distinctive, attractive person. Could anything be more exciting or satisfying?

We must consider age and educational requirements for this work. Check the Department of Public Instruction in your state on the question of age at which you can begin training. Although you need not be a high school or college graduate, it will be much better if you can have at least a few years in high school. In some of the large high schools, courses are now being given in care of the skin and hair. The students have great fun experimenting on each other. Think how helpful that would be in discovering your fitness for this occupation.

What are the actual jobs in beauty work? First is that of manicurist, or you may start out merely shampooing while more experienced operators give the permanents and "sets"—jobs which you will do after you gain experience. In department stores or large beauty shops you will have opportunities to climb into such jobs as assistant-manager or manager, or possibly buyer. There are sales jobs in large establishments, as well, at cosmetic counters—and there is usually a receptionist.

How much capital would you need to start a business of your own? A good deal depends on where and how elaborately you want to start. We know of one young woman who went out to homes giving hair treatments and other services which did not require more equipment than she could carry in her bag. And what a boon she was to convalescents and others who could not go to beauty salons! In some states this "work by appointment," as it is called, must be sponsored by an approved shop which supplies the kit of materials for the operator.

Another woman in our community started in her own home with simple equipment, later moving to a small storeroom, gradually enlarging until today she owns and manages three large and popular salons. Yes, fortunes can be made in this field but many owners may average only a few thousand dollars a year until they have developed a large business.

Here, too, are opportunities for a scientific woman who wants to specialize in skin diseases—but we have discussed that in another chapter.

A skillful beauty operator who has the urge toward social service may find satisfaction in hospital work. Many of the large hospitals maintain beauty shops, especially those with a large number of psychiatric patients. Doctors often prescribe a permanent or a new hairdo as a means of building up the morale of such patients.

In this occupation, there are state laws with rather strict certification requirements. Inquire about them from your school vocational counselor or State Employment Service office before you start your training. By all means try to go to an accepted beauty school rather than learning through apprenticeship.

"Beauty shop owners always send their own children to the best school they can afford," we were told, "because they may miss important points if they learn through apprenticeship."

Courses vary from three-and-a-half to six months, or sometimes longer. Inquire at the nearest beauty school or State Employment Service office for cost of training. Get as much of this training as possible even if you have to pay your tuition on the installment plan or work evenings to pay for it. You can take a daytime job and go to a beauty school at night but you had better be husky if you attempt that plan, or have an easy sitting-down job during the day. Most schools will accept a girl after only a few years in high school but you'll need business training somewhere along the line if you expect, ultimately, to open your own shop. One of our friends in this business figured that her training—which was a thousand hours—cost about five hundred dollars. This included the cost of commuting to school in a nearby city.

Beauty schools teach the following operations: shampooing, scalp treatment, waving, hairdressing, sterilization, tinting, and haircutting. You will learn as well the processes of eyebrow shaping, facial massage, make-up, and manicuring. In classes concerned with business methods you will learn how to buy supplies and manage that shop which you hope one day to own.

Among the interesting and well-paid by-lines for the girl with business ability are advertising, selling, and buying beauty preparations and supplies. If she happens to be gifted with her pen, she may edit a newspaper column on beauty hints or a beauty page of one of the great magazines in the country.

Not long ago, a young cosmetologist gave us her opinion of her work:

"Of course I like it," she exclaimed enthusiastically, and it was the shiny-eyed brand of enthusiasm that is good to see. "It's a lot better than selling things across a counter. You meet all kinds of nice people and there is always the chance of having your own shop and being your own boss. But even if you don't, you'll have a regular salary and earn more in commissions and tips."

"But there must be some unpleasant feature about the occupation," we insisted. "It looks too rosy to be true."

"Usually you're pretty sure of permanent work," she said. "But here in New York, the cheap places cause a lot of trouble. They use inexperienced girls and it isn't fair to the rest of us."

She didn't mention the disadvantage of working in the evening and the infrequent pauses for relaxation during the hours on duty. Another objection that has been mentioned is that training for this occupation cannot be used in any other field of work.

There is little masculine competition here. More than 90 per cent of all operators are women. Men frequently are made managers over the heads of more experienced and competent women, however. But there is no use worrying about that at this stage. Time enough to face that situation when it confronts you.

Despite all disadvantages, you will enjoy interesting contacts with people and the business phases may give you great satisfaction as you discover that you are rendering valuable service. We are sure that you will agree with the person who said:

"I have never known any money makers who seemed to enjoy the process as much as beauty specialists. And I believe the reason is, first, that they are doing things; second, that they are doing beautiful things; third, that they are doing things for other people."

IV

Scientists and Engineers

25. SCIENTISTS

ENDLESS FRONTIERS IN SCIENCE—SCIENCE REMAKING THE WORLD—ADVENTURES IN RESEARCH MAY WIN THE PEACE. These are headlines that show young people how exciting a career in science may be. What are the opportunities for women in the various fields of science? We suggest that you study Bulletin No. 223—*The Outlook for Women in Science*—issued by the Women's Bureau of the U. S. Department of Labor.

Do women have the necessary qualities for scientific work? Patience, for instance, is one of the most important requisites. Well, many women rate far above men in that attribute which is needed in countless ways in any scientific laboratory. Especially in all the minute details of experimental work. If an experiment fails time after time, one must always be ready to go back to the beginning and start over. This indicates the necessity for perseverance and persistence in science; and women are credited with possessing generous supplies of those two qualities. But insatiable curiosity, imaginativeness and creative ability are equally essential for scientific research. One of these creative ladies is credited with coining the famous term "nuclear fission."

In any phase of science intellectual honesty is vital. Disaster will certainly strike the scientist who fails on this point. As in most fields of the world's work, a strong body is a valuable asset. Work on an experiment may keep you on your feet many hours.

Women who have the urge to labor in science must be prepared to study long and diligently. If you've read the life of Madame Curie, you'll understand what we mean. You should read that book before you decide upon a career in science. Even though you may not aspire to such fame, you'll do well to follow Madame Curie's example and study, study, study until you have acquired a Ph.D. degree. Even then you can't stop studying unless you are willing to accept an insignificant place in the world of science.

"A woman who desires to attain eminence in science must expect to work hard for a good many years," we warn you. "If she reaches the rank of full professor in a college or university, it will not be, on the average, until the age of thirty-nine."

In a study of women scientists, it was revealed that among eminent scientists there were ninety-four men for every six women in the field. Nevertheless, the number of women is constantly increasing—particularly in teaching, in laboratory and clinical work, as investigators, editors, and the like.

While a woman may work successfully in any field of science, her chances are best in psychology, only fairly good in the biological sciences and chemistry, and rather poor in physics and geology.

Suppose we turn to the various fields and see what they

have to offer. As we have hinted, teaching is an exceedingly important phase of scientific work, and perhaps there is slightly more chance for women than in the other branches. In the elementary schools women predominate in all the subjects; in high school the competition in teaching science is rather keen, and in college it is extremely stiff. A man will be selected as science teacher nine times out of ten on either the high school or college level and promotions will often go to the masculine members of the faculty regardless of the claims or qualifications of women science teachers. To get to the top as a teacher of science, you will certainly need that ultra-superior equipment we've talked about so much. Yet teaching is really the best place for women in science; they are accepted more willingly there and have better opportunities for advancement, that is, in comparison with laboratory work and the like.

Psychology is a growing field for women as is indicated by the fact that about 30 per cent of the 6,000 members of the American Psychological Association are women. Where do they work and what are the tasks which they perform?

A few hundred of them teach psychology in colleges and universities. Women have much less chance for academic employment than men but, if such employment is once obtained, they have about as good a chance as men for promotion in junior and teachers' colleges, in women's colleges, and in universities (except to the grade of full professor in this latter group). A Ph.D. degree is essential if one wishes to rise above the rank of instructor in a university. A small number of psychologists are employed in guidance centers maintained by colleges and universities.

An area where a considerable number of women are

employed as psychologists is the public schools. The school psychologist is chiefly concerned with emotional problems of pupils, and with helping them overcome difficulties in mastering academic subjects. She observes, tests, makes diagnoses and applies remedial measures. Although there are only about 400 psychologists employed in schools it is estimated that 9,000 are needed.

Non-school places of employment are child-guidance centers, courts, rehabilitation agencies, penal institutions, institutions for the feeble-minded and the insane, social agencies, vocational guidance agencies, business establishments and government agencies such as civil service, Bureau of Agricultural Economics, Bureau of Prisons, U. S. Public Health Service, Air Corps, Army and Navy.

Psychologists who work in clinics are often called clinical psychologists. They specialize in service to individuals. We should distinguish between the expert service rendered by this specialist and that rendered by workers on a lower grade, who are commonly designated psychometrists.

A number of psychologists, commonly called consulting or practicing psychologists, maintain offices where they treat private patients.

The minimum training required for positions is that represented by a Master's degree. For positions of consequence three years of graduate study are required.

In many clinics, fully trained psychiatrists are employed as well as women who have specialized in the study of abnormal psychology. In the chapter on Women Physicians we gave you some idea of the work of a woman psychiatrist.

Among the psychological clinics in which you may find a place are: the clinics in public schools and colleges, the psychopathic clinic, the placement office clinic, the industrial clinic, and the clinic which is connected with the courts to test individuals who run into trouble with the law. Statistical training and courses in educational measurement are required. You must also take plenty of courses in various phases of psychology and in the biological sciences. Here the Ph.D. degree is vitally important.

Workers in a psychological clinic, no matter what kind it is, must be able to win the confidence of its clients. Here accuracy is absolutely essential. Think of the individuals who might be committed unnecessarily to a mental institution through careless mistakes of a psychologist, if such a thing were tolerated. Furthermore, if you go into psychological work, you must remember that each person is a human being with feelings that must not be hurt and quite likely with family ties that mean as much to him as do your own. He is not just an interesting case study for you to experiment upon.

Child development and parent education are developing fields for the psychologist. Here research ability is just as important as in the other branches, as well as the other qualifications we have mentioned.

Almost any of the biological sciences will demand all of that special training we have been urging upon you. First of all, you *must* have a good college training, with biology throughout the entire four years; and you should have had a foundation for it in your high school courses. After college there will be one or more years of graduate study, depending upon the type of work you undertake. You must remember in all your years of study that chemistry and physics are foundation subjects for the biological sciences.

"What do you mean by the biological sciences?" we have been asked.

Suppose we answer that question by examining the contents page of the Women's Bureau Bulletin—*The Outlook for Women in the Biological Sciences*. We'll find general biology, bacteriology, botany, plant pathology, plant physiology, horticulture, agronomy, soil science, zoology, dairy, poultry, and other animal husbandry science.

Another important question is always asked: What are the essential qualifications in the biological sciences? You must possess all the general traits such as patience, intellectual honesty, and others previously mentioned, as well as the willingness to persevere like Pierre and Marie Curie and all other self-sacrificing scientists. In the biological sciences, research will offer you many opportunities, perhaps even more than in teaching. In the chapters on Lady Farmers and Home Economists we have mentioned some of the possibilities for the scientist who has been trained in the biological sciences, such as plant pathologists, nutrition experts, textile testers, and so on. A well-trained research scientist is likely to find opportunities in various government laboratories which employ qualified women for research work.

The college laboratory may be the place for a woman who is heavily endowed with mechanical facility, inventiveness, and ingenuity. She may use a bit of rubber here or a piece of screen there in working out an experiment and suddenly discover that she has a piece of apparatus that is superior to any that is available on the market. We heard of a clever young woman who did that very thing and now she goes about from laboratory to laboratory demonstrating the usefulness of her piece of apparatus, almost forgetting the long years of hardships and struggles she spent to gain her training.

SCIENTISTS

Chemistry is a field where opportunities, even for well-trained women, are less stable than in almost any other phase of science. In the chemistry laboratory, women usually must be superior in training and ability to work hard in order to receive fair consideration. They must be willing to accept criticism and take full responsibility for any errors which they may make.

It has been claimed that women are not adapted to experimental work in the chemistry laboratory because they lack imagination, but there is no real proof that men possess more. You'd better be certain of possessing that qualification, however, before you squander precious years preparing for a career in chemistry. And you must learn to think around the edges of your problem. For instance, there is the case of a young chemist who was working with green tea and noticed that the leaves seemed to be losing their color. Would naturally green tea do that? Of course not! There was but one answer—this was tea that had been dyed illegally. If she had not been an observant, thinking person that tea would have passed muster.

A college education is essential, with courses in all kinds of chemistry, the biological sciences, and as many as possible in cultural and sociological subjects. No knowledge is ever useless; particularly in this science. You can never tell when some little thing will turn your whole experiment into something you hadn't dreamed about—that is, if you are the type of thinking person we've been talking about. A good reading knowledge of French and German is advisable so that you may keep abreast of developments in science abroad. For ultimate success in chemistry, you should aim for a doctor's degree and, by all means, try to have some research experience under someone who has achieved fame in the field of your particular choice.

It would be wise to try yourself out in an industrial or government laboratory before starting this work. Possibly you could act as a volunteer helper in a local public health laboratory. Don't object if they ask you to spend all your time washing bottles and test tubes. Maybe you don't like animals and chickens; possibly cats and rabbits give you asthma. That will be too bad because you'll probably have to take care of the laboratory's menagerie. You'll discover how well you are suited to the work if you can stand the odors, the tiresome attention to detail, and the like.

What are your chances in business, industry, or governmental work? In these days of bureaus and bureaus, there should be plenty of openings in state or federal research laboratories such as public health service, agricultural experiment stations, the U. S. Bureau of Chemistry, etc. Women are eligible to the examinations for all such positions but there's the difficulty of having to be experienced. That's hard on the young graduate who hasn't been able to find a job.

In business and industry, women have the best opportunities where commodities for the home are being manufactured or sold. Textile analysis has developed rapidly, as well as analysis of food, drugs, etc. But even here the research laboratory is largely a man's world. One of the biggest handicaps for the girl beginner is caused by the number of men volunteers who are willing to work for nothing because they know they'll soon have a chance at a better position. A chance that would more than likely be denied to a woman.

Opportunities for women as laboratory technicians have

decided "ups and downs." "Ups" in war times and "downs" when plenty of men are around. The most important personal qualifications are: keen observation, patience, mechanical ingenuity, precision in manipulation, dexterity in using tools, and self-control. No squeamish girl should attempt this work; she'll be unhappy and almost certain to fail. Other necessary traits are neatness, quickness, accuracy, and absolute honesty.

Minimum requirements of the Board of Registry for technicians in the matter of training are: high school graduation; credit of two years' work from a recognized college or university in chemistry, biology, bacteriology, physiology, laboratory demonstration; or graduation from a graduate school of nursing which is recognized by the state board of examiners; minimum of twelve months' instruction in an approved school for technicians or apprenticeship of at least one year under the guidance of a qualified clinical pathologist.

Positions open to trained women technicians are in municipal, state and government civil service in the U. S. Public Health Service, the Veterans Administration, or state public health service. These scientists test microorganisms and tissues, analyze water, milk, stomach contents, and other body fluids, make blood counts, and so on. Similar work is done in large clinical laboratories and university hospitals or college laboratories. But there are usually more trained workers than positions.

One of the chief requirements of a geologist is a strong physique. Give geology a wide berth if you have a weak digestion, dislike climbing, or are afraid of physical discomforts. But there is no field in all the scientific world that can be as exciting and fascinating as geology, if you love it and are fitted for the work. We have several geologist friends who seem to have glorious times together planning field trips or reviewing their experiences.

The preparation for this field is just as serious a matter as for the other sciences. Here, too, you should explore all the possibilities to be certain you are on the right track. Join an exploring party on a short excursion and see what happens. If you are successful on it, then go ahead and acquire all the education and training you can afford. You will need to like mathematics, foreign languages, biology, etc., as well as the various phases of geology.

Our rude awakenings to the importance of conserving our natural resources have developed innumerable opportunities for trained geological workers in government service. There are positions in the U. S. Geological Survey, the Smithsonian Institution, the Soil Conservation Service, etc. This is a growing and satisfying phase of science, but again it's a man's field. In theory all the government positions are open to women but few are awarded them. Men object to women on the excursions, and there are other health hazards and disagreeable features which might deter a woman from anything except teaching the subject. Oil and mining companies are offering many opportunities to the geologist in commercial research but men are usually preferred in these positions because it is the general belief that field work is too hard on a woman. She can, however, study thin slices of rock and the like in a laboratory.

Archaeology and anthropology also demand a strong physique and adaptability because of the hardships of exploring trips.

There are several possibilities in archaeology and anthropology, such as research, museum work, or teaching. Great discoveries have been made by women in both these fields.

Women are usually more successful in museum work, acting as docents or perhaps classifying and preparing material for exhibition. Language ability is necessary here. A museum worker of our acquaintance, who held a doctor's degree and all sorts of academic honors, set herself the task of learning to read Chinese when she was appointed curator of a Chinese collection. Not only languages and that all-important Ph.D. are essential but you'll need an unusually rich cultural background for any kind of museum work. There can be no bluffing or superficiality. Think of the questions that are asked and the lectures to be given!

Teaching offers little to women in archaeology and anthropology because most of the courses are on a high graduate level—where men usually occupy the professorships. There are other phases of educational work, however, which are open to women, such as preparing exhibits to send out to schools, extension work, lecturing and the like. Children's museums are particularly interesting for women who have trained in archaeology and anthropology. Here, again, the gifted pen can be put to good use either in bulletins or small brochures for the museum or in writing children's stories based on objects in the museum or on the adventures of explorers.

So far, comparatively few women have entered pharmacy. Possibly they think of this work in terms of the corner drug store. But there is a fascinating scientific aspect of pharmaceutical work; otherwise why are those four years of intensely technical training required before a license is issued? In a real old-fashioned pharmacy—the kind which is presided over by a dignified, scholarly apothecary—there may be a place as a clerk or in testing medicinal preparations. There might also be a chance to make biological tests. Or you may find a research position in a large manufacturing concern or go out as a saleswoman of drugs and medical supplies. Hospital pharmacies may give you an opportunity to use your training or you could take a civil service examination for a government position such as food and drug inspector or as assistant in such work.

Ownership of a drug store may be the goal of your ambition, even though you must realize what a risky undertaking that would be. In that case you might be wise to open one of those fine apothecary shops which cater only to physicians and patients who want to be certain that their prescriptions are correctly filled or that biological tests are accurately made. Here you may not earn a large income but it is likely to be a dignified and satisfying occupation for you.

Perhaps astronomy is the least promising field for women in all branches of science. Teaching, work in observatories, or in scientific libraries will be the only opportunities for the woman astronomer. But, like geology, astronomy can take hold of you with a grip of iron. More than likely you'll enjoy staying up all night on a thousand to one chance of seeing a new star glimmer in the sky. If you get started on astronomy, you'll probably be so fascinated that nothing will deter you from that chase after a new star—or a new understanding of old constellations.

Research positions for women in astronomical observatories are exceedingly rare because of the limited number of observatories and the feeling that it is a man's world. Only the brilliant highly trained woman will obtain a foothold here. Moreover, very few who do get in will ever reach top positions. After all, how many directors of observatories are there. The absence of a question-mark indicates that this is a purely rhetorical question. We all know that there have been few such personages, so few in fact that it is scarcely worth while to look up the figures. And speaking of figures! You must love them if you insist on becoming an astronomer. Think of the endless and complicated computations that must be made in astronomical measurements.

You might find a teaching position in the field of astronomy but it would probably be combined with teaching other scientific subjects. There are a few libraries in which a woman with research training and technical library training may find a position. But it isn't a promising field—we'll repeat that again. And yet, who can tell about the future? Planetariums are growing in the largest cities and they might well improve the situation for the girls.

Mathematics is a science which can hold more promise for the properly qualified woman than most of the others. If a girl has a gift for mathematics, she is more than likely to be a shark at it. Therefore, if you have that gift, by all means make the most of it, either in teaching or in statistical work.

Teachers of mathematics often command excellent salaries simply because there are so many people who are literally staggered by figures. It's a stupendous task to drag a student with a mathematics complex through even algebra and plane geometry. Trigonometry and the other higher subjects are almost impossible for him unless the teacher has infinite patience and can explain the difficult points in words of one syllable, if such a thing is possible.

In statistical work you'll have a wide variety of choice. On the professional level, the statistician may deal with four types of statistics: vital statistics, which are concerned with population, marriages, births, diseases and deaths; social statistics dealing with housing, delinquency, community problems, etc.; educational statistics which include mental measurements as well as figures dealing with attendance, school costs, and various problems connected with school children; business statistics covering industrial, commercial, financial, and agricultural statistics.

In statistical work you may hold a semi-professional position such as: statistical secretary, accountant, statistical laboratory worker, clerk, editor, or field investigator. There are minor positions which call for statistical skill such as: computer, statistical machine operator, and statistical draftsman.

There are opportunities for statistical workers in every government department from the Department of State down to the least important board. There are jobs in state and municipal governments as well. Then there are various statistical service organizations, state and city boards of education, state and local organizations of various kinds, and social service organizations such as the American Red Cross, the National Association for the Cause and Prevention of Tuberculosis, the American Cancer Society and the like. All of these will need statistical workers. Of course business needs a great many trained statistical workers in manufacturing, trade, banking and finance, insurance, accounting, advertising, trade associations, and on periodicals.

Women are usually in demand for the subordinate positions and sometimes in supervisory positions. But here again they rarely reach the top positions as directors. Many women statisticians admit that this is primarily a man's field.

Among the special qualities required for statistical work are: aptitude for figures, broad general education, ability to write, and training in the techniques of the field. It's helpful also if you have native or acquired skill in mechanical drawing. There really are opportunities for women with keen interest in current social and economic problems, a feeling for facts, and the intelligence to analyze the meaning of these facts.

You will enjoy working with congenial people, the hours are likely to be short and, if you do field work, there will be fascinating contacts with people. On the other hand, some phases of the work may be monotonous, and you run the risk of getting into a rut so deep that only a derrick can get you out.

26. ENGINEERS

WE HAVE FIGURES to prove that a warning against engineering is not ill-advised; less than 200 women competing against more than a thousand times that number of men is what might safely be termed competition of the most difficult sort. Many books on occupations for women sidestep the issue altogether and ignore engineering as a possible lifework for girls; or, if they do mention it, agree that it is a far from hopeful field.

We are including it because of a conversation overheard some years ago in the supplies store of a technical school:

"Are these supplies for yourself?" inquired the curious clerk. The young girl in overalls nodded, and the clerk went on, "Guess you're the first girl this school ever had in engineering—won't you feel lost among all those men?"

"No, indeed," came the prompt reply. "I think it will be lots of fun to show the men that women can learn about electricity and machinery, too. And I've been promised a good position with my uncle when I graduate. He's a very successful engineer."

That's the crux of this matter! Perhaps girls can show the men a thing or two about electricity and all the other technical phases of the work but the difficulty comes "when I graduate." The woman engineer who has no doting uncle or family friend to assure her a job in this business may have a serious time getting a start.

In our local Engineers' Club, the Director of Technical Services, whose job includes finding positions for members who want to make a change, explained that when he offered a man and a woman for an opening—if all things were equal—the man was always chosen. He gave several reasons for this:

"In today's market considerable overtime may be demanded on a rush job. Since labor laws limit the number of hours a woman may work, it is better not to hire women.

"Everything in our profession is set up for men," he went on, "and hiring a woman engineer causes too many complications. In conservative communities, too, something as new and different just isn't done. When I suggest that an employer might try it, he usually decides to wait for someone else to take such a bold step. There seems to be an undercurrent among employers of thinking that the breadwinner should be a man. They believe, too, that it is easier to send a man when travel is necessary for the firm. Now please understand that these are not my opinions—just what employers tell me when they want to hire a new engineer. So you see what a girl faces when she chooses engineering."

Before she even begins a course in an engineering school, a girl must have a better than average high school record in scientific subjects and must have shown the peculiar aptitudes so necessary in the field.

Here, as in some of the other "for men only" professions, a woman once faced considerable discrimination in both class and laboratory. Not so today! If she is admitted to an engineering school, she will be given fair treatment. Most of the men students in one of our largest technical schools were delighted when a girl carried off first honors recently.

Many years ago one of our greatest women scientists was not permitted to study for a doctor's degree in an institute of technology just because she would have been the first person to be granted that degree. Such a distinction could not go to a woman. Today one famous woman engineer insists that in this country "the women in the profession have had only the most kindly and co-operative treatment from the men in the field, and have been given every opportunity for training, for work in the field, for advancement, and for participation in all the activities of the profession."

Perhaps she may be right as far as the welcome is concerned in certain fields, but the fact remains that women are still almost negligible figures in most of the engineering occupations. On the other hand, we find that there is an increasing number of successful women engineers in the newer fields of illuminating, radio, household and industrial engineering. It is more than three decades since we first began to hear of Lillian Gilbreth, the story of whose family *Cheaper by the Dozen* became a best seller. Mrs. Gilbreth—by far the most noted woman engineer in the industrial field—had trained to be a psychologist until she met and married Frank Gilbreth, an up-and-coming industrial engineer. From that day, Mrs. Gilbreth's interest has been equally divided between her family of twelve children and the work of Gilbreth, Inc., famous firm of consulting engineers. The story of their work together may be read in the biography of Frank and Lillian Gilbreth. Countless factories and offices in this country have improved the planning, supervision, and production of their work since these industrial engineers issued their books *Time Study, Fatigue Study,* and others on motion study and industrial management. These books helped in bringing about increased output with a minimum of waste and fatigue.

Perhaps it was the story of this unique woman that lured the girl of our supplies store experience into the profession. Who can tell? But whenever Lillian Gilbreth's success story is told, someone always injects the reminder that it was through work with her husband before his death that she was launched on her spectacular career.

Mrs. Gilbreth insists that the woman industrial engineer must be a mechanical engineer plus; must have "an aptitude for accurate measurement, a willingness to submit to a rigid technical training, strength, endurance, persistence, and the other traits that go with scientific investigation and the application of its results. The engineer must supplement these with a liking for working with human beings, the quality of leadership, and an ability to sell her personality and the things she has to teach." And these must all be supplemented by first-hand experience gained by working in factory, shop, office, or department store.

The work of the industrial engineer is to study "processes and workers in order to simplify work and make it better paying and more satisfying." In other words—*efficiency*. Sometimes the only way to make a start in this profession is by actually working as an operator of a machine in a factory or in a minor position in store or office. Incidentally, you may receive only the minimum wage of such workers despite your years of technical training. But wait until promotion comes your way or you are ready to launch yourself as an independent consulting engineer. A well-known consultant can command an excellent fee.

What does the consulting engineer actually do? The usual procedure is to go into the factory, office, or store; study conditions; advise about improvements which are necessary, and, sometimes, attend to the installation of new machinery or work processes.

This all sounds exciting but we haven't said much about the kind of education required for the engineering profession. Before you attempt to enter a technical school, be sure that you have an analytical mind and a talent for mathematics and science. Then pick out the best school you can that will accept you and prepare yourself for a long, trying four years' struggle with mechanics, economics, mathematics, psychology, and management—in addition to the prescribed technical subjects, laboratory, drafting-room and field-survey work. You won't have a chance to include many "snap" elective subjects in this course and you may need to spend your summer vacations out in industry if you aspire to the field of industrial engineering.

The prospects are not good for women in civil or electrical engineering except for office jobs. Field work with primitive living conditions and the lack of confidence she finds in outside contacts are the chief obstacles to woman's progress in these fields. No matter how well-trained and efficient she has proved herself in working with a small group, men still look askance at the woman civil or electrical engineer when she steps out into strange fields where her ability is not known. In these phases of engineering, office positions offer the best opportunities.

The consulting engineer works long hours, spends much of her time in traveling, and must endure separations from her family. But there are likely to be wonderful contacts in the work, satisfying recognition from her colleagues, and interesting opportunities for lecturing in schools or at conventions in this country and abroad.

V

Literary and Artistic Workers

27. WRITERS, NEWSPAPER WORKERS, EDITORS

WHY SHOULD ANYONE want to write? This query was answered in several ways by a distinguished writer from Great Britain. He said that many people slip into authorship because it looks like an easy and pleasant way of making a living. For instance, he said that Thomas Hardy started writing because he heard that George Meredith made one hundred and twenty pounds on a book. Or, he said, they may have a passion within themselves which must have this sort of outlet; they feel that they have something wonderful to give to the world. Again, vanity may be the driving force within the person who wants to have his superior self permanently memorialized through his writings. And there is the person who has enjoyed a piece of writing so much that he wants to give others the same sort of emotionally satisfying experience. Finally, there is the person who writes because he really *has* something worthwhile to say.

What are the various fields of writing; the requirements and possibilities in each? In the field of creative writing, the writer usually works in a free-lance capacity, selling his products when and where he can. Competition is about as keen here as in any job in the entire world of work, especially for those who want to appear in print in the better-paying periodicals.

Of all forms of free-lance writing, poetry is the least lucrative. Of course, the true poetic genius will not be stopped by anything, but he should have some other means of livelihood. Only rarely is a book of poetry on the best-seller list. Poems may be sold to literary magazines and, if consistently good, may be collected into thin volumes which only lovers of poetry and libraries will buy. Many poets have earned their bread and butter teaching in schools or colleges.

Playwriting may have more possibilities, but it is also a chancy, highly competitive field. A gift for dramatic writing plus a novel idea may lead to a play worth producing on Broadway. Or, if not that good, it may be included in a book of plays suitable for amateur performances. Like the poet, however, the playwright should have other means of support until his smash hit reaches Broadway.

Novel writing usually appeals to the aspiring writer more than any other field because he dreams of one day producing a best-seller. But novel writing is not just sitting down and reeling off a thrilling tale in a few weeks' time. This is proved in a newspaper article on how some of our best-selling novelists have worked. One wrote night after night to produce but six lines and then had to throw them away and make a fresh start. Another said she got a book underway by sitting down at the typewriter, starting a sentence, and then going ahead. On the contrary, Sinclair Lewis prepared a full-length digest for each of his novels in which he outlined the plot and described his characters in detail. He often worked ten hours at a stretch.

Upton Sinclair used the following method: "I shut myself up in a Southern California garden which I seldom leave, except when rain drives me indoors," he said. "In the morning I bring out a little table with a typewriter on it, and sit and hammer out one or two thousand words. In the afternoon I walk up and down and let the morning's stint unroll before my mind's eye. In the evening I revise what I wrote in the morning. In between times I read newspapers and magazines, keeping watch for story material. I seldom see visitors, I go to few shows, and have not been to a party in several years. It is a specialized way of life and not many would care for it."

You must have plenty of imagination if you want to write fiction, plays, or poetry. You will also need an exceptional background of reading in classical and modern literature; and a wide range of information in psychology, history, biography, and science. Better carry a small notebook in which you can jot down clever expressions or ideas which you hear and which you may some day want to use in your play, novel, or poem.

Non-fiction—biography, essays, history, travel books, or books dealing with human problems, personality, social improvements, and political trends—is an important phase of writing. Actually we have almost as many such books on best-seller lists as novels. Think of the success of books like Eisenhower's *Crusade in Europe*, Churchill's *Grand Alliance*, Peale and Blanton's *Art of Real Happiness*, Overstreet's *The Mature Mind,* Gerald Johnson's *Incredible Tale*—to mention only a few. Read these as examples of how to write successfully in these fields, but remember that most successful writing requires maturity, experience, technical and creative ability, and at best a touch of genius.

A witty writer of non-fiction may produce a best-seller such as *The Egg and I* or *Cheaper by the Dozen.* This is exceedingly rare, however, as humorous writing is about the most difficult form you can attempt.

Writing for children is a field of great promise. There is always a place for a writer of real ability in this field, as in any other. But don't make the mistake of thinking that you can write for children if you fail in all other forms. It requires just as much skill, if not more. You must have a thorough understanding of children and be able to meet youngsters on their own ground. You must be able to express yourself clearly, vividly, and forcefully in simple, direct terms suited to the age for which you are writing. It is wise for a free-lance writer in this field to have some other source of income—at least until she is firmly established as a children's book author. One successful writer said: "If you are lucky in writing a book for children that makes an immediate hit, you may be able to make a living as a free-lance writer in the field. It is taking a big chance, though. Most of the time I find it better to work at a part-time job so that I know where my rent and food are coming from. Then I have the intake from books and magazine articles for extras." This is true generally of all writing.

The content of children's books must be considered with the greatest care and it must be suited to a child's understanding and interest. The subject matter should be original and of real worth, never trivial merely because it is written for children. Children deserve the best there is. Think of the importance of developing literary tastes which will last throughout a lifetime.

There is always a chance of finding a market for your writing in children's magazines or of joining the editorial staff of one of the many magazines published by religious denominations for young children, teen-agers, and for young adults. Each of these magazines has its editors and their assistants who select stories, articles, poems and pictures to make up each issue and who carry them through the stages of getting into print. And there are a few commercial magazines especially for children and teen-agers.

One of the interesting personalities among editors of these magazines is Mrs. Ada Rose, editor of *Jack and Jill*. She insists that there should be no taboos in writing for children—that she has none in editing her magazine.

"Any subject, if handled with good taste to meet the needs of children, is acceptable," she says. "Every time I get a letter from an author asking what sort of stories I want, I am tempted to scrawl on the bottom GOOD STORIES, and return it.

"Most authors want to teach too much when they write for children," went on Mrs. Rose, "or they think that a trivial incident is good enough for children. The rules of journalism must never be violated in magazines for children."

If your aim is writing, by all means take your English composition and other English courses seriously both in high school and college. There are, also, writers' conferences, workshops, and various university graduate and extension courses for would-be writers. They can do little for you, however, unless you have a talent to be developed.

Remember, too, that the best source of help is concentrated study of other writers' works. Above all, though, you must gather your material through living yourself and absorbing all you can from every experience. Self-discipline and patience are necessary to keep you everlastingly on the job of writing, rewriting, and rewriting again and again to perfect your work.

Newspaper work probably offers the best opportunity for the young woman who is determined to make a career of writing.

For newspaper work, accuracy, initiative, broad background of knowledge, energy, and perseverance are indispensable. You must have capacity for hard work, a pleasing personality, aggressiveness, self-confidence, interest in and love of people, a sense of humor, and above all a clear, lively style of writing. As Dr. Bleyer, noted teacher of journalism, said:

"You must be curious about everything around you. You must be curious about persons and what they are thinking and feeling and doing. You must be curious about events, their causes and probable results. Unless you have such curiosity, you can never be a successful newspaper writer or editor." An understanding of all you see and hear, ability to select the interesting and significant phases of a day's events, ability to think clearly and to write expressively in simple style are further qualifications insisted upon by Professor Bleyer.

Among newspaper men there is considerable disagreement concerning the value of special courses in journalism as a preparation for newspaper work. Many editors prefer to hire bright young college graduates with general education and train them on the job. These editors have been vindicated by a study which showed that in a period of eleven to fifteen years after graduation the salaries of journalism school graduates were somewhat lower than the salaries of graduates of liberal arts colleges who had learned their trade in a newspaper office.

In either institution your course should include social science, psychology, economics, languages, and as many English courses as you can carry. Through them you will learn correct usage and acquire a flexible and varied style. Despite the figures that are unfavorable to professional journalistic courses, many successful journalists will urge you to take such professional courses as editorial writing, law and ethics of journalism, reporting, copy reading, writing feature articles, special writing for magazines, political writing. In schools of journalism there will be opportunities for practice in writing for college publications or furnishing news items for a school column or educational page of the local newspaper. Indeed, you may begin that sort of writing even in high school days.

The following "factors making for success in journalism" were listed by five hundred successful journalists: "First, broad education, with a preponderance of history, English —both composition and literature, economics, sociology, and philosophy; second, subordination of technical courses in journalism, which should come second to the broader courses of the regular curriculum; third, try-out of the profession practically while studying it theoretically, i.e., in vacation or part-time jobs secured in college years; fourth, excellent health and abundant energy in the constant fight to overcome the effects of irregular hours; fifth, wide reading: literature for style—biography for knowledge of human nature—government and politics for knowledge of the forces behind our government—criticism to understand our complex civilization—and the news should be read—*all* the news."

One important point seems to have been overlooked, and it is far from being a minor consideration—learn shorthand or speed-writing, get yourself a typewriter, and learn to use it expertly. It may be necessary to type on your lap in a swaying train or on an airplane.

James Hilton, author of *Lost Horizon,* tells of his attempts to type on a pitching boat during a stormy crossing of the wintry Atlantic. His greatest problem was in moving the carriage back and forth, a problem which he finally allowed the waves to solve. He simply waited until the tossing boat swung the carriage back into the desired position. That's an example of the sort of ingenuity you'll need for this work.

Let's consider the positions on a newspaper that are particularly suitable for women. If you aim at a job as department editor you may find an opening as: society editor, woman's page editor, club editor, home economics editor, fashion editor, radio editor, children's page editor, school page editor, editor of fiction and special features. Or you may try your hand at society reporting, feature writing, or reviewing books, films, plays, music, art, and so on.

Professor Bleyer tells us that editing a newspaper has two distinct parts: "the writing of editorials, the task of the editor-in-chief . . . ; and the handling of news and non-news features, under the direction of the managing editor." Most of the special editorial positions mentioned as particularly suitable for women come under the managing editor.

The managing editor co-ordinates and supervises all writ-

WRITERS, NEWSPAPER WORKERS, EDITORS

ing departments, plans the make-up of the publication, edits copy, and carries out the policies of the publisher. The news editor plans the lay-out of news items, issues copy to the copy readers, and sends it on to the composing room.

Small daily or weekly newspapers may employ only one general editor who may have to be his own reporter and rewrite man, may write original articles, determine what is suitable for publication, and run the business end as well.

In an occupational brief issued by Uncle Sam's *Roster of Scientific Personnel*, duties of the newspaper reporter are given as follows:

A reporter gathers accurate and significant facts concerning events that are considered "news," and writes interesting, clear accounts of these events for newspapers and magazines. His assignments are apt to be varied, covering the city hall, police court, railway station, or other news sources given him by the city editor. He may cover events of national or worldwide interest in another city, state, or country. He gets his facts by observation, interviewing people, consulting police and other public records, and research in libraries. He may take notes in speedwriting when necessary, and keeps on the lookout for exclusive information on such important events as elections, crimes, or occurrences in local or state politics. He types his stories or submits them to the city editor. A reporter may remain in a news-gathering capacity or, through hard work and competence, eventually may qualify as an editor.

If you are unable to find a post in the editorial or reportorial departments try the business department as an entering wedge. A position as clerk or stenographer in the advertising, circulation, or accounting department is not to be scorned. It may not have the glamour of reporting or editing but there'll be chances for advancement—possibly to be in charge of the local advertising department, to head up the division that secures outside advertisements from agencies and large manufacturers, or to be in charge of the classified advertising department which solicits and arranges smaller advertisements. You may even try your hand at writing the advertisements and thus gain experience that may lead to one of the coveted writing jobs.

If you have no ambition to write, you can advance to administrative positions in the circulation department which has charge of distributing the papers through newsboys, dealers, and by mail. In the accounting department there are always jobs for clerical workers who may win promotion to responsible positions such as cashier, business manager, etc., although men usually capture these jobs.

Is there a place for women in the mechanical end of newspaper work? With the exception of the pressroom where the work is too heavy for women except as press feeders, there are opportunities in the composing room as linotype operators, proofreaders or in make-up work; in the bindery; and a few are employed in the stereotyping rooms and in the photo-engraving department.

In magazine and book publishing there are numerous opportunities. True, you cannot expect to hop right into an editorial chair. You will have to work up here as in any other occupation. You might edge in through the door of stenography or office machine operating. Editorial positions, however, are not numerous, and men occupy a large percentage of them. There are relatively few magazines addressed exclusively to women and each one needs but one editor-in-chief, plus a few assistant editors. Children's magazines are usually edited by women, but here again the field is limited because there are so few publications.

If you fail to find a position as editor, assistant editor, or writer for a magazine, don't give up. You may have an opportunity to become a reader—one of the important persons who give the first reading to the masses of manuscripts that pour into every publishing office. They pick out the few promising manuscripts and pass them on to the editors for final decision.

There are proofreading jobs as well, if you have the accuracy and patience required for such detailed and painstaking work. These positions will give you excellent training and are more than likely to lead to advanced posts.

In book publishing, women are playing an increasingly important part in publicity and advertising, in the exciting business of buying manuscripts and making them into books, in sales promotion and in the usual business routines of a large industry.

You may find an opportunity in preparing announcements and catalogues or writing "blurbs," although this is frequently handled by the editor. There are the usual office positions such as secretarial, typing, operating various calculating machines, and the like.

In a publishing house, the receptionist is an exceedingly important and well-trained individual. It will be her job to protect the editors from wasting time on strange individuals who wander into a publishing house.

Occasionally a woman finds a berth on the sales force but this is rare indeed, unless she is selling subscription sets for children and deals with parents and teachers. The shipping end of book publishing is also a no-woman's land.

On the other hand, children's editorial work is a choice spot for a well-qualified woman, and most large publishing houses have special children's editors.

The editor of children's books must have a thorough knowledge of children's reading tastes and she must also have keen critical ability. It is her job to read and accept or reject manuscripts submitted. After each manuscript has been accepted and prepared for printing, the editor has the responsibility of deciding on the format—the kind of type, the illustrations, the size, binding, and so on. Moreover, she will have to deal with artists as well as authors. She will select the artist and guide him in the preparation of illustrations.

A good general education, including a liberal arts college course, and familiarity with current and general literature are essential for almost every type of work in book publishing. If you aspire to editorship or ownership, a classical education will be helpful. Thorough knowledge of reading tastes and keen critical ability are necessary. This is a field rich in rewards for those who make it their career.

28. ARTISTS, MUSICIANS, ACTRESSES AND OTHERS

IF YOU ARE that rare being who has the spark of genius in some form of art and realizes it, there is little to say because in some way that spark will burst into flame.

Genius—or at least, near-genius in the form of native talent—is the one vital requirement for success in any of

ARTISTS, MUSICIANS, ACTRESSES AND OTHERS

the arts. We know a young girl who had undoubted talent for drawing, but she could do little with it until she had training. It was a hard financial struggle for her to go to art school and during her first weeks there she was continually in the depths of discouragement.

"I'm no better than the other students," she wailed. "They all draw as well as I do. I'll never get anywhere in this art game; might as well pack up and go home."

"I wouldn't do that," counseled an older friend. "Stick to your guns a little longer. You have the right stuff in you —it'll show up soon."

She was right. In a short time the young student began to outstrip her less gifted classmates. At the end of that first year she won first prize in the art school's student exhibition and she continued to be a bright and shining light in all her classes until graduation. Then she turned to commercial illustration and in an amazingly short time was earning upwards of ten thousand a year.

Read the biographies of noted artists, in whatever branch you will, and you will see that courage and perseverance were almost as essential to their success as talent and training. A concert pianist of our acquaintance worked harder than any little "slavey" during her early years of study. She practiced so constantly that she was forced to tape the ends of her fingers. When we watch those fingers skip over the keys today, we wonder how many envious students in the audience would work as earnestly and faithfully to perfect their art. Moreover, an artist in any line must continue to study and practice to maintain perfection. There is no limit to the amount of education and training in any of the arts —and there is no end. When you stop learning, you have taken the first step downhill. Any great painter, singer, or instrumentalist will tell you that simple, homely truth.

What are the chances for women in painting? Given the required degree of talent, can they go as far as men? Of course they can! Look at Mary Cassatt, Georgia O'Keeffe and countless others in our own country.

For inspiring records of successful women artists, read *Girls Who Became Artists*, by Winifred and Frances Kirkland. Here are stories of famous women painters, sculptors, and photographers, and of "how they got that way." There is Wanda Gag, who won fame and a fair fortune against all odds; Pamela Bianco, "Famous Since She Was Twelve"; Margaret Bourke-White, "Photographer of Steel"; Meta Warrick Fuller, "Leading Sculptor of Her Race"; Cecilia Beaux, famous portrait painter; Madame Le Brun, from the days of Marie Antoinette; Malvina Hoffman, whose ability as a sculptor took her around the world in search of all types of human beings. Her work thrills all visitors to the Hall of Man in Chicago's Field Museum. There are stories of others just as inspiring to the would-be artist.

Remember one thing about all these artists—they had the spark of genius else their stories would not be in that book. You may study at the best art schools and work long hours—day and night—but without that spark you cannot reach the heights. Even if you have the necessary talent and training, you will also need all the courage and persistence which you can muster.

For the aspiring artist whose purse is slim, we have good news. Painting is one of the fields of art where you can support yourself almost entirely while you are studying. It is possible to take a few courses at a time and hold a part- or full-time position that will pay your tuition and living expenses. We are not recommending that as the best procedure. If you can afford it, by all means go to the best art school and devote all your time to your studies.

Tales of the glamorous life in the Latin Quarter of Paris lure many art students to France. There it is possible to live and study cheaply—and there it is just as easy to starve. But American schools can do all that is necessary for you if you have the originality, the fertile imagination, and a determination to succeed.

College education is not necessary, although it will give you a useful cultural background. Private art schools or art departments in the universities are the places where you will acquire the fundamental training in form, color, perspective, composition, and so on. After that go where you can see the best pictures and find the most picturesque views to paint. Why do you suppose we find artist colonies on Cape Ann, Cape Cod, near quaint villages in the mountains and by the sea? Visit some of the one-man or one-woman exhibitions of artists who spend the summers in such places, and you will discover why.

In sculpture the examples of Malvina Hoffman and Janet Scudder, as well as others, encourage the girl who has a knack for modeling. Read *Heads and Tales*. It is a fascinating account of Malvina Hoffman's experiences in learning her craft. The story of her trip around the world, in search of models for her figures in the Hall of Man at the Field Museum in Chicago, is as exciting as any travel adventure story you may find.

You will have a harder time making a living in sculpture than in any other phase of art. If you must model, get a regular job and do your sculpturing as an avocation. It is exceedingly difficult to sell your figures because people who might buy a lovely picture or have a portrait painted are likely to exclaim over a beautiful statue and stroll away. As we said before, unless you are a second Malvina Hoffman, you'd better make sculpture a hobby.

During recent years, architecture has become an increasingly good field for women. Today a woman architect, if she is well-trained and the equal in ability of any man, will usually be accepted in this profession on the same basis as a man. In fact, she is often preferred in offices which specialize in residential and apartment house work.

Here, as in many other phases of the fine arts, you may be a free-lance worker. In time of expanding building programs you may do very well as an independent architect. We know one woman architect who does part of her work at home and part in the office of an architectural firm. She is so busy most of the time for them that she has difficulty finding time to work on jobs for individual clients. In bad times, on the other hand, architects are likely to suffer. In fact, our free lancer came out of her school of architecture in the depths of the great depression. She had to forget all her nine years of training to do a clerical job that would provide cash for her living expenses.

After all the years of training you will begin as a draftswoman in an architect's office. In this job, you will spend hours tracing drawings and doing other detailed work which may become monotonous. However, you will probably earn a good salary and will have opportunities to learn much through observation of practices in the office. And, in such a firm, you will gradually take on such responsibilities as designing buildings; conferring with clients; preparing estimates of costs, working drawings, specifications; and even supervise the progress of the building. That's when the job becomes exciting—to see a building grow from your own first idea into a finished home for a happy family.

Now we'll turn our attention to commercial illustration, industrial and costume design, interior decoration, photography, and landscape architecture. In all these fields you'll find that originality, imagination, good taste, color sense, and perseverance are quite as important as in painting, sculpture and architecture. Here again we have the problem of choosing between college and going to art school directly from high school. A junior college course followed by the art school might solve your problem or you could go to a school like Teachers College of Columbia University, Simmons College, Pratt Institute, or to a university which has a good art department. In any of these places you can make a happy combination of college and technical training. There you may have such subjects as: creative design, color and design, drawing and composition, lettering, mechanical drawing, graphic art techniques, costume art, metal work and jewelry, clay modeling, pottery, as well as courses in house design and decoration. Psychology, cultural background courses, and French are also essential— French, particularly, if you are aiming at costume design. Although New York and San Francisco are becoming fashion centers of the world, Paris is still a mecca of all fashion workers and you'll be lost if you can't speak the language. A year of study abroad is extremely important, if you can afford it.

Commercial art is a field where you are more certain of a good bed and a square meal than in any of the so-called Fine Arts occupations. For this work, you will need salesmanship ability, pleasing appearance and personality.

Among the promising opportunities ahead for the commercial artist are those in free-lance magazine illustrating and advertising art, advertising agencies, department stores, and on newspapers. Here you may climb to a position as chief artist, manager of an art department, buyer, or advertising manager. A considerable number of commercial art jobs are available in greeting card and calendar companies.

Here is the story of one young Philadelphia high school graduate who succeeded in commercial art. She is Display Director for a chain of retail bakery and candy shops. "The past year has given me the opportunity to put into practical use the training I received from the Distributive Education course. This training combined with my artistic ability has proved to be an excellent combination for a successful display director. Through the distributive education instruction I have developed a businesslike attitude which has enabled me to cope with the problems in the retail field. Although I always knew that I would go into the commercial advertising field, I never anticipated that I would need the background our retail course offered until I met up with the experiences which I have encountered during the past year. In my present position it is necessary for me to handle the buying of all display fixtures. Also I have meetings with the executives of the organization and hold classes instructing the managers of our stores in display. Any person in the Distributive Education course who wants to go into the field of commercial advertising must have natural artistic ability to begin with. This is an unlimited field with innumerable opportunities for a career. I know from actuality that success does not always come right away—it means you must live your job, taking advantage of every opportunity. If you have the proper qualifications, with a good retail background, there is room for you at the top. While I was a Distributive Education student, I worked as an apprentice in a display department. This gave me a well-rounded background in every type of display. Upon graduation I went into free-lance work for specialty shops. It was at this time that I became interested in confectionery display—a comparatively new field. I picked out the confectioner I wanted to work for—drew diagrams of all their store windows throughout the city and suburbs (22 stores). I spent many months at home designing and illustrating backgrounds for confectionery sales promotion. When I had enough backgrounds illustrated for an entire year's sales promotion, I had the opportunity to meet the president of the firm. He was amazed to think that any outsider would be interested enough in his business to find new methods of sales promotion. He called me in the following afternoon and had me meet the three other owners of the firm. They all agreed the business really needed a person in my field. Therefore, I created my own job, but before I was hired I was given six tests—intelligence, aptitude, color harmony, mechanical construction, design, and lettering. The outcome was very good. I was hired at a much higher salary than I anticipated plus marvelous working conditions."

Again and again we hear that there is a great need for well-trained, capable designers. Especially in the field of industrial design there has been a steadily growing demand for such workers. Machine shops, arts and crafts shops, pottery and china factories offer fine opportunities. Here the young artist will need far more than ordinary ability to draw, paint, and design. Not only will you be called upon to design new products, but you will have the task of redesigning former products so that they will have the eye appeal so important to feminine buyers. In this job you will need to know a good deal about manufacturing processes and about engineering as well. Versatility is an essential qualification, for there will be as varied opportunities as there are different kinds of manufactured products. In all kinds of industrial, textile, or costume design you must actually keep ahead of the times.

Ceramics design is one of the most promising phases of industrial art work in a rapidly expanding and decidedly uncrowded field. The American Ceramic Society reports that there are twice as many jobs as there are people to fill them. Complete ceramic courses are offered at Alfred University, Alfred, N. Y.; Ohio State University, Columbus, Ohio; and Iowa State College, Ames, Iowa. Send for their bulletins if you are interested. The Rochester (N. Y.) Institute has an excellent co-operative course in industrial ceramics.

As in the other art fields, a high school education will be sufficient, although a college background is desirable, but there should be emphasis on mechanical drawing, mathematics, science, etc. Although it is possible to learn on the job in this field, again we urge you to secure the best possible training. And travel is exceedingly important here.

There are almost endless possibilities in the various branches of industrial design; if you fail in one, there's always another in which you may find yourself. If you are fitted for the work, it will give you the greatest joy and satisfaction. There is no limit to possibilities for personal growth and development. If you are working for a large industry, you may be sent all over the country or abroad. The strain of trying to find original ideas is one of the drawbacks, and there is the difficulty of getting started and the necessity for considerable outlay of capital.

Costume design lacks this last disadvantage but it is not a perfect occupation, either. You may have the same fine opportunities for growth, for travel and contacts with interesting people, but you may also run into unexpected and disconcerting difficulties with unreasonable, temperamental employers. You'll find plenty of them in the fashion world. And here is the same nervous strain that comes from striving for originality.

There are two divisions in costume design. First, designing what is known as the "original gown" for custom-made trade. Here the strain is particularly severe because there must be new and distinctive features in each costume, features that will be proof against the copyists.

Second is the designing of costumes for the wholesale trade. Here the artist must create models with features that will have a wide popular appeal. In this field you will need to be familiar with cutting, fitting, sewing, selling, psychology, and the demands of the trade. You must also have creative ability and technical skill with your pencil and brush.

Back of the strikingly styled coats and suits in the Kay-Saks factory at San Francisco's Apparel City is a charming designer. Natalie Yablikoff is her name and how she came to America from Manchuria with the aim of becoming a violinist but turned into a topflight designer is a fascinating story too long to tell in this chapter.

When she discovered that violin study was beyond her slender purse, Miss Yablikoff recalled her joy in designing her own clothes and shoes in her home across the Pacific. She invested all her money in tuition for a fashion school. In four months she had completed the six months' course and found a position as a dress designer. Unfortunately, that brief course had taught her the artistic but not the practical side of her new job. In her first pattern she didn't allow for seams!

In her next job she worked for $10 a week and the promise that she would be taught the basic fundamentals of designing. And then she went back to her original boss and, for three years, created evening dresses, popular and successful for their styling and fit.

Here's how Miss Yablikoff designs. Working on a form, she seems to mold muslin into a graceful feminine suit as a sculptor molds clay into a human, lifelike figure. She likes smooth, continuous lines which decoratively camouflage practical purpose and turns up her nose at lines and darts which look purely utilitarian.

What about her dream of becoming a violinist?

"I am too busy to play the violin." she insists. "It's wrapped in silk now. When I am not asleep, I am thinking of styles. Don't have time to take care of my own hems."

Suppose we turn now to photography, which is one of the most interesting of the arts. Here you may reach heights of fame if you happen to develop a special line such as that of Margaret Bourke-White in her industrial photography and in such assignments as she describes in her *Shooting the Russian War* and *They Called It "Purple Heart Valley."* One of the newer fields such as microphotography may offer opportunities. There are instances of amateur photographers who became adept in this newest phase and finally were given positions of great importance. It has been pointed out again and again that microphotography will eventually be as important to the world as the invention of printing. So it is not unlikely that there

ARTISTS, MUSICIANS, ACTRESSES AND OTHERS

will be new types of positions developing just as they did in the printing business. Keep an eye on microphotography if you are interested in taking up photography as a life work or even as a hobby.

What are the other possibilities in this field? In professional photography there is portrait work, mural photography, commercial photography, and photo finishing, as well as motion picture photography, photostat work, planographing, and the like. Generally speaking, women occupy minor positions in photographic studios, particularly as finishers and developers. But they are constantly advancing into better positions.

Art training is not a requisite for success in photography but it will be helpful. Certainly some training in composition and design is required, as well as the technical training which can be secured in the various schools of photography which have been springing up over the country. So far, a large majority of the workers in this field are forced to learn on the job. During this apprenticeship period the wages are likely to be very small.

Women are working now in almost all branches of photography, although the largest number are in clerical and minor positions. Some are making reputations in preparing photographs for advertising firms. Photo finishing is a good place for women and they are also being employed as photographers in x-ray work, in art museums and libraries, as well as in moving picture laboratories.

Photography can be a fascinating hobby. Camera clubs are flourishing in almost every school and college. And here a girl will have a fine opportunity to discover her fitness for a vocation in photography.

Landscape architecture is a pleasant occupation for the

artistic person who loves the outdoors. If she is blessed with a "green thumb" she can go far and have a joyful time in the going. Her job may be concerned with developing public lands, parks, playgrounds, and other recreation areas, institutional grounds, cemeteries, housing projects, and private residential properties. Land improvement is a possibility. Uncle Sam has opportunities in this line.

Keen imagination is a first requisite so that you can visualize, from a layout on a drafting board, the finished garden, park, recreation field, or even a tiny plot in front of each new home in a large housing development. A knowledge of botany is required and, if you lack the "green thumb," you'll have to hire someone who has such a gift from the gods. Civil engineering skill will be necessary for large-scale developments.

You will enjoy being your own boss if you set up business for yourself, or work in a free-lance capacity on an hourly basis for an established firm. In this event there may be difficulties in dealing with temperamental clients who insist on changes in your cherished plans which you know will ruin the entire project.

Interior decoration and furniture design are two closely allied jobs which offer promise to young women who may not have the talent required to become topnotchers in other phases of the Fine Arts. For interior decoration you must have a keen eye for color harmony, sense of proportion and balance, imagination in visualizing the complete room from your layouts and from samples of materials. Tact and ability to get along with difficult clients will be needed.

Here a college education will be of value but you must have additional training in an art school. This should be followed by years of experience in a well-established interior decoration business if you plan eventually to open your own establishment. Earnings are rather unpredictable as your income will be affected by business conditions. This is decidedly a luxury business.

In furniture design you will need art training in order to sketch your designs. Creativeness is essential but should be combined with practical knowledge of woods, and various new materials such as plastics, plywood, and the like. Furniture manufacturers are likely to snap up a bright young designer who has original ideas and initiative. You can advance rapidly in one of these industries. Here, too, you may do free-lance work and sell your designs through an agency.

If you go into jewelry design, you must be able to originate unique settings for precious stones in rings, pins, necklaces, earrings, and silverware. Four-year apprenticeship with a fine jeweler or with a manufacturing firm may be your means of entrance. Artistic ability and some training are necessary and again—creativeness. Patience, finger dexterity and excellent eyesight are likewise essential—and above all accuracy.

What's ahead for girls in music? First, we'll see what's in store for various types of singers, conductors, or performers on one or more instruments.

If you believe your fortune is in your vocal cords, you may have to earn your living in other lines than music while you are preparing for that hoped-for operatic or concert career, or that break into the radio or the movies as a second Jeanette MacDonald or Judy Garland. We read about girls who have been stenographers, factory workers, waitresses, and the like, while they studied music.

Leading others may mean more to you than being a solo performer. There are choirmasters, leaders of opera choruses or glee clubs, band leaders, and conductors of symphony or other types of orchestras. As a conductor you will need tact and a forceful personality to direct rehearsals and public performances of orchestra or band. It will be your job to select the program, direct the members in playing the compositions, make any necessary announcements or comments, and run the whole show. This involves adequate training in more than one instrument as well as in knowledge of tone of all instruments. Better be sure that you have an accurate ear and "absolute pitch" for this phase of musicianship. Very few women attain these positions.

You will do well to concentrate on one instrument despite the fact that we hear a good deal about musicians who can star on several solo instruments. Consider the piano—no matter how well you perform you'll have to be a second José Iturbi to make a good living as a concert pianist. You may need to add to your earnings by serving as paid accompanist for singers, violinists, or through giving private lessons.

Violinists, too—unless of Kreisler-Heifetz caliber—will find it advisable to join a symphony or radio orchestra. A fine example of this is Evelyn and her magic violin of the famous all-girl orchestra.

What of composing? For all but a budding Carrie Jacobs Bond, this field is not good, though sometimes a newcomer to the field, with little or no training, may write a hit through luck. Music composition is a precarious phase of the arts. There should be creative ability of a high order, a thorough knowledge of the rules of music, harmony,

ARTISTS, MUSICIANS, ACTRESSES AND OTHERS

counterpoint, instrumentation, and orchestration. It will take long years of study to acquire this necessary technical knowledge and to master the secret of using it. The girl who aspires to be a composer should learn to play several instruments. And she should have other financial resources because there are likely to be small money rewards. Of course, there will be the joy that comes from self-expression, but you can't eat that.

If you lack the spark for original compositions, and yet have ability as a composer, you might adapt or transcribe the works of others to suit the needs of particular orchestras or for programs to which the originals were not quite suitable. Jobs along this line are available in radio, movies, music-publishing houses, or with recording companies. And there is the job of librettist. Even if you are not a second Gilbert for a modern Sullivan, you might compose the text for popular tunes or adapt words to an old song.

Now, a few ideas about such jobs in the field of music as music editor, librarian, music critic, and the unusual one of musicologist. Here's what a government occupational brief says about these jobs:

A musicologist does research in the historical origins, creative technique, and scientific bases of music in order to systematize knowledge in the field of music.

A music librarian uses a knowledge of library science in filing and indexing musical documents and recordings in a public, school or college library, and assists students to find them. She may also be employed by large orchestras for filing scores and arrangements and helping to select music appropriate for a particular event.

A music critic uses his literary talents, plus a knowledge of musical technique and sensitivity to musical expression, to write his impressions and criticisms of musical events (concerts, solo recitals, etc.) for newspapers or magazines. He also gives publicity to events of interest to the musical world. The music critic is primarily a journalist and therefore must be a good reporter.

In recent years music appreciation lectures have become increasingly popular. If you are an accomplished pianist, you may be able to present interesting lecture recitals which will feature the works of great composers. Even though you may not be a star performer, you may use recordings of famous artists to illustrate your points. This type of work, again, will scarcely bring in an adequate salary, although it may serve very well as a supplement to other sources of income. Lecture recitals of this sort are included in many college courses in the Fine Arts.

Teaching is by far the most promising field in music. There are more than six thousand music supervisors in the schools of the country and you are fairly certain to find a position if you are a superior person. There are also thousands of private music teachers who have found opportunities particularly in the smaller towns. In large cities the most successful music teachers are well-known artists who combine teaching with a career on the concert stage.

Qualifications for a successful career as music teacher (as given in the yearbook on *Music Education*—National Society for the Study of Education) are:

1. *Musicianship:* Knowledge of the theory and history of music; skill in performance.

(a) For the vocalist: familiarity with the child voice, its conservation and development; acquaintance with the large field of choral literature appropriate for use with choral groups of varying grade levels; ability to adapt materials and teaching

ARTISTS, MUSICIANS, ACTRESSES AND OTHERS 261

methods to the needs of any situation; skill as a vocalist, either for solo or ensemble purposes; authority as a conductor; at least rudimentary skill as piano accompanist.

(b) For an instrumentalist: performing skill on at least two instruments, one a stringed and one a wind instrument; enough familiarity with all instruments to give instructions to beginners; acquaintance with literature, materials, and methods appropriate for the development of instrumental groups ranging from absolute beginners to performers in the most fully developed high school groups; thoroughly developed baton technique; familiarity with the routine necessary to development of marching band.

2. *Personal and Social Qualifications:* Promptness, reliability, tact, co-operation, good nature, industry, creative imagination, initiative, willingness to perform services beyond the terms of the contract.

In your training for teaching music you must meet certain state requirements in liberal arts subjects; in general education, as well as in music education; in theoretical and applied music; in practice teaching; and there are many electives such as music appreciation, choral technique, esthetics, band arranging, composition, physics of music, and the like.

Our government occupational brief takes an optimistic view of opportunities in teaching in high schools, colleges and conservatories although they admit that competition will always be exceedingly keen for the best paying positions.

Music in industry offers a limited number of interesting jobs—chiefly that of full-time director of broadcasting over a manufacturing plant broadcasting installation. Sometimes one person will combine the duties of music director of employee music organizations and that of broadcasting director. The ideal director of plant broadcasting should know people first, and music second; should be trained or experienced in human relations and psychology. Programs must be provided for all shifts of workers based on their own requests and needs rather than on what the director thinks they should have.

If you have musical ability, why not plan to use it as an organist or choir singer? Most organists are employed in churches on an annual basis and, in small communities, may give their services. In addition to playing for one or two services a week, the organist usually trains the church choir and may lead other choral groups in the community. She can become a leader not only in the town's musical life, but in religious and civic affairs and thus serve in a somewhat wider field than some other musicians. After the benediction it will be a satisfaction to realize that joyous notes from your organ will send worshippers out with lighter hearts and with renewed courage to face problems of the coming week.

What about the theater? Superior talent is a "must." Even the greatest amount of talent will not guarantee you success as an actress unless you have intelligence, training, and the courage to work hard and persevere in the face of all sorts of hardships and discouragements. There are certain personality traits that are vital, such as self-confidence, breadth of vision, personal attractiveness and magnetism, and imagination. Acting ability is, of course, essential, as well as an agreeable speaking voice, bodily poise, etc.

One advantage in acting is the freedom from competition with men. They are there, naturally, and in large numbers. But most plays need almost as many women as men. Sometimes there are even more, as in such plays as *The*

ARTISTS, MUSICIANS, ACTRESSES AND OTHERS

Women, The Children's Hour, Pride and Prejudice, and the like. The income of all theater folk is always dependent upon the length of the play's run.

The dance is usually considered a fine art—especially the work of the concert dancer. But this is another precarious career. Again you must have exceptional talent, training, and experience. Usually it requires five years of intensive training to make a concert dancer out of the most promising material. You must be physically strong, graceful, sensitive to beauty, have a keen sense of rhythm, a good stage presence, and personal attractiveness.

If you cannot qualify as a ballet or interpretive dancer, you may find satisfaction in teaching various forms of the dance. There is infinite variety in what you may teach: social dancing, folk dances, ballet, interpretive dancing, etc. In many cities there is a paid supervisor of the dance in community recreational work. There may be opportunities in Y.W.C.A. and other organization work. Incomes of professional dancers are about as variable as those of opera singers, concert pianists, and other artists.

The motion picture field is one of the most difficult and short-lived occupations into which one may go. Of the thousands of girls who pour into Hollywood each year, only a very few find even the smallest kind of job in the movies. If you are determined to try for a career in motion pictures, make your attempt by way of the stage. Begin with school plays and then go on to community or Little Theater productions. Then if you have talent, you may win a part in a professional production and in that case you will not be unknown to the movie producers. Scouts for the motion picture companies study the casts of all plays put on in the large cities and even of many of the Little Theater and Summer Theater plays.

Occasionally we hear of a woman stage manager or director, and what a job it is! She has the responsibility of choosing the play and the cast. She directs rehearsals, decides on stage effects, arranges for publicity, and attends to all the other business details.

Once there was a feeling that women directors could not handle men actors. The near-miracles performed by Margaret Webster in directing plays have certainly corrected that notion. Only recently we heard an authority from the theater world say, most emphatically, that women directors and playwrights are now standing shoulder to shoulder with the men. "In some instances," she declared, "women are slightly better than men—but that may be feminine prejudice." This work is indeed no bed of roses and the salary is well-earned.

Women have always played an important part in theater design and their work is really superior in stage costume design. Exceptional art talent and training are required for success here.

There's no doubt that a career in the arts is difficult, exacting, and sometimes heartbreaking. But if you have great talent, by all means use it for your own satisfaction and for the happiness you can give to others.

29. RADIO AND TELEVISION WORKERS

IF YOU ARE ONE of the increasing number of young people who want to be radio or television entertainers, you must face the fact that overcrowding in this field has been extremely serious for a long time. One radio official once estimated that "of the applicants who are accepted as good radio prospects, only one-half of one per cent may be given a chance before the mike and only two or three out of the whole number may arrive as definite radio personalities in a four- or five-year period."

Sounds bad, doesn't it? Well, we'll offset that gloomy outlook with the more encouraging opinion of a topflight woman radio executive who insists that *if people are really good,* radio wants them either in one of the many jobs behind the scenes such as are offered in any high-powered industry—librarians, secretaries, statisticians, bookkeepers, personnel workers, and the like—or in jobs before the microphone which include singers, musicians, actresses, mistresses of ceremonies. If a person is fully prepared and on her toes when auditions are open for beginners she may make it. This woman cited a number of interesting women who have made places for themselves in radio through their own imagination and vision.

You may read the stories of some of these women in the publication *Women in Radio* issued by the U. S. Women's

Bureau. In the section on *Women in Broadcasting* you will find women in a surprising variety of jobs in radio, such as: Commentator, actress, producer, and director; Employment manager, network librarian, continuity acceptance editor, etc., under *Women in Network Staff Positions*; Time buyer, talent buyer, director of public relations, etc., under *Women in Advertising Agencies*; Free-lance writer, comedy writer, radio columnist, etc., under *Writing for Radio; Teaching Radio; Educational Radio*, and the like.

We cannot discuss in detail each of these phases of radio —and similar jobs in television—but we'll try to give you an idea of what they are like. Suppose we begin with talent occupations which is likely to be the line you are interested in most of all.

If you happen to be one of the rare musicians who has the kind of talent which is bound to bring success, check yourself on such essentials as: tone quality, musicianship, wide and varied repertoire, attractive personal appearance, language ability, and dramatic training. Personal appearance is of major importance for television work or if you appear before large radio studio audiences. And you must secure thorough training if you would be one of the rare musicians who finally make the grade.

In the dramatic field you may have a slightly better chance as television has increased the demand for *good* actresses. If you have recognized talent, you might find a place in one of the regular stock companies which are maintained by the largest broadcasting companies. On the other hand, you might squander years in trying unsuccessfully to break into this field. Here, again, personal appearance, talent, and training for the special field are vital factors. Occasional bit parts may come your way and might eventually help you find a permanent position. Television has made a good memory almost as important as talent. You will be obliged to memorize your parts for television play-acting.

Television has opened opportunities for performers in the "variety show" type of program. Dancers, jugglers, magicians, monologue and comic artists, and many others may have chances that simply did not exist in days of sound projection only. We have been told that some "women comics" are making thirty or forty thousand a year!

Because competition is so keen among radio and television entertainers, suppose we see what else you can do if you are determined to ally yourself with these industries. As we noted before, you need not be an entertainer to get a chance to step before the microphone or camera. If you have the imagination and vision previously mentioned, plus a specialty which appeals to women, you may capitalize on these qualities in a program which is prepared especially for the ladies of leisure or the not so leisurely who do their household chores while they are being entertained or educated by radio. It's a bit difficult to run the vacuum or attend to other work while watching your television screen. Although women may do well as mistresses of ceremonies on daytime programs, men are usually preferred as announcers. On the other hand, many women are highly successful as announcers and as commentators. Women are particularly successful in arranging and directing programs for women listeners. They must have keen understanding of women and of the features that will appeal to them. In television especially, women with home economics training often present pleasing and helpful programs as demonstrators of new equipment, new ways of managing the household, handling a new baby, and the like.

A friend of ours is particularly successful as editor of the woman's page for a small studio. How did she reach her spot in the radio sun? Through *living*—she insists—and more important still through the habit of writing from childhood. Her first work experience was in nursing and surely in that profession she saw much of life—and death. In fact, while a student nurse, a piece of writing about her first experience with death led to much writing, later on, for magazines—articles chiefly about her profession.

Next experience in the world of work for this commentator was running a resort hotel. There she learned to meet people and, in the publicity work for this successful venture, she acquired skill in advertising techniques that led directly to her present radio job. A volunteer publicity job for a Y.W.C.A. membership campaign gave her a chance before a mike. Both stations where she broadcast offered her a job and, when a small station opened nearby, she applied for and got a job as editor of its women's programs. Now she has won several sponsors for the excellent programs which have become popular throughout her locality.

It was this friend who gave us some excellent advice for young women who are interested in a radio or television career. She pointed out that long years of study and work are necessary to become a woman commentator.

"This is a job for the mature woman who has *lived*," she insisted. "And here voice is everything—a pleasing fluid voice with resonance—and never monotonous. It's goodbye to anyone who can't correct a monotonous voice. She had better be a bricklayer. Enunciation and pronunciation are equally important and a wide background is vital—in

RADIO AND TELEVISION WORKERS 269

history, literature, creative writing, advertising, dramatics, psychology, music interpretation and appreciation, languages and speech—in which you must learn how to project your voice. Today, languages are not so important if you are working for a station which gets its materials from big news sources as pronunciation of difficult foreign words will be indicated phonetically.

"A girl will be smart to get a job in a small privately owned station and do anything she is asked to do," went on our commentator. "This may mean news editing, writing commercials, broadcasting commercials, typing the daily log, answering the telephone, preparing script, or meeting people. A girl must be intuitively courteous to everyone she meets in this work and to those out on the air. Every word must be weighed carefully. Courtesy will pay big dividends as we dare not offend anyone. Studying and writing movie scripts will help in teaching how to create suspense. In other words, the job of a commentator entails endless hours of work."

She explained also that interviewing on the radio is an art in itself. Kindness to nervous guests that will put them at ease is essential. Most important of all is to draw out everything that is in them.

"You must drain them dry in the first five minutes or you have failed," she insisted.

"There are not so many 'thou shalt nots' in a small station," she went on. "You will have much more latitude than in big studios where everything must be okayed. Many big-time radio women began in the bush leagues and rose by sheer merit. You may get in by the help of someone whom you know but unless you have what it takes you won't last. There are definite microphone techniques which are learned only by experience. The more you study radio work in schools the more you may have to unlearn when you get on an actual job," were her final words of advice.

If you aspire to program production in either radio or television, by all means study play producing in college and take part yourself in all dramatic activities. This will help you to learn how to handle people. Dramatic training and speech courses are invaluable if you want to produce radio or television shows. Director of auditions, continuity editor, or musical director are other types of directorial positions which are open to a few properly qualified women.

But suppose you can't find a spot before the mike or camera; is there any other place for you in radio or television? Of course there is, as we indicated at the beginning of this chapter. A stenographer, filing clerk, or other office employee may learn much about the radio or television business. One girl stenographer we know came into a station just to punch a typewriter and now she often pinch-hits in reading commercials. Does she get a thrill out of that! On the other hand, you might be well content in a clerical position and eventually work up to a responsible post with a good salary and opportunities for extensive service. Assuming, of course, that you can produce what it takes to get there.

There are also possibilities in personnel work, as a statistician, or as a research worker whose business it is to discover how well Mr. and Mrs. America and their small fry like the programs, and, what is still more important, how much of a sponsor's products are sold through airwave advertising. Here again you must have plenty "on the ball" if you want to reach high places.

You might be a receptionist or hostess in a broadcasting

studio, conducting tours through the station, directing people to offices, and so on. An artists' bureau to supply entertainers for emergencies on radio or television is a possibility —although a rather remote one. Acting as a script agent is another chance that may be equally slim.

A girl with training in both music and library techniques may find a fascinating position in the library of a large broadcasting station. Although the majority of stations are not large enough to maintain such services, there are several fine libraries—chiefly of music—in New York's great stations. A special knack for careful indexing and filing is vitally important for this work. Think of the thousands of songs and instrumental scores that must be stored and yet be available at a moment's notice. Material which will be needed by writers of advertising copy or entertainment scripts must also be readily available. A librarian who is not right on her toes won't last long here. She must be even-tempered and unperturbed, in addition to having actual research ability. She must not get excited when she is rushed. And, right here, we might emphasize that nervous people are not welcome in any phase of radio or television.

Although almost as difficult to enter as the entertainment field, script writing is still considered hopeful for the writer who can produce unique and popular work that is suitable for radio or television. Here you may sell your work either as a free-lance script writer or you may be employed as a continuity editor or as an advertising copywriter. That is, if you have the talent and previous experience. Because television is still in the development stage, the truly creative young person has an opportunity to start something entirely new and thus win fame and fortune.

A girl with super sales ability may find a place in the

radio-television industry selling time to advertising agencies, or she may deal directly with the advertising manager of a large firm which wishes to appear on the air. However, opportunities in this line are rather limited for girls and women.

We have said nothing about the mechanical or technical end of radio and television for the simple reason that technicians are almost exclusively men. There is no place for girls here except, perhaps, in certain phases of research—or in time of war when women have to take over in fields otherwise almost "for men only." Men are the ones who operate the control rooms, produce sound effects, and attend to the machinery which transmits the program afar. Women may break into these phases eventually—but not yet.

During our search for new material for this edition, we interviewed the educational director of a big-time broadcasting company on possibilities for girls in a radio or television career. Replying to our query concerning what to pass on to our readers, he confirmed the advice of our woman commentator.

"Tell them to forget it unless they are super," he said. "And they must be willing to work harder than they have ever worked before. Nor must they give up if things turn against them. Girls who think they can get into the entertainment field through a secretarial door would be far wiser to stay outside until they have perfected their own art and have made a reputation in their line elsewhere."

VI

Farm and Home Workers

30. LADY FARMERS

NOT SO LONG AGO agriculture would have been considered a "for men only" profession. But within the last two decades so many women and girls have found it a satisfying vocation that we are including it.

Before you think of taking up any branch of agriculture as a vocation, be sure that you can qualify for it. There is no place in the world where a misfit can find less happiness. A person who has grown up in the city and knows nothing about country life can be intensely unhappy in the solitude of a farm. In these days of radios, television, automobiles, fine roads, and local meetings, there is less danger of that, but if you really enjoy city life you'd better try yourself out with at least a full year on a farm before you spend time or money on preparing for a career in agriculture.

If you are afraid of hard work and long hours, get yourself a job far from a busy farm. It has been said that a farmer's work is never done. But if you are fond of animals, enjoy watching things grow, and find your own company fairly satisfying, there's no reason why you should not consider some phase of farming.

You need to be a good student, though, willing to study long enough in school to secure the best preparation, and then to go on studying all your life. Because that's exactly what you will have to do. Think of the bulletins, booklets, and circulars that are issued from the U. S. Department of Agriculture, the Bureau of Animal Husbandry, various state departments, government experiment stations, and so on! They will keep your mind at work; they cannot be neglected by anyone who wishes to be successful in agriculture.

The subjects you will study if you go into this field will keep your mind busy too. Among the technical courses will be: agronomy, soils, farm equipment, farm crops, plant breeding, care of live stock, dairying. Short courses are available in agricultural schools and colleges which will be useful if you cannot take the full course which leads to a degree. Among them are general agriculture, farm management, market gardening, animal husbandry, and the like.

If you want to be a farmer you will be wise to select one of the phases of agriculture that you can handle easily, and for which you will have sufficient capital. Most women cannot run the general type of farm unless they employ a man to manage it for them. Certainly they cannot do the heavy work. If they do, they will surely pay for it in the long run. However, there are women who have managed large farms with marked success.

Horticulture is a branch of agriculture in which women are frequently successful. Take up raising fruits, nuts, flowers, berries and you may find yourself with a profitable business. It is not wise to attempt too much, however. Find a specialty that appeals to you and stick to it. If you have a passion for roses, learn all you can about raising roses and then devote your life to it. Experiment and try to develop new climbers or a special prize-winning variety that will bring you fame. Here—as in almost every other business—it's the old story of having something, or doing something, just a shade better than anyone else is doing it. Think of the trade names of certain roses and what they mean. People will send from all parts of the country if you build up a reputation for your brand of rosebushes that will thrive anywhere.

There is the story of a woman who had a different kind of specialty. She grew pecans in one of our southern states. Faced suddenly with the need to support herself, she had nothing except a lovely old southern home and a few acres of ground, situated near a flourishing little railroad center. Against the advice of all her friends, she planted a grove of pecan trees, eking out a scanty living by means of a part-time position in the town until the trees began to bear. When the buyers discovered that this woman's nuts were too large to pass through the largest hole of their grading machines, they scrambled to buy her crop and secure an option on succeeding crops.

Poultry-raising is another branch of agriculture where women have been successful. Raising chickens and other fowls has always been a side line for the farmer's wife— one of those little jobs she does when she isn't baking, churning, cleaning, sewing, cooking for a crew of hungry farm hands, and so on. But this work can be turned into a very profitable business that can absorb all one's time. Moreover, it can be done on a small scale just to add a little to the family income, or perhaps in the backyard so that there will always be fresh eggs and a chicken handy if unexpected company arrives.

If you want to make a living at poultry-raising, you must be sure that you like chickens, turkeys, ducks, and geese, and don't mind the labor of taking care of them. For they must have regular feeding and constant care to protect them from vermin and diseases which may break out in the flock. If you are careless on this point, the entire flock can be wiped out before you know it. Read *The Egg and I* by Betty MacDonald and you will realize what we mean. You should take a four-year course in poultry husbandry at a good agricultural college, if you are in earnest about making this your life work. There you will get a thorough training and six months' practical experience before you can graduate.

You must be careful in the choice of your poultry farm, and must provide comfortable, economical, convenient houses for the fowls. In some places this business has become highly mechanized—almost an egg factory. The eggs drop on a moving belt and speed-up of laying is secured through the use of special lighting devices that fool the birds into thinking one day is two. It doesn't sound humane but undoubtedly it is good business.

The choice of the breed of poultry (especially chickens) you want to raise is vitally important. Drive through the country and keep an eye out for the various kinds of chickens you will see. A huge flock of white Leghorns will tell you that the breeder cares only for the production of eggs. Our egg factory owner will be likely to raise this kind. Don't stop there to purchase a fresh-killed chicken for your Sunday dinner; drive on until you find a flock of plump Plymouth Rocks, Rhode Island Reds, or the like. Then you will have an idea about the kind of fowls you should raise if you want to market both eggs and chickens.

Your best opportunity in poultry-raising is to start a business of your own. Although you will run the risk of an uncertain income and the danger of losing your flock if disease strikes, you have more than an even chance of making a success. Women are not welcomed on large poultry farms no matter how well-trained and capable they are, unless the farm is large enough to need clerical service. But there are positions for college-trained women in government service here as well as in other branches of agriculture. Their work is usually in laboratories or on experimental poultry farms.

The uncertain income and the need to be constantly on the job are the chief drawbacks in poultry-raising. On the other hand, it is a growing industry and the work is healthful and pleasant. Small capital is required and quick returns can be expected. One word of warning—if you have the slightest tendency toward asthma, have tests made to see that feathers do not affect you. This is not a joke—it can be deadly serious if you happen to be allergic to feathers.

Although the romantic days of the pretty little milkmaid are no longer with us, dairying offers many opportunities to women. Mechanical milkers have supplanted them in the barns but there is still much that they can do, particularly in clerical work on a large dairy farm, in a managerial capacity, or as owners. Although men dislike working for a "lady boss" they will stand it here more easily than on a general farm or in stock raising. Women are supposed to know more than men about the value of milk in the diet, about making fine grades of cheese and butter, and so on.

A high school education may be sufficient for running a dairy farm, especially if you can take a dairying course in a vocational agriculture high school. But it is much wiser to take the special training given in state agricultural colleges. You can get along if you take a correspondence course from the state college, but nothing can take the place of actual study under well-trained teachers and practical experience on an experimental farm. The standard curriculum in this field includes biology, zoology, botany, chemistry, dairy husbandry, agricultural economics, farm management, farm mechanics, etc.

Here again, you must like the animals you are working with and must be liked by them. It is generally agreed that the quantity and quality of the milk can be affected by persons working with the cows.

And now we come to the best field of all for outdoor girls. Bee-keeping is rapidly becoming an important industry. More than a hundred million pounds of honey are sold each year, bringing in an income that may be close to twenty million dollars. And there certainly is a shortage of honey in the country. We Americans are noted for our sweet tooth, and honey in the diet can satisfy that craving as well as furnish other dietary values.

Raising bees is not a hard job, either. The industrious, independent little workers take fairly good care of themselves. Give them good strong hives, situated in a sheltered spot, and your only worries will be capturing bees when they swarm, extracting the honey, bottling, and marketing it. It is suggested that the honey producer should sell her honey under a special brand. If she has a particularly fine grade of table honey, she'll be able to sell all she has—and quite likely at fancy prices. It is possible, too, to stress medicinal values if your bees can gather nectar from blossoms that have curative properties.

Here again, you must have a love for the outdoors. Bees can be extremely fascinating, you will discover, if you'll take the trouble to study them and their habits. You must be strong, because there will be some heavy lifting, unless you hire help for this. And you will need the usual intelligence, resourcefulness, and—for the marketing end—real business ability.

Although the majority of bee-keepers have learned on the job, agricultural schools are now stressing the necessity for special training. You might get experience by taking a position in a large apiary but, here again, women are not likely to be employed except in a clerical capacity.

What about the scientific phases of agriculture? They are not very good for women—yet. But later on there may be more opportunities, particularly in teaching. Soil service is a vitally important branch of the government's efforts to aid farming, because everyone admits that the prosperity of the country depends largely upon the fertility of the soil. Millions of people are living on land that is too poor to provide an adequate income, but soil science is coming to the rescue. No phase of government work is growing more rapidly. The Soil Conservation Service is now a permanent part of the U. S. Department of Agriculture and is offering many fine opportunities to scientifically trained young people.

Many types of positions are available in the Federal Service. In the chemistry and soils branch of the Soil Survey Division, they range from junior soil surveyor, assistant soil surveyor, up to senior soil scientist and chief of the division; in the Soil, Chemistry and Physics Division, there are positions from junior physicist and junior chemist up to senior chemist and chief of the division. Other positions in the Federal Service are in the Bureau of Plant Industry, the Resettlement Administration, and the Tennessee Valley Authority. Appointment to all these positions is through civil service examination.

The various states employ soil scientists in colleges, universities, and experiment stations as laboratory assistants, field assistants, instructors, assistant, associate, and full professors. There are openings for trained soil scientists with commercial concerns as salesmen, demonstrators, laboratory technicians, and soil chemists. Salaries vary according to the size of the firms; there are some star performers who are paid munificent salaries. Scientific positions are also available with private owners of large plantations, orchards, and large estates. Here the positions may be: agronomist, pomologist, citriculturist, soil chemist, and soil surveyor. The salaries are usually very good.

The work of these soil scientists is performed both in laboratories and in the field; usually the field work is too strenuous for girls. Workers in the Bureau of Chemistry and Soils map soils, take samples in the field, classify them, and prepare reports that are issued in bulletin form. In the Soil Conservation Service, they determine the extent of erosion and outline methods of control; for commercial fertilizer concerns, they demonstrate proper use of fertilizer and determine the plant food content in the fertilizer sold. In college, these scientists teach classes in soils and conduct experimental research in agricultural problems as related to soil management, or they may specialize in laboratory and field work dealing with applied problems in soil chemistry and physics, soil bacteriology, or plant nutrition.

Practically all positions in this field require a four-year college course with the major in the field of specialization. A Master's degree is essential for most of the college positions and a Ph.D. is desirable. A strong physique is important because there is a rigid physical examination. Experience in farming and plant culture is also a valuable asset.

Among the necessary qualifications for work in this phase of agriculture is ability to handle people easily and secure their co-operation; you will need to be almost as diplomatic as in the field of foreign service. For that reason courses in psychology should be included in your college courses.

Teaching agricultural subjects is considered one of the most promising fields in teaching. Since the passage of the Smith-Hughes Act, agriculture has been taught in all grades of the public schools and in extension and vocational agriculture schools. Teachers must have had a four-year course which includes agricultural subjects as well as methods of teaching. Men are preferred for these positions, although women are eligible and are frequently highly successful, especially if they have had practical farming experience.

The extension phase of agricultural work has been discussed in the chapter on Home Economists.

The beneficial effects of outdoor life are the chief attraction of any branch of agricultural work, as well as the independence which one may have in most phases. And there is promise of better things to come through the scientific research and experimental work which we have described in considerable detail. Don't expect an easy life, though. You won't get it.

For additional information on opportunities for girls and women in various fields of agriculture, write to Polly's Career Market, *Farm Journal*, Philadelphia 5, Pa.

31. HOMEMAKERS

WHY IS HOMEMAKING generally omitted from lists of occupations for women? Probably because most occupations lists include figures relating only to persons gainfully employed and housewives are not thought of as gainfully employed unless they are actually holding down a full- or part-time job in addition to the business of making a home.

There's a strange attitude toward the work of housewives. How many husbands believe that this is a real job? The housewives themselves may be to blame for the condescending attitude toward their business. Listen carefully to any quiz hour on radio or television. "And what is your occupation?" will be the question. "Oh, I'm just a housewife," is likely to be the apologetic reply. When that tone is used, the quizzer's reply is almost invariably in the same vein, "Well, we're always glad to have housewives on our program," but usually there will be more than a hint of condescension as though he's thinking, "Poor thing—just a housewife—hmmm—we can't expect much from her."

Too many girls approach the job of homemaking with the idea that they need no special preparation for it. They do not consider this a real career. They may feel that a girl can learn all she needs to know from her mother. Or, at any rate, there's always a delicatessen around the corner to provide food. However, girls like this are becoming fewer and fewer. And the world will be the happier for that. High school and college courses in homemaking have had a decided effect and excellent books are appearing constantly on the topic of marriage and homemaking.

The homemaking course offered in three vocational schools in Philadelphia, which is typical of many others, prepares girls not only for efficient management of their own homes but for paying positions which will enable them to earn a cash income until they are ready to become homemakers. They learn the social importance of education for family life as well as specific trades related to foods and clothing.

Emphasis is first placed on the girl herself, her personal problems of grooming, health and behavior. Problems of living in the home follow, including child study, care of the house, furnishing, entertaining, managing, and family relationships. The wise use of leisure, consumer buying and home nursing are also included. In clothing classes the selection, making, and care of personal and family clothing are all considered. In foods classes the planning, preparation, and serving of meals is stressed.

Each student is required to demonstrate the preparation of food, the operation of a piece of household equipment, and some phase of clothing construction. In the last year vocational guidance aims to help the girls solve future occupational and personal problems.

Child care is another course that will be helpful to the future homemaker. As nursery governesses, they learn the care and guidance of children of nursery age, including the preparation of food; the repair and laundering of clothing; the care of rooms; fundamentals of sewing; the selection and use of toys, books, clothing, and furniture.

Although reading the right books can be exceedingly helpful to a prospective homemaker, the very best preparation for this vital task is to train for it as seriously as you would for any other profession. How many girls give as careful thought to their fitness for marriage as for any other career? Too few, if the increasing number of divorces and separations is evidence. There are certain qualities that you must have to be a successful homemaker just as in any occupation. First of all, you must be physically fit, for homemaking is a wearing job. Countless labor-saving devices have lightened the burden of housework, but it is still not easy for the majority of wives. A delicate, complaining wife and mother may cause untold misery to the members of a family. Physical health, however, is not the only consideration. Mental health is equally important. If there is the least taint of mental trouble in your family or in that of the man you would marry, think twice or more, before you marry. It isn't fair to the possible children of such a union. Even if there is no actual mental trouble, you must do everything in your power to maintain a good mental balance. A course in mental hygiene will give you the right preparation for that.

Tolerance, fairness, understanding, generosity, kindness,

sympathy, and so on are vitally important to the potential homemaker. Above all, be sure that homemaking will keep you interested and happy.

And that brings us to the most controversial subject in this entire book—marriage and career, or shall we say marriage versus career?

Some time ago, we listened to a radio discussion of the question, "Shall married women work?" It was a heated discussion. There was a politician who wanted to legislate against women in government service. He had some excellent arguments in favor of his point, as everyone admitted. But it was pointed out that this had been tried in the depression of the 1930s and had been so unsuccessful that the bill (the famous no. 213) was repealed. A foreman in a factory was another opponent of women working after they married; he was the traditional "woman's place is in the home" type. The best arguments in favor of women working after marriage were produced by a member of the Business and Professional Women's Club who had proof that 90 per cent of the married women who were working were forced to do so by economic necessity.

Each case is different simply because every individual is different, and each individual must decide for herself in such a serious matter as this. If we make laws that keep all married women out of the world's work, think of the creative ability that may be stifled. Remember that Madame Curie was a married woman and that many another contributor to science has been a married woman. Yet there is much to be said against the young married worker who is merely working so that she can have an extra fur coat, and has little or no interest in what she is doing. We don't like that sort of thing any better than the employer who is forced to contend with it until he can stand it no longer.

However you settle this problem of working after marriage, use good common sense and you'll probably make a suitable adjustment. If you continue to work because your career means too much to you to sacrifice it, make a sensible arrangement so that you can give all your mind and thought to your work while you are on the job. It's the divided interest that employers complain about and which makes it harder for other women to combine marriage and career. Use your head in making your choice of a career, if you contemplate matrimony. We have pointed out that certain professions go better with marriage than others; don't forget to investigate that. It is not a minor consideration.

Perhaps part-time work may be the solution for you. We have a list of possibilities for part-time positions for either the married woman or for the student who must work her way through college. Under home economics there are cooking, housework, dietitian, waitress, cafeteria work. All these can be on a part-time basis and in many cases employers are happy to have married women. Care of children, nursing, plain sewing, or dressmaking may be other means of helping out the family income. In office work, you may find a part-time position as cashier, bookkeeper, typist, stenographer, or operator of a new-type office machine. If you are a trained and experienced teacher, there may be substitute work for you in teaching any subject which you are capable of handling. Library work holds many part-time opportunities for girls who can do the work, and research, translating, editing, scoring tests, tabulating, etc., may provide opportunities. If you own a car, you may use it in taking invalids or old people out for rides—for a consideration, of course.

Religious work can be a satisfying outlet for your energies, either in a part-time paid position or a volunteer undertaking. You can teach in the church school, do social service work, act as part-time church secretary, and the like. Here again there are ways of turning an honest penny and, at the same time, having most of your time free to study or to devote to your family.

32. HOUSEHOLD WORKERS

WHAT'S THE MATTER with household work for the girl who must earn a living as soon as she can leave school? Certainly there is no field less crowded at present. The title "servant," however, has been driving more and more girls toward stenography, a factory job, or almost any field of work except this important one of keeping household wheels turning. There has long been a social stigma attached to that term but, today, conditions are changing as many homemakers are realizing that this stigma complicates their "servant problem." *Household worker* or *Housekeeper*—please note the new titles—may become a promising occupation for girls if these ladies are successful in their efforts to raise standards of this vocation.

Shortly after the turn of the century, when the condition of household workers was often deplorable, an interesting experiment called the Household Aid Company was started in Boston. The purpose was "to study at first hand the problems of household labor under modern conditions by furnishing household labor by the hour." The sponsors of the plan hoped to develop household work as an attractive profession with regulated hours, decent wages, and improved living conditions. The company operated somewhat like certain employment agencies of today which send out trained workers for household work. The sponsors wanted to dignify domestic service by thus sending out well-trained girls on an hourly basis. Their idea was that these workers would be accepted on the same basis as the plumber, the electrician, or anyone else who took part in keeping household wheels turning smoothly. Unfortunately, that worthy project fizzled—we do not know why.

Back in the mid-thirties the National Council on Household Employment was formed for the same purpose—to help raise standards in such matters as pay, lack of privacy, social stigma, long and uncertain hours, and lack of freedom; all drawbacks which had been responsible for the unpopularity of domestic service as an occupation.

Only a few years ago, the chairman of this Council wrote hopefully of the future—insisting that household workers would soon have the economic status of factory or office workers. She looked forward to new conditions for household workers such as: a clear-cut employer-employee basis with the same hours, pay, freedom and respect that they would have in a factory, store, or office; the title of "household assistant" or "housekeeper"—instead of "maid" or "servant"—depending on duties, training, and experience.

"She will work a five-and-a-half- or six-day week," this writer says of the future household worker. "Her time off will be sacred. She'll quit at her agreed time each evening, even though your husband misses his train and gets home late for dinner. She will not live in, except in rare instances. If she does, she may agree to ten hours a week 'on call' evenings in return for her room. Working an eight-hour shift, she won't be there at both ends of the day. Either you'll get up mornings to prepare breakfast, and have the evening to relax; or you'll sleep late, but serve your own dinner and wash the dishes.

"By putting housework on a business basis," concluded this writer, "we'll get more and better service crowded into fewer hours, we'll end the mutually degrading mistress-maid relationship and we'll find new privacy and a more intimate family life. In short, by freeing domestic workers from their old servitude, we shall free our homes as well."

Figures from the U. S. Census Bureau indicate that would-be employers of these "household assistants" had better take steps to increase the popularity of the occupation else they will be left without their assistance. Every time we have a national emergency, girls leave this type of work and flock into war work. Although their numbers, on the whole, have increased steadily since the census takers first began to count women workers separately, there has been a decided decrease in the number of women in such jobs as chambermaid, cook, maid, and general servant in the private home during years that opportunities have increased in factories, shops, and offices.

Maybe you won't agree that housework is "in itself a desirable and suitable occupation for the girl who can't get into the 'white collar' class," but if the conditions that make it distasteful to the modern working girl are changed, you may discover that it is just that.

"But what can anyone do about those conditions?" you ask.

"Training—and then more training," is our reply.

By that we mean training employers as well as the workers. On this point we'll quote from a government publication, *Duties and Responsibilities of the General Household Employee*: "The employer needs training which will enable her: to understand better what is fair and reasonable for her to expect or require of her household employees as to quality and quantity of work; to realize what 'living' conditions she should provide; the wages she should pay; the hours of work she should require and the time off she should allow. In addition, she needs training which will help her to develop greater ability in personnel management, and a more socially-minded attitude toward household employment."

On the other hand, "the employee needs training which will enable her: to become more skillful in manipulative activities; to understand and care for children; to plan and manage her time to good advantage; to develop desirable personal qualities and health practices; to use and care for modern home equipment intelligently; and to develop a more professional attitude toward her work."

The lack of trained workers has always been a serious handicap. But that problem is being attacked with vigor and enthusiasm by a number of agencies which are aiming at the objective of a nation-wide program for better training facilities for girls who might be induced to go into household work.

As Josephine Perry declared in her book, *The How and*

Why of Home Etiquette, "To be an ignorant girl hired as an untrained scullion in a slovenly kitchen *is* degrading. To be a skillful, well-trained woman capable of assuming the responsibilities for service in a household is a vocation with many compensations."

Moreover, it is a hopeful sign that pride in their work is gradually developing from household workers' own study of their problems. They are beginning to realize that they will be taken at their own face value and that they can change the attitude of people toward them and their work, just as the nurses improved their situation. We have admitted all the time that present conditions are far from desirable in this field but we are hopeful of better things in the future. Perhaps one of you girls will be the Florence Nightingale of this vocation.

But the desire for training must come from yourselves. Some employers may be interested in improving the training situation but the majority will be indifferent. Go to a Y.W.C.A. Industrial Club and watch the domestic workers change their point of view. At first they'll complain about their unhappy condition, then they'll start talking about standards—what they should be and what employers have a right to expect. The next step will be trying to measure up to those expectations by training for household work and attacking it in a different and more professional spirit.

The girl with a gift for cooking can go far. Guests who taste her delicious meals are likely to attempt to lure her away from their hostess. If she is an exceptional chef, she may receive offers from restaurant or tearoom operators. She might save enough to start a small catering business of her own or open a tearoom or restaurant.

Another possible business of your own is a training school

for prospective household workers. The constant demand for trained workers in this field should bring success, especially if the school is run in connection with an employment agency.

Consider this about household work. Less than a century ago the practice of nursing was in even worse repute than housework today, chiefly because persons hired to care for the sick were untrained. Yet, due to the example of well-educated Florence Nightingale and others who followed her, the profession of nursing has become a skilled and honorable one. Wages, hours, and duties are clearly defined and the social inferiority stigma of Florence Nightingale's time has completely disappeared.

That is why the titles "household worker," "housekeeper," and "infant's nurse" have made this occupation very different from the days of the "hired girl" and "domestic servant." To deserve the new titles, however, and the dignity that goes with them, girls must be willing to take special training. No longer can a girl step out of her mother's kitchen—especially if it is an old-fashioned one—and win instant success as a paid household worker.

In the past, inexperienced household workers were usually trained by the hapless employer who could not afford experienced help. All too often this was slipshod training. Today, on the contrary, training may be secured at school in home economics courses, in vocational schools, or at training centers operated by such community agencies as the Y.W.C.A.

One thing is certain—there will be no monotony in the days of a young household worker. Almost anything can happen in the course of a single day—from rescuing the baby from a neighbor's lily pond to catching a burglar in the act of stealing the family silver. Preparation of food is likely to be the chief job if the house is equipped with the latest household appliances. Menu-planning and marketing may be part of the daily work, if the household worker can prove to her employer that she is capable.

Household tasks have been lightened by labor-saving devices once undreamed of, but now as common as plumbing. No need to worry about what may be happening to a meal while other work is under way, or if you are caught in a long line at the supermarket. It will be simmering, roasting, or baking at the correct temperature under the control of gadgets that will not let the food burn the moment your back is turned. Cleaning and laundry work, too, are done with a minimum of effort in the modern home.

Are you wondering what kind of person is needed for this type of work? As in every other field, there are certain definite characteristics that lead to success. The results of a study made in 1938 indicate that employers prefer girls who are dependable, efficient, good-tempered, honest, willing, agreeable, neat, clean, and intelligent in caring for children—and, of course, good cooks are always successful. Other reasons listed for satisfaction with workers were: "that they took a personal interest in their work and in members of the family; that they were cheerful, capable, intelligent, and expeditious in their work; that they were quiet and thoughtful and took the initiative in the performance of their duties." Now, that is the sort of girl you should be—or turn yourself into—for success as a household worker. Then you can go far and enjoy the going as well.

But is household work in the private home the only opportunity in this field? Far from it! Think of the hotels, clubs, schools, office buildings, and all sorts of institutions employing large numbers of such workers. Yet the figures indicate that only a comparatively small proportion of the women engaged in household work are in these positions. Hence our emphasis on work in the home. But often a route for promotion begins in the home. In the institutions there are more opportunities for advancement: to the position of head maid, supervisor, assistant housekeeper, or eventually housekeeper. There is more prestige in such positions as well. But we'd like to warn you here and now that the highest positions which call for executive ability and scientific knowledge usually have good salaries and social prestige which attract trained home economists.

Here is the way one woman felt about her job as a household worker: "I like cooking and tried to do my work as my employer taught me," she declared.

"Before long I was accepted as a member of the family. I sewed and offered to stay nights with the children and take them on picnics. I took great satisfaction in arranging flowers after my rooms were clean, in putting a tasty meal on the table, in doing a job as it should be done. I have known and worked with girls who were resentful because they thought their employers were unfair and because they felt that the employers considered themselves superior. But I found that if a girl took pride in her work, used good language and had good habits, she would be treated with respect. I am married now and I know that I learned more about homemaking by working in a pleasant, well-regulated home than I would have in any other way. If I had to support myself again, I would go into housework for the pleasant home and congenial work it provides."

33. HOBBIES AND THE STAY-AT-HOME WORKER

THERE WAS ONCE a busy professor whose days—and many of his nights—were devoted to his beloved work. "Hobby! What nonsense!" he would snort. "Haven't time enough for my work as it is. What on earth would I do with a hobby?" But the inevitable day of retirement came to him, just as time brings all things to an end for all of us. And what happened? Life became suddenly flat, tasteless; there was nothing interesting to do; but luckily for that gentleman he had a sensible wife. Very subtly and cleverly she stirred up his interest in Oriental art. Together they studied book after book on the subject, haunted auction sales to add new treasures to a constantly growing collection of beautiful objects, and spent hours in the Oriental sections of the city's great museums and department stores. No longer was life flat and uninteresting. A hobby had saved the situation—and fortunately it had not come too late.

The moral of that "true life story" is: start early on your quest for a hobby. It's like learning to drive a car or play a musical instrument, the older you are the harder it may be for you. Not that we are implying that hobbies are difficult to acquire. All you need is to find something that truly interests you for its own sake and then let yourself go. Behold! You'll have a hobby. But don't let yourself go too far.

It's the easiest thing in the world to allow a hobby to absorb too much of your time. A hobby horse has to be held in check just like any other beast or it will surely run away with you.

"What kind of hobbies are there?" you inquire. Suppose you look over several issues of the various hobby magazines. Or, better still, visit a hobby show; it's the best place to discover the infinite variety from which you may choose.

Here's a partial list of the hobbies you'll find in almost any show: collecting shells, various kinds of birds, tropical fish, wild flowers and ferns, butterflies and other insects, rare editions of books, antique glass and china, miniature rock gardens, dolls from all lands, postcards from here and there, coins, stamps, old photographs or cartoons, all kinds of objects having historical significance, souvenir spoons, music boxes, toy birds and animals, theater and concert programs, old etchings and prints. Among other kinds of hobbies are puppets, wood-carving, hand-made furniture, pottery, hammered-brass, jewelery, pets, gardens, fancy embroidery, genealogy, etc.

Any one of these may some day turn out to be a real lifesaver for you. Suppose we consider what gardening can do for the city-dweller. Don't scoff at the idea. Look over the roof gardens on the top of New York City's skyscraper apartment houses or at the pathetic little window-boxes bravely flaunting a few scrawny branches and pale dwarfed blossoms; these are hobbies to someone. Who knows how much release they have given to harassed souls? It takes no stretch of the imagination to picture the stodgiest worker in an office as a gay, happy gardener in his tiny suburban plot somewhere on Staten Island or up in Westchester County.

If gardening can't make a new person of you, why did a group from one of our great city colleges start a country club thirty miles from the city and there portion out small flower gardens to its members? And how those gardens became the pride and joy of the gardeners! In the summer session's bedlam, what a relief it was to drive that thirty miles of lovely parkways and then dig, dig, dig—and pull weeds until tense nerves relaxed and beads of perspiration carried off all the pent-up irritation of the week.

But relief from nervous tension is not all one gains from a gardening hobby. Far from it! Get two or three amateur gardeners together and listen to them talk. Or if you lack friends yourself, get a little garden and see what happens. Suppose you are lucky in developing a new flower or plant, what offers you'll have to trade for the prize plants belonging to your neighbors. Moreover, there is nothing more satisfying than the sheer joy one gets from giving bouquets to associates who may have a different kind of hobby.

In times of uncertainty, a hobby may be your best friend. It was certainly that to a young Navy officer who was floundering badly after his return from service in World War II. He had lost all interest in his pre-war profession and daily life seemed bleak to him. Turning to his almost forgotten hobby of making bits of furniture, he tried his hand at a rather ambitious piece of fine living-room furniture. His young wife took one look at the sheen on the finished work and said, "This is it." Today, that young man has a flourishing business and specializes in reproductions of colonial furniture which are eagerly snapped up by some of the best city interior decorators and dealers in fine furniture.

There are innumerable tales like that in villages, towns,

and cities from sea to shining sea in these United States. We think one of the most interesting is the story of a middle-aged immigrant to this country who was stranded with nothing except a stamp collection which he had hoarded since early childhood. To keep from starving, he began to sell some of his stamps. Today one of the finest office buildings in a great metropolis is the scene of his business activities; we've bought stamps from him and we know what a fine business he has developed—all from a boyhood hobby.

Suppose your life takes a sudden turn which forces you to stay at home. Gone will be your dreams of rising to positions of great responsibility and dignity in the outside world. Possibly an invalid mother requires your presence at home or perhaps the children of a widowed brother. You may have a hobby that can be used in this difficult situation.

We read again and again about women with prize-winning recipes which are used only for family and neighbors or to win prizes at the county fair. What that will mean if these women are forced to earn a living—and can't leave home! Fine jellies, cakes, candies, cookies, pickles, and the like will sell as fast as they can be made. Go to a woman's exchange in any city and you'll discover ways of making money without leaving your own cookstove, sewing-machine, or fireplace. Hand-hooked rugs are an ever popular means of adding to the family purse, but only in rare instances can you earn a satisfactory living that way. This kind of home-work should only be depended upon to supplement a too frail income.

One thing the stay-at-home worker should understand very thoroughly: to make a success of anything at home your service or product must be *superior*. Remember the old adage: "If you write a better book, or preach a better sermon, or build a better mousetrap than your neighbor, the whole world will make a beaten path to your door."

A woman of our acquaintance cooked better food than any of her neighbors and her fame spread over the small city where she lived. Others wanted a chance to enjoy the delicious dishes she prepared and she was finally induced to cater for occasional banquets. She loved doing it and it didn't take her away from her invalid husband very often. Moreover, she was able to give him luxuries that had previously been denied. Later, when she no longer needed to stay at home, she developed a catering business on a grand scale and soon became one of the substantial business women of the city.

Another stay-at-home worker went in for making old-fashioned dresses for elderly ladies who simply couldn't find a thing ready-made in the shops. Think how much joy she gave those conservative old ladies, at the same time adding a tidy sum to the family cash-box!

Suppose you are extremely fond of children, especially babies, and yet you are forced to remain at home for one reason or another. Why not try to have a few babies in to play with during the day? Many a working mother would welcome such a suggestion and would gladly pay you a small fee for the care of her child. A day nursery can be a very happy solution to the earning problem of someone who cannot leave home.

We might go on and on with suggestions of ways and means such as these but instead we'll refer you to a few books that will give you further help. You will find them in the reading list for this chapter.

VII

Workers for Uncle Sam

34. GOVERNMENT WORKERS, POLITICIANS, AND DIPLOMATS

THE U. S. GOVERNMENT service offers splendid opportunities to the young people of today. Old residents of Washington, D. C., who resent the recent influx of workers, feel that the whole country has marched on the nation's capital and the figures that give the increases in government positions almost verify their fears. Today there are more than two million government employees scattered throughout the country and in our possessions beyond the seas.

What chance is there for women to secure one of these positions? Very good indeed! Today the women have an even chance with the men at a wide and fascinating range of clerical, professional, and scientific government positions. But it was not always so. Katherine Lenroot tells us that "In the late eighteen-fifties a woman, Clara Barton of Civil War fame, was employed as a clerk in the Patent Office, and in 1862 Jennie Douglas was appointed to cut and trim paper currency. The faithful performance of these women, the first to be employed by the United States Government, opened the doors of Federal service and was the beginning of a demonstration of capacity and fitness which finally led to the appointment of a woman to the Cabinet." With the exception of positions such as foresters, railway mail clerks, and firemen, girls may hope for positions in any branch of government service, if they are properly qualified. Statistics show that there are almost as many women as men in government work in Washington; outside the capital men far outnumber them but only because of the larger numbers of soldiers, sailors, marines, coast guardsmen and the like.

Is there discrimination against women in the Government? Although appointive offices with their large salaries once were given mostly to men, a constantly increasing number of women are winning appointive and elective offices in these United States.

Changes have also taken place in the civil service in this matter of equality of opportunity for men and women. Once there were countless cases of discrimination against women in obtaining promotions to higher positions in certain fields. Even if there is still a long way to go there has been great improvement here.

At times there has been determined opposition to the employment of married women. There was even a regulation that forbade the employment of women in government positions. War conditions quickly changed that and today you will find *Mrs.* on the labels beside many a door in Washington office buildings. Instead of regulations against married women, they are accepted everywhere and even granted maternity leave.

For the various kinds of positions in the government you will need all the qualifications mentioned in the chapters on each particular field. In addition, there must be very special ability and experience if you expect to hold some of the highly specialized positions for which there is keen competition.

Since the majority of government positions open to women are under civil service, you should make a thorough study of all the announcements issued by the Civil Service Commission. Check yourself with the qualifications demanded and decide for which field you can qualify. Then study the educational requirements and fill in what you lack. Perhaps then you can try the examinations which are given in most large cities. However, don't rush too fast. You may find it wiser to wait until you have a few more years of experience before taking the examinations. A glance at the relative importance of the three points—qualifications, training, and experience—will give you an idea of the best course to pursue. Be wary of schools that advertise themselves as ready to train you for civil service posts. Be sure to investigate them very thoroughly and check their standing with Departments of Education, local Chambers of Commerce, the Better Business Bureau, and such organizations, before you enroll. There are impostors here as in every other business. Remember that the U. S. Civil Service offers no correspondence courses and there is no school that may rightfully guarantee employment in the civil service.

Clerical positions, although in the lowest bracket of government service, may be used as a fine opening wedge and be a starting-point for a career of distinction. Look at the huge office buildings in Washington, or at their pictures if you are too far away to visit your nation's capital, and consider the number of file clerks, stenographers, mail clerks, and so on who are working in these offices. These employees have shorter working hours than in almost any other work of similar nature in the country. Would you like to know what many of these clerks are doing after hours? The ambitious young clerks are most likely attending late afternoon and evening classes in the nearby universities—preparing themselves for the professional or scientific positions in the various bureaus. But even if they are satisfied to remain in the clerical divisions, they have a chance to climb to administrative positions if they have the ability, the perseverance, and the personalities that will make them eligible for promotion when vacancies occur above them. The work is usually performed in pleasant surroundings with agreeable associates; indeed, they are likely to be as congenial as you will find anywhere in the business world. Many girls with a superior background take jobs as typists or general office workers in the hope of advancing to more responsible positions. This hope has been realized in many cases. Again and again college women have done well and risen to top posts.

In the professional and scientific branches of government service there are almost unlimited opportunities for properly qualified workers. In the scientific and technical fields—especially in research—there is less attention to sex than in other branches. Here it is expected that women will make a career of their work and thus be more permanent than office workers who are likely to work only until they marry. Women have been placed in research and other scientific jobs that once belonged exclusively to men. "Most of them are doing able work," was the pleased comment of the Civil Service Commission official who gave us this information.

Experts are needed to test all sorts of materials—foods, soils, water, etc. Well-trained women will find opportunities in home economics, child welfare, library work, agriculture, nursing, teaching, social work, and in many other fields. Here they will find little, if any, discrimination in the matter of promotion to higher positions.

After you have safely passed a civil service examination, your name may remain on the eligible list for a considerable time. But don't be discouraged—the appointment may come when you least expect it. Even then you are not in for life; you will face a year's probationary period during which your every move is watched. If you surmount that hurdle, your appointment becomes permanent and you'll be established for life, unless there are unusual economic or political upheavals. At any rate, you will have the right to appeal to the Civil Service Board if there is an unjustified attempt to remove you from your position. There's no chance of being fired just because the boss doesn't like the shape of your nose or the color of your hair. Only flagrant inefficiency or one of the above-mentioned upheavals can disturb your security. That's why pessimistic friends may advise you to get a job with Uncle Sam.

Promotion within the government service is usually made on the basis of merit, although this is not true in all departments. Politics still play a considerable part, and occasionally whim and favoritism in recommendations for promotion may penalize deserving workers who are eligible for vacancies higher up. There is always the possibility of transfer from one department to another as a means of advancement, especially for those girls in Washington who have secured further training in the after-hour classes. While salaries in government service are never very high, they compare favorably with compensation received for similar work outside.

One of the greatest advantages of government work is the retirement arrangement which assures every employee a fairly adequate pension or retirement allowance after sixty-two. The security and stability of government service lure many workers from jobs that are likely to disappear under bad economic conditions. The hours are shorter than in many occupations and working conditions are usually attractive. Patriotic, idealistic young women will find plenty of chances to work for Uncle Sam as nurses, librarians, social workers in Army, Navy, and Veterans' hospitals, or in other welfare and scientific posts. Ambitious girls will be attracted by the opportunities for study and research in Washington and in the government laboratories all over the country.

Government service has its drawbacks just as any other work. You may chafe under strict regulations that are necessary in any big organization, whether in private industry or the government. You may feel that you are not allowed to express your own individuality in your work or that there is no recognition for original investigations and ideas. During recent years, however, the award system has become general throughout the government agencies to offset this once serious drawback in government work.

There are many and varied opportunities awaiting you if you choose to serve Uncle Sam. Your own state, county, or city may also have public service positions and many of them may be open to the person who can pass the local civil service examinations. In preparing for such examinations, get all the general education you can; then, when you have decided on the field you want to enter, check educational requirements and try to meet them. Meanwhile, you should try to gain some actual work experience in the field of your choice as this will add many points to your score in the examinations and might well be the deciding factor when your name is submitted to the employing officer. Write to the U. S. Civil Service Commission, Washington, D. C., or call at the nearest regional office to ask for full information about positions that are likely to be open in the field in which you are interested. You will be told when and where examinations are to be held. Then, it will be your task to prepare so well that you will not only pass but win a top position on the eligibility list.

We suggest that you study Bulletin #230 of The Women's Bureau—*Women in the Federal Service* (Part I—*Trends in Employment*; Part II—*Occupational Information*).

Today, women are becoming quite a force in politics— local, state, national, and international. Of course, we are a long way from the feminists' dream of a woman president; and perhaps there will not be a woman member of the Cabinet soon again, but you must admit that women are entering the Senate, Congress, and various state elective offices.

It is not easy for those women, however. Men may make idiots of themselves with few comments made; but let a luckless woman make one minor mistake! The world hears about it promptly and how men chortle and chuckle. "Just like a woman," they say.

To be a successful Congresswoman, a woman must have developed executive ability and an abundance of tact and

GOVERNMENT WORKERS

diplomacy. Psychology may turn out to be the most helpful study she has had when she deals with her constituents. There are times of terrific pressure, such as the closing days of a session when the strain is exceedingly wearing on the hardiest constitution. But if she "can take it," a woman—especially if trained in law—can make a name for herself in politics. Moreover, she will have an opportunity to use all her sympathy and humanitarian ideas in trying to promote better social legislation that will improve the condition of the underprivileged in the nation.

Here is the way several women politicians reached high places. Mrs. Margaret Chase Smith, from Maine, became in 1948 the first Republican woman elected to a full-fledged term in the United States Senate and the only woman elected to a full six-year term without first being appointed. In 1930 she married Clyde H. Smith, a former state Senator and became active in politics when elected to the Republican State Committee. In 1936, when her husband was elected to the U. S. House of Representatives, she worked as his secretary and office assistant, managing the office work, handling mail, and doing research on the subjects of various bills. When her hubsand died in 1940, she was elected to fill his unexpired term, and she has been re-elected to every Congress since then. In 1944 she served as one of 13 advisers to the U. S. Government delegation to the International Labor Conference meeting in Philadelphia.

The Women's National Press Club gave Mrs. Smith their Politics Achievement Award for 1948, and the Associated Press named her the 1948 "Woman of the Year." Many other honors have come to her since then and now she is being mentioned as a candidate for Vice-President of the U. S. A. This could make her the first woman president.

While she is a champion of women, Mrs. Smith says she is not a feminist. She believes that "a woman's viewpoint should be objective and free of any emphasis on feminine interests." It is important, though, she thinks, for more women to qualify for public office, for responsibility for good government rests equally on men and women. She adds that "we can't all be Members of Congress and the Senate, but there must be good people working all down the line, on school boards, civic organizations, community chest boards, church groups, and community projects . . . We must remember that America has been made great, not from Pennsylvania Avenue in Washington, but from the Main Streets in our villages."

Mrs. Mary T. Norton—unofficial "dean" of Congresswomen—has served in the U. S. House of Representatives continuously since 1924. Probably Mrs. Norton's best-known work is associated with the important House Labor Committee which she headed for 10 years. She helped steer through Congress many major labor laws. In 1945 she was appointed Government Representative and Adviser to the International Labor Conference in Paris, France. Like Mrs. Smith, this noted woman politician has received many awards—notably in 1946 when the Women's National Press Club selected her as one of the ten outstanding women of the country and the outstanding woman in Government for that year.

You need not be middle-aged to become a legislator. Mary Shadow, youngest representative in the Tennessee State Legislature, was elected at the age of twenty-three. In college she had majored in political science and taught

GOVERNMENT WORKERS

this subject and history at Tennessee Wesleyan College in Athens. She says this about her reasons for entering politics: "My mother and father were always active in community affairs and have been appalled by the lack of interest on the part of most people in our government set-up. In college I saw my chance to study toward the end that I might be able to help, and political science seemed to be the field most sparsely settled, and touching the most lives." She insists that "politics are necessary to the American way of life" and that "the welfare of the individual is not to be separated from that of the group."

"Some of the few women who have been in the Service have done such excellent work that the admission of more is possible," was the prediction concerning opportunities for women in Foreign Diplomatic Service more than a decade ago. Even though women are still only a small per cent of the workers in this field you may indeed have a chance to see the world via a typewriter or stenographer's notebook at the expense of your Uncle Sam.

For the benefit of those girls who may one day find themselves in that exclusive small per cent, we'll tell you about the qualifications, training, and opportunities in the diplomatic and consular service. In the diplomatic service, which deals primarily with international politics, one must be far above the average in tact, language aptitude, good judgment, adaptability, tolerance, ability to make friends, and in willingness to conform to the old maxim, "When in Rome, do as the Romans do."

It's the only sure way to get along. A polished social manner which comes from a good social background is a decided asset to the aspiring young diplomat. The social side of diplomatic service is vitally important; hence the stress on the social graces.

It goes without saying that a thorough education is essential. The rigid examinations for appointments will eliminate you if you cannot measure up on that score. Subjects included in the examination are: international law, diplomatic usage; modern languages; natural, industrial, and commercial resources and commerce of the United States; American history, government, and institutions; modern history of Europe, South America, and the Far East. You are likely to find in many universities and colleges all the courses necessary to prepare you for these examinations.

Top ambassadorial posts are filled by Presidential appointment and confirmed by the Senate. Hence, these examinations are not required of the few and far-between ladies who represent us in these top posts in faraway lands. This fascinating field of work consists of representing this great country of ours abroad and defending our interests in other lands. One false step or careless remark might easily plunge the entire world into a disastrous war. Once, men were afraid to take a chance on women for this work until they gained a reputation for holding their tongues. Lately, however, the men have made so many boners that it behooves them to forget that restriction against women.

The task of looking after the interests of American citizens and American travelers abroad is by no means a small part of the diplomatic corps' duties, despite the fact that the consular service shares in this responsibility. How to handle delicate situations that may arise in this line is one of the many lessons that may be learned in the Foreign Service School in Washington, D. C. Persons who pass the civil service examinations for foreign service are required to spend a specified period in this school before they receive appointment as regular officers of the service.

Anyone who comes through that course safely deserves something better than the lowest rank in the diplomatic officer corps but all must pass through that rank. Then will come promotion through other officer ranks to the top one which is just below that top ambassadorial post previously mentioned. Positions below the rank of minister or ambassador are: the Counselor of the Embassy, several Secretaries varying in degree of importance, the military and naval attachés with their assistants, the commercial attachés, and, last of all, the clerks, stenographers, filing clerks, and other office employees.

The consular and foreign trade services differ from the diplomatic service in that they deal exclusively with matters of international trade, although they also share the responsibility of protecting the lives and property of American citizens abroad. Women are eligible to consular posts just as they are in the diplomatic corps, but how often do they get them? It's news when a woman is appointed as vice consul or if a woman consul retires from service.

Qualifications and training similar to those mentioned for the diplomatic service are required for the consular service, but more emphasis should be given to commercial subjects. Here the various ranks are consul general and consuls (who are appointed by the President with the approval of the Senate), the vice consuls, interpreters, student interpreters, and various consular agents. Examinations for the consular service differ slightly from those for the diplomatic corps.

In spite of difficulties in getting a job in foreign service we must admit that if you do get in you'll have a delightful life with foreign travel and contacts with all sorts of stimulating people. But you must be willing to adapt yourself to different climates, long hours, and hard, exacting work. Also, discipline is very strict. A call to go to a distant country may come at a moment's notice and go you must. Often it is necessary to leave friends and family for years; perhaps to live with strangers who will never accept you graciously or may even endanger your life. Investigate all such possibilities thoroughly before venturing into a career in foreign service.

35. WACS, WAFS, WAVES, MARINES

HERE'S A BRAND-NEW career field for women of today and tomorrow. New, except, of course, for those in the nursing profession. And—if you choose a career in the Armed Services, *and* are good enough to be chosen by them—you'll find that the ceilings of opportunity are almost unlimited.

Have you felt the urge to fly to faraway places? Then listen to the director of women in the Air Force. "The opportunity of serving as an integral part of the United States Air Force affords the women of America a rare privilege never before accorded in the history of our country," says Colonel Geraldine May. "Upon the Air Force team falls the responsibility of providing air power to guard, with vigilance, the security of America. Young women who qualify may become members of the Air Force on a basis of full equality. We welcome those who are sincerely interested in pursuing a career which will contribute immeasurably to maintaining the peace."

Colonel Mary A. Hallaren, Director, Women's Army Corps, tells girls that a career in the WAC "carries with it that intangible feeling of belonging—that comradeship which goes with being a part of the Army, as well as that very real and tangible security that goes with the rights and benefits of the service. Standards for enlistment and appointment in the Women's Army Corps must be high, for the women who enter the service today will provide the leadership of the future."

Here are the special qualifications:

Age—18 to 34, inclusive. (18 to 21 must have parents' consent.)

Education—New enlistees must be high school graduates. (Waived for women with prior service in the Armed Forces.)

Citizenship—Must be a U. S. citizen.

Marriage—Must be single, if without previous military service. No dependents.

Health—Must be in good physical condition as determined by a physician's examination.

Mental Aptitudes—Must pass a test for normal mental aptitudes.

Period of Enlistment—Women may enlist in the Army for 3, 4, 5, or 6 years; or in the Air Force for 4, 5, or 6 years.

"How do I go about enlisting?" may be your question. Find the nearest main Army or Air Force recruiting office and ask for an interview. There you will fill out an application and, if you meet initial specifications, you'll be advised when and where you may take mental and physical examinations. If you are qualified you may be selected for the next basic training group after your name has been placed on the eligibility list for consideration. Won't you keep an eagle eye out for the mailman to bring your notification and further instructions? These will mean, for the lady soldier, ten weeks at the basic training center at Camp Lee, Virginia; or, for the would-be WAF, eleven weeks at Lackland Air Force Base in Texas.

With only a few exceptions, this course is similar to basic training for men—learning the background of the Army or Air Force, becoming familiar with the customs and courtesies of the Services, studying administration and supply, as well as close order drill, and a physical training course which includes swimming. The aim of the course is to help the new recruits get acquainted and understand their part in the U. S. Army or U. S. Air Force.

Jobs open to Army and Air Force women include: technicians in medical field and physical sciences; operators and installers in communications; clerks, stenographers, librarians, and many other jobs in administration; in photography, public relations, personnel work, mechanical trades, supply, statistics and finance—and so on. Actually there are more than four hundred non-combatant jobs in the Army alone that women can do and, in which, under a Career Management Plan, they may advance in their chosen field of specialization from apprentice to supervisory status.

If you want to advance more rapidly or want to continue your education, you may take extension courses through the United States Armed Forces Institute and earn up to two years' college credits. Opportunity is also given to all qualified WACs and WAFs to go to Officer Candidate

School. College graduates and other educationally qualified women may apply directly from civilian life. Ages: WAC, 19-28; Air Force, 20½-26½.

How would you like to train for the nursing profession and then join the oldest of all women's military services, the *Army Nurse Corps?* You see, an Army Nurse must be a graduate registered nurse, able not only to assume full responsibility for the nursing care given to patients in Army medical installations, but to teach and supervise non-professional aides. Advanced courses given in a number of specialties equip her to teach in such specialties as operating room, anesthesia, and psychiatric sections.

When Army nurses are attached to the U. S. Air Force, they have many of the same duties in Air Force hospitals. Some will care for the sick in flight and travel with the Military Air Transport Command.

In the Women's Medical Specialist Corps of the Army are dietitians, physical and occupational therapists who help keep our Army and Air Force in tip-top physical and mental condition. After a trained dietitian has been inducted into Army life, her first assignment will probably be to a general or large station hospital; her job to assist the Chief Dietitian (a Captain or a Major) in charge of hospital food service by planning nutritious menus, and training personnel in sanitation, food handling and waste control.

A trained physical therapist will—upon prescription of a medical officer and under the supervision of the chief physical therapist—administer treatments employing electrotherapy, heat, ultra violet, massage, muscle re-education and other therapeutic exercises for patients recovering from disease and injury. Occupational therapists will practice their special profession in the same way. Their knowledge of anatomy, physiology and psychology combined with skill in crafts will be scientifically applied in the treatment of such patients.

The Army tells you that "Your country's Services are constantly aware of the need for experienced and competent leaders. Women with ambition and superior abilities may go far in the many new Army and Air Force career fields. There is no finer mark of professional ability and prestige than the insignia and uniform of a commissioned officer in the U. S. Army and U. S. Air Force."

Moreover, in any branch of the Armed Services, you will be certain of well-kept, attractive quarters, the finest foods available, free dental and medical care, 30-day vacations with special extra passes when necessary. And each post has chapels in which services are held by Protestant, Catholic, and Jewish chaplains.

Do you lean to the Navy's blue? Then here's the story of life as a WAVE recruit at the Great Lakes U. S. Naval Training Center. The first week is devoted to a special processing to assist the recruit in bridging the gap between civilian and military life. Haircuts, medical and dental examinations, medical shots, classification tests, uniform issue, fitting of the first Navy blue suit, instruction in stowing gear into individual lockers, learning to make a bunk, greetings from almost everyone on the station—and so on. By the end of that first week, the recruits are more than ready to welcome the standard schedule which will last during the next nine weeks. Here's a schedule of the routine daily activities Monday through Friday during those weeks:

0500 Waking of the galley detail.
0520 Galley detail muster and leaving for galley.
0600 Reveille and reveille muster.
0600-0740 Ablutions, dressing, barracks details, morning mess.
0740 Morning quarters.
0805-1135 Four 45-minute class periods with two 5-minute breaks, and one 20-minute break during which the smoking lamp is lighted.
1135-1300 Mail call, noon mess, noon quarters.
1300-1630 Four 45-minute classes divided like the morning sessions.
1630-1730 Mail call, evening mess.
1730-2000 Area liberty, except on Wednesday nights which are field nights to prepare for the weekly Thursday inspection.
2000-2100 Barracks details, personal chores.
2100-2120 Prepare for bed.
2120 Tattoo.
2130 Taps and bunk check.

On Saturday morning the schedule is the same except that Personnel Inspection plus a lecture or a movie replace the usual classes. Then comes area liberty. On Sunday reveille is an hour later but you wash, dress, make your bunk, muster and march to breakfast as usual. After attending church service, area liberty begins, interrupted only by noon and evening musters for meals.

In the classes will be instruction in drill, health or swimming, jobs and training, personnel, ships and aircraft, naval history, and naval organization, with one period each day allowed for administrative matters and study. One of the most interesting and important of these classes is *Jobs and Training* where the recruit learns about the ratings open to women. This is important because approximately 60 per cent of them will be sent to specialist schools after the training period. Information given in this course gives the recruits a basis for discussing with the classifier the particular field they want to select.

Finally the great day of graduation arrives and you pass in review before the Captain. The WAVE with the highest standing is given an identification bracelet and a Meritorious Mast. Your company dance is that night and the next morning you have your last breakfast with your classmates, finish packing, log out, grab your bags and run for the train.

During your two-weeks recruit leave you will delight in showing off your bright uniform. Then off to the new station where, after checking in, you meet the other WAVEs who will be your friends and fellow-workers.

Here's how one recruit ended her first letter to the home folks:

"Most of the officers are really swell. They are much nicer than I expected. So are our barracks.

"It's almost taps so I'll close now. This is a wonderful life even though it's so different from anything I've experienced before."

What about entering as an officer? Here are the qualifications for commissions as Ensign (Line) in the U. S. Navy:

Age—21-25.
Education—Graduate of an accredited college or university.
Citizenship—Native-born citizen of the United States, or naturalized for a period of at least ten years.
Mental and moral fitness must be established as well as an aptitude for the Naval service.
Marriage—Unmarried at time of appointment.
Dependents—No children under 18 years of age regardless of custody.

Minimum Physical Standards—Must be at least 5 feet tall and must weigh at least 100 pounds with weight in proportion to height and age. Both eyes must be at least 15/20 and must be correctible to 20/20 with glasses. Must have at least 18 vital serviceable permanent teeth; must have sufficient teeth in functional occlusion to insure satisfactory incision and mastication; and must not require immediate dental work.

All applications are sent to the Navy Department for consideration by a selection board; names of selected women must be approved by the President and their commissions confirmed by the Senate before they are sworn into the Navy. Moreover, all commissions are probational for the first three years. There is a five-months indoctrination course before these Ensigns will be ordered as junior officers to various shore activities for duty in connection with Personnel, Public Relations, Training, Publications, Intelligence, Communications, Logistics, Operations, or any similar type of duty where there are authorized billets for military personnel. After a period of active duty further specialized training may be requested and, if the needs of the service permit, preferences of the individual will be considered in making assignments.

How would you like to join the group of women who did one of the finest jobs of all during World War II? Women Reserve Marines released enough regular Marines to form an entire division which made a big name for itself in the Pacific. And they had a fine tradition back of them in the Marinettes of World War I, who were the forerunners of the Women Reserves of 1943 and the regular Women Marines of today and tomorrow.

What a selected group these girls are! Their number is so small that it takes an almost super-girl to qualify, especially on the point of excellent character. Twenty to thirty years are age qualifications. You must be single and with no dependents at time of enlistment, be a high school graduate and a citizen of the United States. Although a background in clerical and administrative work is desirable, it is not essential.

As a Marine, you will serve in such "billets" as: stenographer, administrative clerk, statistical clerk, classification specialist and clerk typist. These duties will take you to such cities as New Orleans, San Francisco, Washington, D. C., New York, and over 35 other cities within the continental limits of the U. S.

Life in the Marine Corps is pleasant. You live and work in attractive surroundings, probably sharing quarters with other women Marines with whom you work. Monday through Friday, your day ends at 4:30 P.M. Your time after work and on the weekend is your own; *and* there will always be someone ready to take in a movie with you or any of a dozen other pastimes. Moreover, even as a private in the Corps, you will earn a higher net income than girls in comparable civilian jobs. In addition to your salary you'll receive free food, quarters, hospital and dental care. On top of this you are allowed an annual uniform allowance for the purchase of those smart Marine uniforms. The 30-day vacation is given here as in all branches of the Services. Here, too, you may earn promotions which mean more pay and responsibility. And after twenty years' service, you may retire with a lifetime income.

There are a very limited number of openings for officers in the Women Marines. High professional standards are required of these officers as well as the ability and education to serve in executive positions where leadership and responsibility are necessary.

36. NEW HORIZONS FOR GIRLS AND WOMEN

CHOOSING A CAREER is indeed serious business for the teen-ager who is beginning to look around the world of work in search of the best niche for herself. And it is equally serious business for college girls—from "frosh" to "grads"—who have been looking but are still uncertain and unprepared for what lies beyond the new horizons that have opened to them during the years.

"Today too many girls just flock into the softest jobs at highest pay with no thought of the future," was the sad and too true comment of a counselor, when employment was at its peak during war preparations. We admit that this is the situation with the majority of girls and women at any time of full employment. And those are the girls who are likely to work just enough to "get by" on the job—and no more—with little pride in work well done. Very few of them will study and think about their future work or will be eager to do their best.

Nevertheless, it is reassuring to remember that "the hope of the world is in its minorities" and that our hope for the future lies in the minority of girls who put service first in planning their careers. We'd be willing to guarantee a happy future to any girl who approaches her life work in that spirit. She would undoubtedly hold her job indefinitely and advance rapidly in it. The girl who sets her mind on a goal of service and steers straight for it will eventually arrive there. She will force her way. There may be unavoidable delays but everything she does will help in some way toward the end for which she aims. That is, if she does not get discouraged and allow herself to be permanently sidetracked from her objective.

It is for these girls that we'll take a look at the past in each of the major fields of work. Perhaps they will find help there in career planning. In many instances we find that only a small minority of women fought the battles that opened new opportunities for their daughters—and for you working girls and women of today and tomorrow. Are you fearful of what lies beyond the horizon for you? Then you should find inspiration and encouragement for meeting crises in your lives from our look at the past.

First, a few figures about the number of women in various occupations today. In such jobs as stenography, nursing, teaching, bookkeeping, and selling more than 250,000 women have been counted. Maybe that sounds overcrowded to you who consider preparing for one of these occupations. On that point we'll quote the U. S. Women's Bureau:

"Large numbers mean more jobs open each year as workers leave—and more likelihood of employment almost anywhere." You are warned, too, that there is some danger of unemployment if you prepare for occupations in which there are less than 5,000 women. Among these are actresses, radio commentators, photographers, lawyers, psychologists, airplane stewardesses. In between these two extremes are occupations with 25,000 or more women, such as: social workers, musicians, college instructors, religious workers, medical and laboratory workers, buyers, department heads,

NEW HORIZONS FOR GIRLS AND WOMEN

and owners of retail stores. One of these might hold your best chance for the future.

Think next whether or not the job you are considering is chiefly an occupation for men. You must decide for yourself how much courage, initiative, and patience you have if you want to follow the lead of pioneer women who broke into fields that have always belonged mostly to men.

Women are only five per cent of all dentists, clergymen, physicians, engineers, pharmacists, lawyers, chemists, architects, veterinarians, draftsmen, airplane pilots, insurance agents, meteorologists, and certified public accountants. On the other hand, women are more than seventy-five per cent of all librarians, professional nurses, home economists, medical-laboratory technicians, teachers, dental hygienists, physical and occupational therapists, stenographers, milliners, and demonstrators.

In the occupational group labeled *Guardians of Health* there was plenty of pioneering. It was Nurse Florence Nightingale and Doctors Emily and Elizabeth Blackwell who broke down barriers against women in these fine professions and made the way easier for others to enter the related professions of dentistry, osteopathy, veterinary medicine, physical and occupational therapy, and other fields. A few actual figures from our Census Bureau will show us just how and when the ladies started to go places and do things in these professions.

Back in 1870, when Uncle Sam first began to count the pretty noses of his feminine workers, there were only twelve hundred nurses, twenty-five dentists, and slightly more than five hundred physicians. There were too few in other health-guarding lines to be counted at that time. Now, we have about four hundred thousand nurses working in over a half-dozen phases of this noble profession and in hospitals and other medical service centers all over the world.

The number of women physicians has gone up to nearly eight thousand but dentists and osteopaths have increased to only a few more than a thousand. We must admit that cash earnings in this occupational group are not high, but we need not remind our serious girls that rewards in any phase of health-guarding are far, far beyond cash returns. There is such "psychological income" as: joy in helping the ill in mind and body to regain perfect health, restoring to use maimed or helpless arms and legs, assisting those with imperfect vision to see better and thus increase their usefulness and happiness, and healing dumb animals who are in pain. In fact, just having a part in the improvement of the world's health may be all the reward you want.

Among the *Women Who Mean Business,* clerical workers and secretaries have climbed since 1870 from less than a thousand to approximately two million in 1950. That's what the invention of the typewriter and all the later office machines did for women, for it took their nimble fingers to run these machines efficiently. We don't know much about the pioneering girls who were lured from their homes into the business world to operate those new machines. We do know, though, that the first of these workers were often looked down upon by their former schoolmates. Husbands and fathers were ashamed to admit that wives or daughters "had to work" as very few were bold enough to start a business career just because they chose that means for service instead of teaching or nursing which were the only acceptable lines of work for women in the early days.

Think of the big jump in numbers of these workers!

NEW HORIZONS FOR GIRLS AND WOMEN

Only 930 clerical workers and secretaries in 1870 up to more than a million immediately after World War I. About 800,000 joined these typists, secretaries, and others from 1920 to 1940.

Women in department and other retail stores, in wholesale, real estate, and insurance selling increased from about nine thousand in 1870 to nearly 900,000 in 1940 and in 1950, 1,500,000.

Wars and inventions of new machines opened new opportunities to factory workers as well—especially to those blue-jeaned women, young and middle-aged, who trooped into munitions factories during World War I and II.

Back in the seventies, most of the factory jobs for women were in textile and clothing manufacture—over 100,000 in textiles and nearly 200,000 in clothing. The textile girls, more than quadrupled by 1940, are now 521,000 in number. Clothing workers rose to 727,000. Back in those days nearly nine thousand worked in footwear manufacture but they did much of their work (stitching uppers) at home. More than 100,000 were operating new types of machines in this industry by 1940 and in 1950, 685,000.

Wars and new inventions gave glass, metal, and electrical workers chances that had been almost nil in the seventies. Today electrical and metal figures are zooming upward with 260,000 in electrical and 97,000 in metal. These girls have made good, too.

All these girls and women flocking into offices, stores, and factories brought a need for women personnel workers to keep them happy and satisfied on their jobs. Advertisers were needed, too, to keep the jobs going, bankers to take care of the workers' financial needs and to provide cash for operation and expansion of the industries and other businesses. Transportation and communication workers had their big share, too, as did the lady bosses in top management jobs. These bosses rose from about 8,000 in 1870 to well over 300,000 in 1940 and 1950 listed 946,000. Back in 1910 the figures on lady bankers were over two thousand. By 1930 these financial wizards numbered over eight thousand but lost several thousand according to later reports. Women advertisers were not even mentioned specifically in census figures until 1940 when they had less than four thousand.

The most spectacular increase of all was among communication workers—especially the girls of the switchboards. All this was owing to Messers Alexander Graham Bell and Samuel F. B. Morse—and those who followed these pioneers in the all-important business of getting widely separated peoples together for business, other economic, and social purposes. Telephone and telegraph operators rose from only 321 in 1870 to over 200,000 in 1940 and 628,000 in 1950.

In any phase of the world's work the *Women Who Mean Business* can make or break our future. The girls who go abroad to work are our representatives. Even the clerk on the lowest rung may be an ambassador of good will—especially in our embassies. Often they are the only persons callers will meet.

Right in the U. S. A., too, the business women have a vital part in production and distribution of products from farms and factories—not only to maintain our high standard of living but to help raise the standard in all other nations. Isn't that thought quite a satisfactory "psychological income" which should keep girls happy even on the most monotonous jobs in office, store, or factory?

When we talk about jobs for girls and women in which *People Are Their Business* we have the teachers, the social workers, ladies of the law, ministers and other religious workers, librarians, home economists, recreation leaders, and beauticians. Back in 1870 it was quite genteel for a woman to make a living as a teacher, even though the majority of teachers in that long ago time taught only because they had not been able to catch a husband. Nearly 85,000 women did this and teaching has remained a heavily "ladies first" occupation ever since those days. By the booming twenties, we had more than 645,000 teachers—a number that climbed to 822,000 in 1940 and to 950,000 in 1950.

Social workers—as a distinct professional group—started with only 65 in the seventies. This did not include those ladies behind the scenes who did endless hours of unrecognized and unpaid social work. Among these was splendid Jane Addams who was not only unpaid but gave all her personal fortune to her life work. By 1920, this had become a real profession with more than 28,000 workers—a figure which, like the 65 of 1870, included religious workers as well. By 1940, that figure had climbed toward 49,000 and it is still rising. It has taken women like Marion Talbot, Sophonisba Breckinridge, Edith and Grace Abbott of the University of Chicago and women of their stature elsewhere in the training phases of social work to gain respect and recognition for this splendid profession.

The ladies of the law were not counted until 1910 and then had only 558. They gained about 1,200 by 1920 and rose to 4,500 in 1940. Though a small group, these women have accomplished a great deal of good, especially those who have achieved high places as justices and judges.

VOCATIONS FOR GIRLS

Women ministers and other religious workers scarcely counted at all back in the early days. They were just part of those 65 social workers, as we noted above. Among the pioneers here were a number of great women who opened new political, social, and economic horizons for their sisters, daughters, and for others to follow into the future; such women as Anna Howard Shaw whose pioneering against tremendous odds opened doors for the 3,300 women ministers of 1940 and the added ones counted in 1950.

Librarianship has been one of the fastest growing professions for girls and women. From a count of 43 in 1870, librarians numbered over 34,500 by 1940 plus the more than 16,000 attendants and assistants who were counted separately. This is an expanding field; experts predict that many more recruits to this profession will be needed than are being prepared right now.

Home economists date only from the early 1900's. We know a good deal about such early workers in this field as Ellen Richards and Mary Hinman Abel who ran a demonstration program called the "Rumford Kitchen" at the Chicago World's Fair of 1893. And there were annual gatherings of women—like Mrs. Richards and Mrs. Abel—and some men at Lake Placid which preceded the founding of the American Home Economics Association. And it is a leaflet from this association which insists that "No other profession offers richer variety of occupations or greater personal satisfactions," and that there is a niche "for practically every type of girl: the artistic, the scientific, the homebody, the business-minded, the fashion fan, the bookworm, the girl who yearns to teach or to do radio work, and the girl who wants to make this a better, happier world."

Recreation leaders have been included with physical education teachers until recent years. Now they are developing into a separate and distinct profession with high standards. The constant variety in this job is worth more than cash returns to recreation leaders as is also the exhilaration in seeing fine results from the games and other recreational activities which they have planned.

The beauticians, who accomplish more for women than people realize, jumped in numbers from about 1,500 in 1870 to more than 218,000 in 1940, with increases in 1950. Criticisms are often leveled at American women for the vast sums they spend on beautification but our beauticians can point to many of their clients who began their climb to high places only after they had become well groomed. Stores, offices, and other places of employment have no room for unkempt women. Those "vast sums" were often decidedly well spent for the careers of the spenders.

Nowhere in the world of work—except perhaps as *Guardians of Health*—can girls find more chances for satisfying work than in these professions where people are their business. In many cases, salaries are so inadequate—especially in beginning jobs—that the "psychological income" will be about all that is left after living expenses and taxes have been paid. Here, you will not only help in the improvement of the health of the world but of the morale as well.

Women scientists and engineers have not been plentiful in numbers down the years but what a job some of the great ones have done! Not a single woman chemist was listed in 1870. There were just 49 in 1880, a jump to 253 in 1900, close to 2,000 at each census count in later census reports.

In this field wars opened more and more opportunities to women scientists and it has been admitted that women physicists "had a real share in the fundamental research that made possible developments in atomic energy, radar, and electronics. Astronomers, as well, though less directly connected with the military effort, helped to solve problems of air navigation by adapting findings from the study of such stellar problems as direction and time.

"Other scientists aided the war effort by transferring to the closely related fields of mathematics and physics when the shortage of technically trained persons became acute early in the war."

Girls in such scientific jobs as laboratory technicians and laboratory assistants were not clearly counted in this work until 1930 when there were 8,000. In Uncle Sam's count of 1940 they were 23,000.

Women engineers in 1940 added up to slightly less than 800 and, surprisingly, the largest numbers of these technical ladies were in civil, electrical, and mechanical engineering. Over a hundred were surveyors, seventy-four each in industrial, mining, and metallurgical engineering. Chemical engineers had the fewest numbers—only fifty-nine.

The women who have made the fine arts their business have had a good many ups and downs statistically. Back in 1870, there were 6,000 music teachers and other musicians. By 1910, they numbered 84,000; then down in 1940 to 66,000. Artists and art teachers accounted for less than 500 women in 1870; but they have increased in number to exceed 20,000.

Actresses, dancers, and other entertainers were 800 in 1870; went up to 28,000 in 1940.

Women in the field of writing have never figured large

in numbers but, like the women scientists, their contributions have often outdistanced those of many men. Take Harriet Beecher Stowe and her powerful *Uncle Tom's Cabin* for example. In the seventies there were 115 of these ladies; they went up to 2,000 in 1910. It has been up-and-down for these women, too, with 5,000 in 1930, 4,600 in 1940. Editors and reporters grew in numbers from only 43 in the seventies to 16,000 in 1940.

In all phases of the fine arts, women may have many heartaches as they try to make a place for themselves but, when they do, there are satisfactions as rewarding as you can find anywhere in the world of work.

Radio and television workers, perhaps, have the greatest satisfactions from their work as their audience grows and grows. Here are a few ideas about that from a commentator friend. First is the exhilaration of sending your message to a large audience; then the challenge to increase the number of your listeners; the stimulus of drawing out guests in interviews on the air; the satisfaction of meeting an obligation to the public, for radio is a terrible weapon for propaganda; the self-expression found in a polished performance and the fun of using all your ingenuity which is often taxed to the limit in varying programs.

Included among the *Farm and Home Workers* are the lady farmers, the homemakers, household workers, hobbyists and stay-at-home workers. Distinct census figures aren't easy to present in most of these lines, except that of household worker.

When Uncle Sam began to hand out "homestead acres" to pioneering families, women played such a courageous and colorful part that hundreds of novelists have used these brave women as heroines. Later on, their work became so drab in many sections of the country that all who could left for more exciting work in towns and cities. Back in 1910, Uncle Sam counted more than twice as many women as farm workers than in 1870. After that, their number went down until by 1940 there were actually fewer of these workers than there had been in 1870. In 1950 we have 660,000.

We'll quote a Women's Bureau writer about the situation among household workers: "the fifty years from 1870 to 1920 was a period during which service occupations both in private and public housekeeping appeared to be increasingly unpopular among women workers. From nearly one half of all working women in 1870, women service workers in private or public housekeeping dropped to less than one third by 1890 and continued downward to less than one sixth in 1920." In 1950, there were 3,700,000 or only one sixth of all workers. Demand for such workers has dropped somewhat, too, as families have become accustomed to smaller homes and apartments equipped with labor-saving devices.

Changes in the occupations of laundresses and other cleaning workers have come since inventions of power laundry and home washing machines. Many women who worked as laundresses in private homes in the early days transferred to commercial laundry and cleaning establishments. The number of laundresses and of women in laundering, cleaning, and dyeing establishments was over ten times greater in 1930 than in 1870.

Last, but far from least—both in numbers and in importance—are *Workers for Uncle Sam.* Here are the girls and women civilian workers, most of them working in Washington, who receive a fortnightly pay check from Uncle

NEW HORIZONS FOR GIRLS AND WOMEN 333

Sam, and the women in military uniforms. Until World War II the girls of the Army, Air Force, Navy and Marine Corps were nil except for nurses, a few other medical service workers, and a fair number of clerical workers who stayed on in their jobs after World War I or came in during the twenties and thirties. Women of the Armed Forces are now 23,000, according to latest word from the U. S. Women's Bureau.

We suggest that you study very thoroughly a publication of this same Women's Bureau if you would join the ranks of civilian workers for Uncle Sam. This is a publication in two parts titled Women in the Federal Service. Part I tells about the progress that has been made by women in civil service jobs—how they gained equal pay with men, won admission to all examinations, and made other gains through the years since the first pioneering women broke down the barriers that were very high and firm against them. Trends in employment are stressed, especially since the great influx of girls into Uncle Sam's employ during World War I. The second part of this publication is even more significant as it deals chiefly with women who have reached top-salaried positions, describes those positions with training and experience required for them, amounts of these top salaries and, most important of all, just what per cent of women have climbed to the top in each field of work.

Since Uncle Sam offers opportunities to women in practically every line of work today, it will be a good idea to visit the nearest office of the Civil Service Commission and ask for information about examinations in the field which you are considering as a possible career. Or send to the

Commission in Washington for a copy of its pamphlet which describes all opportunities.

Once Uncle Sam's workers received such small pay checks that they had to be satisfied with "psychological income." Not so today. A recent change in the classification act has stepped up all salaries and made it possible to advance on merit through the regular grades to top positions in which salaries compare favorably with any paid for similar work in non-government jobs.

Remember, too, that in all the jobs for Uncle Sam, the non-cash rewards may be even higher than elsewhere. Often he provides equipment for research and other opportunities in the various occupations that will make your work far more effective than you had ever hoped it would be. And maybe here you can help in the big challenge which Lady Astor cynically handed to women "to make the world safe for the men."

We hope that our look at the exciting progress that women have made across the years will help you prepare for the fascinating horizons of which the girls of the seventies had not even dreamed. However, if you are still uncertain about your choice of a career and feel that you need more detailed information than we have been able to present, read as many of the books as you can in the reading lists. And, by all means, explore all other avenues of help. If you are still in college, you will have the placement bureau there to help you. And there are other agencies prepared to help you, such as the Y.W.C.A., the Business and Professional Women's Clubs and similar women's service organizations, and such government agencies as the State Employment Service.

Business schools, art schools, and other specialized training schools will also do all they can to help their students find their first jobs and move to better ones as they gain experience. If you join one of the professions, there is usually a national association which operates a placement service for its members. Nursing organizations, the American Association of Social Workers, the American Library Association, and many others like them are active in such work.

Maybe you are one of those who feel that in uncertain times it doesn't matter much which career you choose. Forget it! We are pretty sure our pioneering women of the past decades didn't worry about the disasters that might befall them. They were too busy on their own big jobs. You must learn not to worry, as nothing can impair your efficiency or warp your personality more easily. We suggest following the precept of Pope Pius XI, who said:

"Tomorrow is in God's hands, in whose better could it be?"

Keep that thought in mind and all your powers will be concentrated on doing each day's work to the best of your ability and none of them will be wasted in worrying about the future.

READING LISTS

ON CHOOSING A VOCATION

Brooke, Esther E. *Guide to career success.* Harper.
Careers for women. Syracuse University, Syracuse, N. Y.
Chambers, M. *Youth-serving organizations.* American Council on Education, Washington, D. C.
Edlund, S. W. and M. G. *Pick your job and land it.* Prentice-Hall.
Forrester, Gertrude. *Occupational pamphlets; an annotated bibliography.* H. W. Wilson.
Frankel, Alice H. *Handbook of job facts.* Science Research Associates, Chicago.
Hamman, Mary. *The Mademoiselle handbook.* McGraw-Hill.
Leach, Ruth M. *Jobs and the woman.* National Association of Manufacturers, New York, N. Y.
Kahm, Harold S. *Careers for modern women.* Knickerbocker Pub. Co.
Kitson, Harry D. *How to find the right vocation.* Harper.
———. *I find my vocation.* McGraw-Hill.
Lingenfelter, Mary R. *Vocations in fiction.* American Library Association.
Lyle, Betty. *And so to work.* Woman's Press, New York, N. Y.
Longarzo, L. Cornelius. *Vocational guide for women.* Catholic Youth Organization of the Archdiocese of New York, Inc., New York, N. Y.
Rahn, A. W. *Your work abilities, how to express and apply them through manpower specifications.* Harper.
U. S. Women's Bureau. *Bulletins.* The Bureau.

NURSES

Deming, Dorothy. *Careers for nurses.* McGraw-Hill.
———. *The practical nurse.* Commonwealth Fund.
Eberle, Irmengarde. *Nurse! The story of a great profession.* Crowell.
Institute for Research, Chicago. *Nursing as a profession.* The Institute.
Schulz, Cecilia L. *Your career in nursing.* McGraw-Hill.
Stewart, Isabel M. *Education of nurses.* Macmillan.

Sutherland, Dorothy G. *Do you want to be a nurse?* Doubleday.
U. S. Women's Bureau. *Outlook for women in occupations in the medical and other health services.* By Marguerite W. Zapoleon. (Bulletin 203-3. Professional nurses.) Govt. Print. Off.

BIOGRAPHY

Kenny, Elizabeth, and Ostenso, Martha. *And they shall walk.* Dodd, Mead.
Merrick, Elliott. *Northern nurse.* Scribner.
Newcomb, Ellsworth. *Brave nurse.* Appleton-Century.
Nolan, Jeannette C. *Clara Barton of the Red Cross.* Messner.
———. *Florence Nightingale.* Messner.
Richards, Laura E. *Florence Nightingale.* Appleton-Century.
Williams, Beryl. *Lillian Wald, angel of Henry Street.* Messner.
Williams, Blanche C. *Clara Barton: Daughter of destiny.* Lippincott.
Yost, Edna. *American women of nursing.* Lippincott.

Marshall, Marguerite M. *Wilderness nurse.* Macrae-Smith.
Wells, Helen. *Cherry Ames; private duty nurse.* Grosset & Dunlap.
———. *Cherry Ames; veterans' nurse.* Grosset & Dunlap.

FICTION

Boylston, Helen D. *Sue Barton* series. Little, Brown.
Deming, Dorothy. *Penny Marsh* series. Dodd, Mead.
———. *Ginger Lee, war nurse.* Dodd, Mead.
———. *Pam Wilson; registered nurse.* Dodd, Mead.
———. *Anne Snow, mountain nurse.* Dodd, Mead.
Gardner, Mary S. *Katharine Kent.* Macmillan.
Johnson, Martha. *Ann Bartlett* series. Crowell.
Lansing, Elisabeth H. *Nancy Naylor* series. Crowell.
———. *Rider on the mountains.* Crowell.
Mallette, Gertrude E. *Into the wind.* Doubleday.

PHYSICIANS

Institute for Research, Chicago. *Medicine as a career.* The Institute.
Klinefelter, Lee M. *Medical occupations for girls: Women in white.* Dutton.

Moon, George R. *How to become a doctor.* Blakiston.
O'Hara, Dwight. *Medicine.* Bellman Pub. Co.
Rifkin, Lillian. *When I grow up I'll be a doctor.* Lothrop, Lee & Shepard.

U. S. Women's Bureau. *Outlook for women in occupations in the medical and other health services.* By Marguerite W. Zapoleon. (Bulletin 203-11. *Women physicians.*) Govt. Print. Off.

Mallette, Gertrude E. *Single stones.* Doubleday.
Sterne, Emma G. *Amarantha Gay, M.D.* Dodd, Mead.
Truax, Rhoda. *This dynasty of doctors.* Bobbs-Merrill.
Worth, Kathryn. *Middle button.* Doubleday.

BIOGRAPHY

Baker, Rachel. *First woman doctor.* Messner.
Barringer, Emily D. *Bowery to Bellevue.* Norton.
DeKruif, Paul H., and DeKruif, Rhea. *Life among the doctors.* Harcourt, Brace.
Kerr, Laura. *Dr. Elizabeth.* Nelson.
Knapp, Sally E. *Women doctors today.* Crowell.
Ross, Ishbel. *Child of destiny.* Harper.
Van Hoosen, Bertha. *Petticoat surgeon.* Pellegrini & Cudahy.

FICTION

Carfrae, Elizabeth. *Fish in the sea.* Putnam.
Chandler, Caroline A. *Dr. Kay Winthrop, intern.* Dodd, Mead.
———. *Susie Stuart, M.D.* Dodd, Mead.
———. *Susie Stuart, home front doctor.* Dodd, Mead.
De Leeuw, Adele L. *Doctor Ellen.* Macmillan.
Felsen, Henry G. *Davey Logan, Interne.* Dutton.
Hamilton, Kay. *Doctor on Elm Street.* Macrae-Smith.
Hobart, Alice T. *Yang and Yin.* Bobbs-Merrill.

DENTISTS

Institute for Research, Chicago. *Dentistry as a career.* The Institute.
Rome, Florence L. *Dentist.* Occupational Index, Inc.
Science Research Associates, Inc. *Occupational brief: Dentists* (No. 112). The Associates.

U. S. Women's Bureau. *Outlook for women in the medical and other health services.* By Marguerite W. Zapoleon. (Bulletin 203-10. *Women dentists.*) Govt. Print. Off.
Woodhouse, Chase G. *Dental careers.* (Kitson career series.) Funk & Wagnalls.

DENTAL HYGIENISTS

American Dental Association. *The dental hygienist.* The Association.

Institute for Research, Chicago. *Dental hygiene as a career.* The Institute.

Horner, Harlan H. *Dental education today.* University of Chicago Press.

Rome, Florence L. *Dental hygiene.* Occupational Index, Inc.

Rome, Florence L. *Dental technician.* Occupational Index, Inc., New York University.

U. S. Women's Bureau. *Outlook for women in the medical and other health services.* By Marguerite W. Zapoleon. (Bulletin 203-10. *Dental hygienists.*) Govt. Print. Off.

Woodhouse, Chase G. *Dental careers.* (Kitson career series.) Funk & Wagnalls.

OSTEOPATHS, OPTICAL WORKERS, VETERINARIANS

OSTEOPATHS

American Osteopathic Association. *The osteopathic profession and its colleges.* The Association.

———. *Osteopathy as a profession.* The Association.

———. *Women in osteopathy.* The Association.

Belleau, Wilfred E. *Osteopathy as a career.* Park Publishing House, Milwaukee, Wisc.

Carey, Robert E., ed. *Osteopathy as a career.* New York State Osteopathic Soc.

Greenleaf, Walter J. *Osteopathy.* (U. S. Office of Education, Guidance leaflet No. 23.) Govt. Print. Off.

Institute for Research, Chicago. *Osteopathy as a career.* The Institute.

OPTICAL WORKERS

American Optometric Association, Inc. *Optometry.* The Association.

Ewalt, H. Ward, Jr. *Optometry.* Bellman Pub. Co.

Institute for Research, Chicago. *Opticians and optical mechanics.* The Institute.

———. *Optometry as a career.* The Institute.

Science Research Associates, Inc. *Occupational briefs: Opthalmologists* (No. 221); *Optometrists* (No. 114). The Associates.

READING LISTS

VETERINARIANS

Institute for Research, Chicago. *A career in veterinary medicine.* The Institute.

Fiction

Paschal, Nancy. *Magnolia Heights.* Nelson.
Thompson, Mary W. *Pattern for Penelope.* Longmans, Green.
———. *Crossroads for Penelope.* Longmans, Green.

PHYSICAL AND OCCUPATIONAL THERAPISTS

PHYSICAL THERAPISTS

American Physiotherapy Association. *Physical therapy, a service and a career.* The Association.
Daly, Maureen. *High school career series: Physical therapy* (No. 11). Ladies' Home Journal.
Hennessey, Thomas F. *Physiotherapy.* Bellman Pub. Co.
Rome, Florence L. *Physical therapy.* Occupational Index, Inc.
U. S. Women's Bureau. *Outlook for women in the medical and other health services.* By Marguerite W. Zapoleon. (Bulletin 203-1. *Physical therapists.*) Govt. Print. Off.

OCCUPATIONAL THERAPISTS

American Occupational Therapy Association. *Occupational therapy, a pioneering profession.* The Association.
Steele, Evelyn, and Blatt, H. K. *Careers in social service.* Dutton.
U. S. Women's Bureau. *Outlook for women in the medical and other health services.* By Marguerite W. Zapoleon. (Bulletin 203-2. *Occupational therapists.*) Govt. Print. Off.

Fiction

Cobb, Meta R., and Hudson, Holland. *Joan chooses occupational therapy.* Dodd, Mead.
Stern, Edith M., and Cobb, Meta R. *Betty Blake, O.T.* Dodd, Mead.
Thompson, Mary W. *Hillhaven.* Longmans, Green.

Biography

Williams, Beryl E. *People are our business.* Lippincott.

CLERICAL WORKERS

Cooley, Robert L., Rodgers, R. H., and Belman, H. S. *My life work; office and store occupations.* McGraw-Hill.
Niles, Henry E., and Niles, M. C. *Office supervisor.* 2d ed. Wiley.
Potter, Thelma M. *An analysis of the work of general clerical employees.* Teachers College, Columbia University.
San Francisco Employers' Council. *Office workers.* The Council.
Schloerb, Lester J., and Medsker, Leland I. *Clerical occupations.* Science Research Associates.

FICTION

Lawrence, Josephine. *Tower of steel.* Little, Brown.
Raymond, Margaret T. *Linnet on the threshold.* Longmans, Green.

SECRETARIES

Becker, Esther R. *Secretaries who succeed.* Harper.
Institute for Research, Chicago. *Private and social secretaryship as a career.* The Institute.
———. *Commercial and trade association secretaryship as a career.* The Institute.
Langston, Mildred J. *Secretarial science.* Bellman Pub. Co.
Maule, Frances. *Road to anywhere.* Funk & Wagnalls.
———. *She strives to conquer.* Funk & Wagnalls.
Pierce, Joseph A. *Negro business and business education.* Harper.
Pratt, Margaret. *The successful secretary.* Lothrop, Lee & Shepard.
Purvis, Elgie G. *Secretaryship as a career field.* National Council of Business Schools, Washington, D. C.
Scott, Louise H., and Belcher, E. C. *How to get a secretarial job.* Harper.
Smedley, Dorée, and Robinson, Lura. *Careers in business for women.* Dutton.

FICTION

Cuthrell, Faith B. *Job for Jenny.* Rinehart.
Gibbs, Blanche L., and Adams, Georgiana. *Shirley Clayton, secretary.* Dodd, Mead.
Macdonald, Zillah K. *Marcia, private secretary.* Messner.
Mallette, Gertrude E. *Mystery in blue.* Doubleday.

SALESWOMEN

de Schweinitz, Dorothea. *Occupations in retail stores.* International Text Book.
Institute for Research, Chicago. *Candy store operation as a career.* The Institute.
———. *Food shops and small grocery operation as a career.* The Institute.
———. *Merchandising as a career.* The Institute.
———. *Salesmanship as a career.* The Institute.
Ivey, Paul W. *Salesmanship applied.* McGraw-Hill.
McFerran, Doris A. *Careers in retailing for young women.* Dutton.
Maule, Frances. *Selling—a job that's always open.* Funk & Wagnalls.
Pierce, Joseph. *Negro business and business education.* Harper.
Richert, G. Henry. *Retailing principles and practices.* Gregg Publishing Co.
———, and Humphrey, Clyde W. *Retailing as a career.* Gregg Publishing Co.

Smith, Paul E., and Breen, George E. *Selling in stores.* Harper.
Thal, Helen M. *Careers for youth in life insurance.* Institute of Life Insurance.
Woodhouse, Chase G. *The big store.* Funk & Wagnalls.

FICTION

DeLeeuw, Adele L. *Future for sale.* Macmillan.
———. *A place for herself.* Macmillan.
———. *Title to happiness.* Macmillan.
Pennoyer, Sara W. *Polly Tucker, merchant.* Dodd, Mead.
Urmston, Mary. *Quite contrary.* Doubleday.
Whitney, Phyllis A. *Star for Ginny.* Houghton Mifflin.
———. *Window for Julie.* Houghton Mifflin.

BIOGRAPHY

Beasley, Norman. *Main Street merchant.* McGraw-Hill.

GIRLS AT MACHINES

American industries series. Bellman Pub. Co.
Institute for Research, Chicago. *Manufacturing as a career.* The Institute.

Science Research Associates. *Occupational briefs.* The Associates.
Textile Information Service. *Your career.* The Service, 551 Fifth Ave., N. Y. C.

U. S. Women's Bureau. *Earnings of women in selected manufacturing industries.* (Bulletin No. 219.) Govt. Print. Off.

———. *Women's occupations through seven decades.* By Janet M. Hooks. (Bulletin No. 218.) Govt. Print. Off.

FICTION

Priestley, John B. *Daylight on Saturday.* Harper.

Raymond, Margaret T. *Bend in the road.* Longmans, Green.

BIOGRAPHY

Antin, Mary. *Promised land.* Houghton Mifflin.

THE LADY BOSS

Peterson, Florence. *Careers in labor relations.* Science Research Associates.

Smedley, Doree, and Robinson, Lura. *Careers in business for women.* Dutton.

FICTION

Chidester, Ann. *Long year.* Scribner.

DeLeeuw, Adele L. *Place for herself.* Macmillan.

BIOGRAPHY

Taves, Isabella. *Successful women.* Dutton.

Williams, Beryl E. *People are our business.* Lippincott.

PERSONNEL WORKERS IN BUSINESS AND INDUSTRY

Amiss, John M., and Sherman, Esther. *New careers in industry.* McGraw-Hill.

Institute for Research, Chicago. *Careers in the U. S. Employment Service.* The Institute.

———. *Industrial personnel work as a career.* The Institute.

Smythe, Doree M. *Careers in personnel work.* Dutton.

Sorenson, Clark C. *Personnel administration.* Bellman Pub. Co.

Strang, Ruth, and Hoppock, Robert. *Guidance and personnel services.* Occupational Index, Inc., New York University.

Western Personnel Service. *Personnel work.* Western Personnel Institute, Pasadena, Calif.

ADVERTISERS

Davis, Edwin W. *Advertising as an occupation.* Science Research Associates, Inc.

Institute for Research, Chicago. *Careers for women as advertising copy writers.* The Institute.

———. *Careers for women in advertising art.* The Institute.

Lyon, Marguerite. *And so to Bedlam.* Bobbs-Merrill.

McBride, Mary M., ed. *How to be a successful advertising woman.* McGraw-Hill.

Rome, Florence L., and Hoppock, Robert. *Advertising.* Occupational Index, Inc.

FICTION

Grumbine, E. Evalyn. *Patsy breaks into advertising.* Dodd, Mead.

———. *Patsy succeeds in advertising.* Dodd, Mead.

Hutchinson, Dorothy D. P. *Nathalie enters advertising.* Little, Brown.

———. *Nathalie moves ahead in advertising.* Little, Brown.

BIOGRAPHY

Hopkins, Claude C. *My life in advertising.* Harper.

LADY BANKERS

Campbell, Dorcas. *Careers for women in banking and finance.* Dutton.

———. *Your career in banking.* Dutton.

Griffin, Albert. *Banking.* Bellman Pub. Co.

Institute for Research, Chicago. *Banking as a career.* The Institute.

Occupational Index, Inc., New York University. *Occupational abstracts: Banking.* The Index.

Quigley, John J. *The loan industry.* Bellman Pub. Co. (American industries series No. 12.)

Science Research Associates. *Occupational brief: Bank workers.* The Associates.

Smedley, Dorée, and Robinson, Lura. *Careers in business for women.* Dutton.

FICTION

Bell, Thomas. *There comes a time.* Little, Brown.

Marquand, John P. *Point of no return.* Little, Brown.

TRANSPORTATION AND COMMUNICATION WORKERS.

TRANSPORTATION

Baker, Morris B. *Airline traffic and operations.* McGraw-Hill.

Burger, Samuel. *Careers in aviation.* Greenberg.

Carlisle, Norman V. *Your career in transportation.* Dutton.

Institute for Research, Chicago. *Careers for women with the air lines.* The Institute.

——. *Careers in travel service.* The Institute.

Lent, Henry B. *Eight hours to solo.* Macmillan.

Lindbergh, Anne S. M. *North to the Orient.* Harcourt, Brace.

——. *Listen, the wind.* Harcourt, Brace.

Meyer, Dickey. *Girls at work in aviation.* Doubleday.

Peckham, Betty C. *Women in aviation.* Nelson.

Science Research Associates. *Occupational brief: Railroad workers.* The Associates.

Shields, Bert A. *Air pilot training.* McGraw-Hill.

Tipton, Stuart G. *Air transportation industry.* Bellman Pub. Co.

U. S. Women's Bureau. *Women in aviation.* By Frances W. Kerr. Govt. Print. Off.

Western Personnel Service. *The carrier traffic manager.* Western Personnel Institute.

Fiction

Cavanna, Betty. *A girl can dream.* Westminster Press.

Hager, Alice R. *Janice, air hostess.* Messner.

Lindbergh, Anne S. M. *The steep ascent.* Harcourt, Brace.

O'Malley, Patricia. *Wings for Carol.* Greystone.

Simmons, Margaret I. *Sally wins her wings.* Crowell.

Willson, Dixie. *Hostess of the skyways.* Dodd, Mead.

Biography

Adams, Jean, and Kimball, Margaret. *Heroines of the sky.* Doubleday.

Garst, Doris S. *Amelia Earhart, heroine of the skies.* Messner.

Knapp, Sally E. *New Wings for women.* Crowell.

Moody, John. *The railroad builders.* Yale University Press.

Pease, Herbert L. *Singing rails.* Crowell.

COMMUNICATION

Baltimore Department of Education. *The telephone operator.* The Department.

Robbins, Zila, and Medary, Marjorie, eds. *All in the day's work.* Appleton-Century.

Science Research Associates. *Occupational brief: Telephone* and telegraph operators. The Associates.

Smedley, Dorée, and Robinson, Lura. *Careers in business for women.* Dutton.

U. S. Women's Bureau. *Typical women's jobs in the telephone industry.* (Bulletin 207.) Govt. Print. Off.

U. S. Women's Bureau. *The woman telephone worker.* (Bulletin 207-A.) Govt. Print. Off.

TEACHERS

American Council on Education. *The crisis in teaching.* The Council.

———. *Teachers for our times.* The Council.

Bowers, Harold J. *Let us consider teaching.* Ohio State Department of Education, Columbus.

Burton, William H. *Teaching.* Bellman Pub. Co.

Butler, Vera M., Jewett, Ida A., and Stroh, Mary M. *Better selection of better teachers.* Delta Kappa Gamma Soc., Austin, Tex.

Evans, Eva K. *So you're going to teach.* Julius Rosenwald Fund, Chicago.

Frazier, Benjamin W. *Teaching as a career.* (U. S. Office of Education Bulletin no. 11.) Govt. Print. Off.

Greenleaf, Walter J. *Teachers are needed.* Govt. Print. Off.

Houle, Cyril O. *Teaching as a career.* Science Research Associates, Inc.

Institute for Research, Chicago. *Teaching as a career.* The Institute.

Pratt, Margaret, Grover, Frederick O., and Rifkin, Lillian. *When I grow up, I'll be a teacher.* Lothrop, Lee & Shepard.

Stroh, Mary M. *Find your own frontier.* Delta Kappa Gamma Soc., Austin, Tex.

FICTION

Aldrich, Bess S. *Miss Bishop.* Appleton-Century.

Boyce, Burke. *Miss Mallett.* Harper.

Chase, Genevieve. *Four young teachers.* Dodd, Mead.

Dalgliesh, Alice. *Silver pencil.* Scribner.

Erdman, Loula G. *Fair is the morning.* Longmans, Green.

———. *Separate star.* Longmans, Green.

McCormick, Alma H. *Merry makes a choice.* Little, Brown.

Rosenheim, Lucile G. *Kathie, the new teacher.* Messner.

Singmaster, Elsie. *You make your own luck.* Longmans, Green.

Stone, Elinore C. *Laughingest lady.* Appleton-Century.

Urmston, Mary. *Forty faces.* Doubleday.

BIOGRAPHY

Byers, Tracy. *Martha Berry, the Sunday lady of Possum Trot*. Putnam.

Perry, Bliss. *And gladly teach*. Houghton Mifflin.

Peterson, Houston, ed. *Great teachers portrayed by those who studied under them*. Rutgers University Press.

SOCIAL WORKERS

American Association of Schools of Social Work. *Social work as a profession*. The Association, Chicago.

American Association of Social Workers. *Personnel—training, recruiting*. The Association, New York.

——. *Social work as a profession*. The Association, New York.

Brown, Esther L. *Social work as a profession*. Russell Sage Foundation.

Family Welfare Association of America. *Family case work*. The Association, New York.

Hutzel, Eleanore L. *Policewoman's handbook*. Columbia University Press.

Institute for Research, Chicago. *Social work as a career*. The Institute.

Lerrigo, Ruth, and Beull, Bradley. *Social work and the Joneses*. Public Affair Committee, Inc., New York.

Steele, Evelyn M., and Blatt, Heiman K. *Careers in social service*. Dutton.

White, R. Clyde. *Social work*. Bellman Pub. Co.

FICTION

Boylston, Helen D. *Sue Barton, visiting nurse* (and sequel). Little, Brown.

Kasius, Cora. *Nancy Clark, Social worker*. Dodd, Mead.

BIOGRAPHY

Addams, Jane. *Twenty years at Hull House*. Macmillan.

——. *Second twenty years at Hull House*. Macmillan.

Williams, Beryl. *Lillian Wald, angel of Henry Street*. Messner.

Wise, Winifred E. *Jane Addams of Hull House*. Harcourt, Brace.

LADIES OF THE LAW

Daly, Maureen. *High school career series: Law.* Ladies' Home Journal, Philadelphia.

Fenning, Karl. *Patent law as a profession.* Bellman Pub. Co.

Institute for Research, Chicago. *Law as a career.* The Institute.

Selina, Ruth. *Lawyer.* Occupational Index, Inc.

University of Chicago Law School. *The study and practice of law.* The University Press.

FICTION

Train, Arthur C. *Tutt and Mr. Tutt* (and sequels). Scribner.

BIOGRAPHY

Bowen, Catherine D. *Yankee from Olympus.* Little, Brown.

Train, Arthur C. *My day in court.* Scribner.

RELIGIOUS WORKERS AND MINISTERS

Nichols, James A., Jr. *Religion.* Bellman Pub. Co.

Science Research Associates. *Occupational brief: Clergyman and religious workers.* The Associates.

FICTION

Barber, Elsie M. O. *Wall between.* Macmillan.

Turnbull, Agnes S. *Rolling years.* Macmillan.

White, Nelia G. *No trumpet before him.* Westminster Press.

BIOGRAPHY

Floyd, Olive. *Doctora in Mexico.* Putnam.

Graham, Abbie. *Grace H. Dodge.* Woman's Press.

Miller, Basil. *Ten girls who became famous.* Zondervan Pub. House.

Shaw, Anna H. *Story of a pioneer.* Harper.

Spence, Hartzell. *One foot in heaven.* McGraw-Hill.

LIBRARIANS

American Library Association. *Books and people; a career in library service.* The Association.

──. *Training for library work.* The Association.

Institute for Research, Chicago. *Librarianship as a career.* The Institute.

Klaw, Alma A. *Librarian.* Occupational Index, Inc., New York University.

Rossell, Beatrice S. *Public libraries in the life of the nation.* American Library Association.

Savord, Ruth. *Special librarianship as a career.* Institute of Women's Professional Relations, Connecticut College, New London, Connecticut.

Stebbins, Kathleen B. *Challenge of special librarianship.* Special Libraries Association, New York City.

Wheeler, Joseph L. *Progress and problems in education for librarianship.* Carnegie Corporation.

FICTION

DeLeeuw, Adele L. *With a high heart.* Macmillan.

Dickson, Marguerite. *Turn in the road.* Nelson.

Fargo, Lucile F. *Marian—Martha.* Dodd, Mead.

Lingenfelter, Mary R. *Books on wheels.* Funk & Wagnalls.

Provines, Mary V. *Bright heritage.* Longmans, Green.

Waite, Helen E. *Butterfly takes command.* Macrae-Smith.

BIOGRAPHY

Dawe, George G. *Melvil Dewey, seer, inspirer, doer.* Lake Placid Club, N. Y.

Rider, Fremont. *Melvil Dewey.* American Library Association.

HOME ECONOMISTS

American Home Economics Association. *Along the home economics highway.* The Association.

Bane, Lita, and Chapin, Mildred R. *Introduction to home economics.* Houghton Mifflin.

Brumbaugh, Aaron J. *American universities and colleges.* American Council on Education, Washington.

Healey, Katheryne T. *Home economics.* Bellman Pub. Co.

Hostetter, Helen P. *For you—a career in home economics.* American Home Economics Association.

Institute for Research, Chicago.

Dietetics as a career. The Institute.
Institute for Research, Chicago. *Home economics as a career.* The Institute.
———. *Restaurant management as a career.* The Institute.
Maule, Frances. *Careers for the home economist.* Funk & Wagnalls.
Smedley, Dorée, and Ginn, Ann. *Your career as a food specialist.* Dutton.

FICTION

Eells, May Worthington. *Sally* series. Dodd, Mead.

RECREATION LEADERS

Blank, Helen R. *Recreation.* Occupational Index, Inc.
Butler, George D., ed. *Playgrounds, their administration and operation.* Barnes.
———. *Recreation areas.* Barnes.
Grandofsky, Jack. *Industrial recreation.* Occupational Index, Inc.
Institute for Research, Chicago. *Recreation leadership as a career.* The Institute.
National Recreation Association. *Recreation leadership as a field of work.* The Association, New York.
———. *Recreation leadership standards.* The Association, New York.
Science Research Associates. *Occupational brief: Recreation workers.* The Associates.

BEAUTICIANS

Baltimore Department of Education. *The cosmetologist.* The Department.
Bander, Irving L. *Beauty culture.* Bellman Pub. Co.
Gordon, Edith E. *Establishing and operating a beauty shop.* (U. S. Department of Commerce. Industrial, small business series, No. 25.) Govt. Print. Off.
Institute for Research, Chicago. *Beauty shop management as a career.* The Institute.
Pierce, Joseph A. *Negro business and business education.* Harper.
Science Research Associates. *Occupational brief: Barbers and beauticians.* The Associates.

FICTION

Leech, Margaret. *Manicure; a short story.* (In Best short stories of 1929; also, O. Henry Memorial Award—Prize stories of 1929.)

SCIENTISTS

Carlisle, Norman V. *Your career in chemistry.* Dutton.
Coith, Herbert S. *So you want to be a chemist.* McGraw-Hill.
Institute for Research, Chicago. *Biological work as a career.* The Institute.
———. *Career as a laboratory technician.* The Institute.
———. *Exploring as a career.* The Institute.
———. *Geological work as a career.* The Institute.
———. *Statistical work as a career.* The Institute.
Pollack, Philip. *Careers in science.* Dutton.
Steele, Evelyn. *Careers for girls in science and engineering.* Dutton.

FICTION

Allee, Marjorie H. *The great tradition.* Houghton Mifflin.
———. *Jane's island.* Houghton Mifflin.
Turner, Mary E. *Karen Long, medical technician.* Dodd, Mead.

BIOGRAPHY

Benchley, Belle. *My friends, the apes.* Little, Brown.
Crowther, James G. *Famous American men of science.* Norton.
Curie, Eve. *Madame Curie.* Doubleday.
Ditmars, Raymond L. *Making of a scientist.* Macmillan.
Jaffe, Bernard. *Crucibles.* Simon and Schuster.
Levinger, Elma E. *Albert Einstein.* Messner.
Robinson, Mabel L. *Runner of the mountain tops.* Random.
Rourke, Constance M. *Audubon.* Harcourt, Brace.
Rukeyser, Muriel. *Willard Gibbs, American genius.* Doubleday.
Wood, Laura N. *Louis Pasteur.* Messner.
Wright, Helen. *Sweeper in the sky.* Macmillan.
Yost, Edna. *American women of science.* Stokes.
Zinsser, Hans. *As I remember him.* Little, Brown.

ENGINEERS

Brown, Esther L. *The professional engineer.* Russell Sage Foundation.
Carlisle, Norman V. *Your career in engineering.* Dutton.
Engineers' Council for Profes-

sional Development. *Engineering as a career.* The Council, 29 West 39th Street, New York 18, New York.

McHugh, Fred D. *How to be an engineer.* McBride.

Steele, Evelyn. *Careers for girls in science and engineering.* Dutton.

Stewart, Lowell O. *Career in engineering.* Science Research Associates.

———. *Career in engineering—requirements and opportunities.* Iowa State College Press, Ames, Iowa.

U. S. Women's Bureau. *The outlook for women in architecture and engineering.* (Bulletin 223-5.) Govt. Print. Off.

Williams, Clement C. *Building an engineering career.* McGraw-Hill.

BIOGRAPHY

Bishop, Joseph B., and Farnham. *Goethals, genius of the Panama Canal.* Harper.

Gilbreth, Frank B., and Carey, E. G. *Cheaper by the dozen.* Crowell.

WRITERS, NEWSPAPER WORKERS, EDITORS

Brande, Dorothea. *Becoming a writer.* Harcourt, Brace.

Institute for Research, Chicago. *Journalism as a career.* The Institute.

———. *Publishing as a career.* The Institute.

Lent, Henry B. *"I work on a newspaper."* Macmillan.

Logie, Ione R. *Career for women in journalism.* International Textbook.

Milwaukee Journal. *Journalism as a career.* The Journal.

Peacocke, Emilie H. *Writing for women.* Macmillan.

Robinson, Mabel L. *Writing for young people.* Nelson.

FICTION

Best, Allena C. (Erick Berry, pseud.) *Forty-seven keys.* Macmillan.

Bugbee, Emma. *Peggy covers the news* (and sequels). Dodd, Mead.

Connolly, Vera. *Judy Grant: editor.* Dodd, Mead.

Dalgliesh, Alice. *Along Janet's road.* Scribner.

Hogeboom, Amy. *Ann comes to New York.* Lothrop.

McIlvaine, Jane S. *Front page for Jennifer.* Macrae-Smith.

Mallette, Gertrude E. *Private props.* Doubleday.

———. *Unexpected summer.* Doubleday.

Van Gelder, Robert. *Front page story.* Dodd, Mead.

Varga, Margit. *Carol Brant, picture magazine reporter.* Dodd, Mead.

Whitney, Phyllis A. *Silver inkwell.* Houghton Mifflin.

BIOGRAPHY

Baker, Louise M. *Out on a limb.* McGraw-Hill.
Eaton, Evelyn S. M. *North star is nearer.* Farrar, Straus.
Ferber, Edna. *A peculiar treasure.* Doubleday.
Hinkley, Laura L. *Ladies of literature.* Hastings House.
Jackson, Phyllis W. *Victorian Cinderella.* Holiday.
Jordan, Elizabeth G. *Three rousing cheers.* Appleton-Century.
Kipling, Rudyard. *Something of myself.* Doubleday.
Miller, Henry Wise. *All our lives.* Coward-McCann.
Rinehart, Mary R. *My story.* Rinehart.
Ross, Ishbel. *Ladies of the press.* Harper.

ARTISTS, MUSICIANS, ACTRESSES, AND OTHERS

Biegeleisen, Jacob I. *Careers in commercial art.* Dutton.
Brosnac, Ethel. *How to make money in commercial art.* McBride.
Chambers, Bernice G., ed. *Keys to a fashion career.* McGraw-Hill.
Denis, Paul. *Your career in show business.* Dutton.
Epstein, Beryl W. *Fashion is our business.* Lippincott.
Institute for Research, Chicago. *Photography as a career.* The Institute.
Johnson, Harriett. *Your career in music.* Dutton.
Lariar, Lawrence. *Careers in cartooning.* Dodd, Mead.
Lescaze, William H. *On being an architect.* Putnam.
Leyson, Burr. *Photographic occupations.* Dutton.
Martin, Charles J. *How to make modern jewelry.* Simon and Schuster.
Taylor, Deems. *Music to my ears.* Simon and Schuster.
Traube, Shepard. *So you want to go into the theatre?* Little, Brown.

FICTION

Boylston, Helen D. *Carol Page* series. Little, Brown.
Bro, Marguerite H. *Sarah.* Doubleday.
Cather, Willa S. *Song of the lark.* Houghton Mifflin.
DeLeeuw, Adele L. *Clay fingers.* Macmillan.
———. *Curtain call.* Macmillan.
———. *Year of promise.* Macmillan.
Dickson, Marguerite. *Lightning strikes twice.* Nelson.
Gallagher, Louise B. *Frills and thrills.* Dodd, Mead.
Hayes, Helen, and Kennedy, Mary. *Star on her forehead.* Dodd, Mead.
Headley, Elizabeth. *Take a call, Topsy.* Macrae-Smith.

READING LISTS

Janney, Russell. *Miracle of the bells.* Prentice-Hall.
Mallette, Gertrude E. *Inside out.* Doubleday.
Pelus, Marie-Jeanne. *Opera ballerina.* Dodd, Mead.
———. *Yankee ballerina.* Dodd, Mead.
Swarthout, Gladys. *Come soon, tomorrow.* Dodd, Mead.
Urmston, Mary. *Plain clothes Patricia.* Doubleday.
Walden, Amelia E. *Sunnycove.* Morrow.
Whitney, Phyllis A. *Ever after.* Houghton Mifflin.

BIOGRAPHY

Burke, Billie, and Shipp, Cameron. *With a feather on my nose.* Appleton-Century.

Ewen, David. *Story of Irving Berlin.* Holt.
Hansen, Karen (pseud.). *Flight agaist the wind.* Odyssey.
Harvey, Ruth W. *Curtain time.* Houghton Mifflin.
Lawrence, Marjorie. *Interrupted melody.* Appleton-Century.
Newcomb, Covelle. *Secret door.* Dodd, Mead.
Scott, Alma O. S. *Wanda Gag; the story of an artist.* University of Minnesota.
Skinner, Cornelia O. *Family circle.* Houghton Mifflin.
Trapp, Maria A. *Story of the Trapp family singers.* Lippincott.

RADIO AND TELEVISION WORKERS

Crawford, John E. *Television.* (Occupational abstract No. 74.) Occupational Index, Inc.
Dunlap, Orrin E. *Future of television.* Harper.
Institute for Research, Chicago. *Careers in radio.* The Institute.
Jones, Charles R., ed. *Your career in motion pictures, radio, television.* Sheridan.
Knight, Ruth A. *Stand by for the ladies!* Coward-McCann.
Science Research Associates. *Occupational brief: Radio jobs.* The Associates.

FICTION

Olds, Helen Diehl. *Come in, Winifred.* Messner.
———. *Lark, radio singer.* Messner.
Hargrove, Marion. *Something's got to give.* Sloane.

BIOGRAPHY

Dunlap, Orrin E. *Radio's 100 men of science.* Harper.
Everson, George. *Story of television; the life of Philo T. Farnsworth.* Norton.

LADY FARMERS

Duryee, William B. *Farming for security.* McGraw-Hill.
——. *A living from the land.* McGraw-Hill.
Greenberg, David B., and Corbin, Charles. *So you're going to buy a farm.* Greenberg.
Institute for Research, Chicago. *Animal husbandry as a career.* The Institute.
——. *Careers in the florist industry.* The Institute.
——. *Farm management as a career.* The Institute.
——. *General agriculture as a career.* The Institute.
McMillen, Wheeler. *New riches from the soil.* Van Nostrand.
Robbins, Zila, and Medary, Marjorie, eds. *All in the day's work.* Appleton-Century.
Spence, Hartzell. *Happily ever after.* McGraw-Hill.
Teller, Walter M. *Farm primer.* McKay.
Tetlow, Henry. *We farm for a hobby and make it pay.* Morrow.
Tetlow, Henry. *On Medlock farm.* Morrow.
U. S. Dept. of Agriculture. *Shall I be a farmer?* Superintendent of Documents.
Waring, P. Alston, and Teller, W. M. *Roots in the earth.* Harper.

FICTION

Carroll, Gladys. *As the earth turns.* Grosset.
Corey, Paul. *Corn Gold farm.* Morrow.
Davis, Lavinia R. *Come be my love.* Doubleday.
Garst, Doris S. *Wish on an apple.* Abingdon.
Johnson, Enid. *Cowgirl Kate.* Messner.
——, and Peck, A. M. *Big bright land.* Messner.
Paschal, Nancy. *Clover Creek.* Nelson.
Scarborough, Dorothy. *In the land of cotton.* Macmillan.
Tunis, John R. *Son of the valley.* Morrow.

HOMEMAKERS

Canadian Youth Commission. *Youth, marriage, and the family.* Ryerson Press.
Gilbreth, Lillian E. *Home-maker and her job.* Appleton-Century.
Groves, Ernest R., Skinner, E. L., and Swenson, S. J. *The family and its relationships.* Lippincott.
Justin, Margaret M., and Rust, L. M. O. *Today's home living.* Lippincott.

READING LISTS

Landis, Judson T. and M. G. *Marriage handbook.* Prentice-Hall.
Landis, Paul H. *Your marriage and family living.* McGraw-Hill.
Ray, Randolph. *Marriage is a serious business.* McGraw-Hill.
What today's woman should know about marriage; by the editors of *Today's Woman.* Farrar, Straus.

FICTION

Aldrich, Bess S. *Mother Mason.* Appleton-Century.
Bianco, Margery W. *Winterbound.* Viking.

BIOGRAPHY

Homer, Sidney. *My wife and I.* Macmillan.
Parker, Cornelia S. *American idyll.* Little, Brown.

HOUSEHOLD WORKERS

Institute for Research, Chicago. *Executive housekeeping as a career.* The Institute.
Miller, Frieda S. *Can we lure Martha back to the kitchen?* U. S. Women's Bureau.
New York State Department of Labor—Division of Industrial Relations. *Domestic service employment in New York State.* The Department.
Wisconsin State Board of Vocational and Adult Education. *Occupational opportunities for young women trained in vocational homemaking skills.* The Board.
Science Research Associates. *Occupational brief: Household workers and hotel workers.* The Associates.
U. S. Bureau of Labor Statistics. *Employment outlook in hotel occupations.* Govt. Print. Off.
U. S. Women's Bureau. *Old age insurance for household workers.* Govt. Print. Off.

FICTION

Bianco, Mrs. Margery W. *Other people's houses.* Viking.
Boo, Mrs. Sigrid. *Servants' entrance.* Simon and Schuster.
Lawrence, Josephine. *A good home with nice people.* Little, Brown.

BIOGRAPHY

Dickens, Monica. *One pair of hands.* Harper.

HOBBYISTS AND STAY-AT-HOME WORKERS

Collins, A. Frederick. *How to ride your hobby.* Appleton-Century.

Lampland, Ruth. *Hobbies for everybody.* Harper.

Zarchy, Harry. *Here's your hobby.* Knopf.

FICTION

Hall, Esther G. *Sharon's career.* Random.

GOVERNMENT WORKERS, POLITICIANS, AND DIPLOMATS

Chapman, Paul W. *Jobs in rural service.* Science Research Associates.

Childs, James R. *American foreign service.* Holt.

Institute for Research, Chicago. *Careers in government service.* The Institute.

——. *Consular and foreign trade service as a career.* The Institute.

——. *Politics as a career.* The Institute.

Liebers, Arthur. *Careers in federal service for the college trained.* Wilcox and Follett.

Science Research Associates. *Occupational briefs: Diplomatic service workers.* (No. 92); *Politicians.* (No. 106.) The Associates.

Spero, Sterling D., ed. *Government jobs and how to get them.* Lippincott.

U. S. Civil Service Commission. *Working for the Federal Government.* Govt. Print. Off.

U. S. Women's Bureau. *Women in the Federal Service.* (Bulletin No. 230.) Govt. Print. Off.

White, Leonard D. *Government career service.* University of Chicago Press.

FICTION

Keyes, Frances P. *Parts unknown.* Messner.

BIOGRAPHY

Bryan, Florence H. *Susan B. Anthony.* Messner.

Kerr, Laura N. *Girl who ran for president.* Nelson.

Roosevelt, Eleanor R. *This I remember.* Harper.

WACS, WAFS, WAVES, MARINES

Banning, Kendall. *The fleet today.* Funk & Wagnalls.
Baumer, William H. *How to be an Army officer.* McBride.

FICTION

Jacobs, Helen H. *"By your leave, sir."* Dodd, Mead.
White, Barbara. *Lady leatherneck.* Dodd, Mead.

INDEX

Abel, Mary H., 190-198
Accountants, 64, 66
Actresses, 262-263
Addams, Jane, 156
Addressograph operator, 63
Advertisers, 115 ff.
Agricultural workers, 273 ff.
Air hostesses, 134
Anesthetists, 16
Anthropologists, 222-223
Architects, 248
Artists, 244 ff.
Astronomers, 224-225
Aviators, 135-136

Bankers, 125 ff.
Barton, Clara, 300
Beauticians, 206 ff.
Beaux, Cecelia, 246
Beekeepers, 278-279
Biologists, 217-218
Blackwell, Elizabeth and Emily, 23, 24, 323
Bleyer, W. G., 238, 240
Bookkeepers, 64
Botanists, see Biologists
Bourke-White, Margaret, 254
Brown, Lela T., 44
Buck, Pearl, 176
Buyers, department store, see Saleswomen

Camp Fire Girls, 195
Camp workers, 204
Candy makers, see Confectionery industry workers
Cashier, bank, 127
Cataloguers, 185

Charters, W. W., 68, 69, 72
Chemists, 219-220
Child development, 217
Choosing an Occupation, 4 ff.
Civil Service, 159, 300 ff.
Clerical workers
 in business, 55 ff.
 in railroad, 132-133
Commentator, 268-270
Commercial artists, 249 ff.
Commercial demonstrators, 194-195
Comparison shoppers, 82-83
Composers, 258-259
Confectionery industry workers, 102
Consular Service, 309-312
Counselors, 152
County demonstration agents, 194
Court reporters, 66
Curie, Marie, 214, 218
 Pierre, 218

Dairy farmers, 277-278
Dancers, 263
Dental hygienists, 36 ff.
Dentists, 30 ff.
Department store workers, see Saleswomen
Designers, 251 ff.
 ceramic, 252
 commercial, 250 ff.
 costume, 253-254
 furniture, 257
 industrial, 252
 jewelry, 257
Dietitians, 195-196, 198
Diplomats, 309-312
Distributive education, 59-60, 78-81, 250
Diversified occupations classes, 59-60

INDEX

Draftswomen, 248
Dramatists, see Playwrights

Eastman, Linda, 188
Editors, 243-244
Employment agencies, 9, 114-115
Employment managers, 112
Engineers, 227 ff.
Errand girls, 57

Farm and Home workers, 273-298
Field Museum, Chicago, 246-247
File clerks, 61-62
"Floater" in banking, 130
Food workers, 196
Foreign Service, see Government workers
4-H Clubs, 195
Future Retailer Clubs, 79

Gardening, 274-275
  as a hobby, 297
Gardner, Florence, 123
Garland, Judy, 257
Garment industry workers, 92 ff.
Geologists, 221-222
Georgia State College for Women, 79-81
Gilbreth, Frank and Lillian, 230
Gildersleeve, Virginia, 159
Girl Scouts, 161, 195
Government workers, 300 ff.
Graphotype operators, 63

Hallaren, Colonel Mary, 313
Hardy, Thomas, 233
Hilton, James, 240
Hobart, A. T., 29
Hobbies, 295 ff.
Hoffman, Malvina, 246, 247
Home demonstration worker, 194
Home economists, 189 ff.
Homemakers, 282 ff.
Horticulture, workers in, 274-275
Hotel workers, 293-294
Household workers, 287 ff.
Hull House, 157

Illustrators, see Artists
Income tax experts, 128-129
Insurance saleswomen, 88
Interior decorators, 256-257

Journalists, see Newspaper workers

Kaempffert, Waldemar B., 139
Key-punch operators, 64

Laboratory technicians, 220-221
Lady Boss, The, 103 ff.
Landscape architects, 255-256
Lawyers, 162 ff.
Lenroot, Katherine, 300
Lewis, E. F., 29
Lewis, Sinclair, 235
Librarians, 177 ff.
Library of Congress, 179, 185
Linotype operators, 242

MacDonald, Betty, 276
Mail clerk, 57, 62
Marines, 319-320
Marlowe, Christopher, 184
Mathematicians, 225
Maule, Frances, 56, 71, 127
May, Colonel Geraldine, 312-313
Merchandising, see Saleswomen
Meredith, George, 233
Methodist Church, 167
Millinery workers, 100 ff.
Mimeograph operators, 63
Ministers, 172 ff.
Missionaries, see Religious workers
Mistach, Wanda A., 55
Models, 84
Morse, Samuel F. B., 139
Mossman, Lois, 146
Motion picture workers, 263-264
Multigraph operators, 63
Museum workers, 223
Musicians, 257 ff.

New England Kitchen, 190
Newspaper workers, 238 ff.

INDEX

Nightingale, Florence, 12
Non-fiction writers, 235-236
Norton, Mary T., 308
Novelists, 234-235
Nurses, 12 ff.
  institutional, 16-17
  private duty, 16-18
  ocean liners, 21-22
  public health, 18-19
Nutritionists, see Home economists

Occupation, investigation of an, 5 ff.
Occupational therapists, 53-55
Oculists, 44
Office machine operators, see Clerical workers
Office managers, 66-67
O'Keeffe, Georgia, 246
Optical workers, 44-46
Opticians, 45
Optometrists, 44-45
Osteopaths, 41 ff.

Pastor's assistants, 168
Perry, Josephine, 290-291
Personal shoppers, 83
Personnel workers, 109 ff.
Pharmacists, 223-224
Photographers, 254-255
Physical therapists, 51-55
Physicians, 23 ff.
Planetariums, workers in, 225
Playground supervisors, see Recreation leaders
Playwrights, 234
Poets, 234
Policewomen, 161-162
Polier, Justine Wise, 166
Politicians, 306-309
Polly's Career Market, in *Farm Journal*, 282
Poultry farmers, 275-277
Power machine operators, 92 ff.
Printers, 242
Probation workers, 160-161
Psychiatric social workers, 160
Psychiatrists, 28-29
Psychologists, 215-217

Publicity workers, see Advertisers
Publishers, 242 ff.

Radio and Television workers, 197, 265 ff.
Readers' advisers, 186
Real estate saleswomen, 89
Receptionists, 57, 62, 243
Recreation leaders, 199 ff.
Religious workers, 167, 287
Richards, Ellen H., 189, 190, 198
Ross, Ada, 237
Rumford Kitchen, Chicago, 190

Saleswomen, retail, 74 ff.
  "outside," 86 ff.
Scientists, 213-232
Scudder, Janet, 247-248
Sculptors, 247-248
Secretaries, 68 ff.
Securities saleswomen, 128
Self-analysis, 7
Shadow, Mary, 308-309
Shaw, Anna Howard, 172-174
Shoppers, see Saleswomen
Shorthand reporters, 66
Sinclair, Upton, 235
Smith, Margaret Chase, 307
Social secretaries, 71
Social workers, 156 ff.
Soil Conservation Service, 279
Starbuck, Katherine, 72
State Employment Services, 9, 210
Statisticians, 64, 225-227
Stenographers, 61-62
Stewardesses, see Air hostesses
Still, Dr. Andrew, 41
Stylist, 82

Teachers, 142 ff.
Telegraph
  clerks, 140
  operators, 140-141
Telegraphers, 140
Telephone
  operators, 136-139
  order clerks, 81-82

Teletype operators, 63
Television workers, 265 ff.
Typists, 61, 63

UNESCO, 160
Urban, Frances, 192-193

Veterinarians, 46-51
Vining, Elizabeth J. G., 156
Vocational counselors, 149 ff.

WACs, WAFs, WAVEs, 312 ff.
Warren, Althea, 188
Webster, Margaret, 264
Whitley, I. B., 68-69
Winsor, Beatrice, 188
Woolworth, F. W., Company, 10-11
Writers, 234 ff.

Yablikoff, Natalie, 253-254
Y.W.C.A. workers, 161, 168 ff., 181, 263, 292